Affectionately dedicated to
Morley and Jean Kennerley

Maurice Collis

Nancy Astor

Futura
Macdonald & Co
London & Sydney

A Futura Book

First published in Great Britain by
Faber & Faber Limited

First Futura edition 1982

Copyright © Maurice Collis 1960

ISBN 0 7088 2166 9

Filmset, printed and bound in Great Britain by
Hazell Watson & Viney Ltd, Aylesbury, Bucks

Futura Publications
A Division of
Macdonald & Co (Publishers) Ltd
Holywell House
Worship Street
London EC2A 2EN

Contents

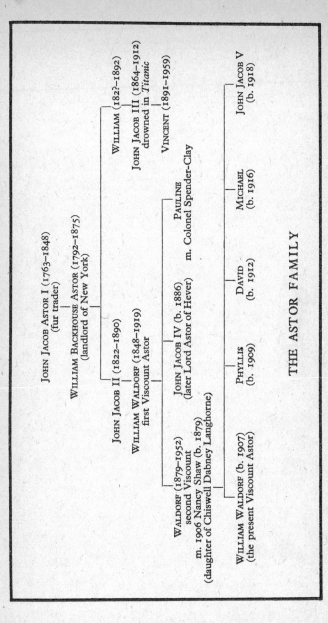

JOHN JACOB ASTOR I (1763–1848)
(fur trader)

WILLIAM BACKHOUSE ASTOR (1792–1875)
(landlord of New York)

JOHN JACOB II (1822–1890)

WILLIAM WALDORF (1848–1919)
first Viscount Astor

WALDORF (1879–1952)
second Viscount
m. 1906 Nancy Shaw (b. 1879)
(daughter of Chiswell Dabney Langhorne)

WILLIAM WALDORF (b. 1907)
(the present Viscount Astor)

PHYLLIS
(b. 1909)

DAVID
(b. 1912)

MICHAEL
(b. 1916)

JOHN JACOB IV (b. 1886)
(later Lord Astor of Hever)

PAULINE
m. Colonel Spender-Clay

JOHN JACOB V
(b. 1918)

WILLIAM (1822–1892)

JOHN JACOB III (1864–1912)
drowned in *Titanic*

VINCENT (1891–1959)

THE ASTOR FAMILY

Foreword

Lady Astor has been on the scene of this world for eighty years. For a great part of that long period she has been much in the public eye. Two countries have found her career astonishing; her native land America, where she lived from 1879, the year of her birth, until 1906 when she married the second Viscount Astor; and her husband's country England, the place of her chief activities. Her celebrity rests mainly on what she did between 1919, when she took her seat in the House of Commons (the first woman ever to do so) and 1945 when she retired from politics after representing Plymouth (Sutton Division) for over twenty-five years, the voters' choice in seven consecutive elections. Her compatriots became very proud of her; no other American woman had ever done the like. Supported in this way by two countries, she became an international figure.

In the pages which follow an attempt is made to explain how she managed to accomplish this. The various steps will be clear enough. It will appear, however, that it was less what she did than what she was that made her. She was an original. In Parliament she was not like the other women there; in society there was no other hostess of her sort. Among several characteristics peculiar to herself, which will appear as the narrative unfolds, she had two which particularly marked her off: she was a great wit, wonderfully droll and stimulating; and she had a great heart. These two qualities are seldom seen in conjunction; great wits tend in general to be hard and dry; women of heart are rarely noted for lightning repartee. The combination has the advantage that it takes the sting out of wit, without making it less forceful; and by purging the heart of over-sweetness gives it the more power. But while Lady

Astor's secret will be seen to lie here, her temperament is so spontaneous, natural and unexpected that it defies tight classification. There remains a mystery, for you cannot altogether explain an original personality.

This book is in no sense a full biography. But as far as it goes it is authentic. It rests on what Lady Astor has told me and what I have heard her say to others over a course of years. It also rests on material which her son, the present Viscount Astor, has allowed me to see and a quantity of information which he has given me. I have also benefited by talks with other members of her family, notably her son, David Astor, and her niece Mrs Lancaster, and also with her friend the Hon. Mrs Mildmay-White. The authenticity of the book, however, owes more to Lord Astor than to anyone else, for besides helping me with the documentation he read the typescript and made suggestions where he thought what I had written could be made more correct. I must also thank his secretary at Cliveden, Miss Thom, who was always ready to help, and Mr J. J. Astor's secretary at Plymouth, Miss Knight, who took a great deal of trouble on my behalf when I visited that town. I am particularly indebted to Miss Jones, Lady Astor's secretary, who made suggestions so valuable that without them I don't know how the book could have been written.

Maidenhead, July 1959   MAURICE COLLIS

CHAPTER 1

Beginnings in Virginia

To begin with, Lady Astor will have to be called Nancy Langhorne, for that was her name. Her father, Chiswell Dabney Langhorne, owned, as a young man, a large tobacco estate in Virginia, a slave plantation in the old style. The Virginian planters were not unlike the English landed gentry in their way of life. With the enfranchisement of their slaves after the Civil War the resemblance became closer. But the transition from slave to free labour was a painful experience.

The victory of the North ruined Langhorne. In the course of the war, at the age of twenty-two, he had married Nancy Witcher Keene, a girl of sixteen, belonging to a Virginian family of Irish extraction. Now he and his young wife, bereft of money, slaves and plantation, had to face the realities of a new era. He was a man of resilient character, able and amusing. Nevertheless, the difficulties which faced the Virginian gentry in this black period were so great that for the best part of fifteen years he lived a precarious existence. Of the various jobs he had, one was auctioneer of horses, another handyman in a hotel. It seems, however, that he was very lucky at cards. To say that he lived on his winnings would be to exaggerate. But recalling that time Lady Astor has said: 'He told us that after the Civil War he played poker and was so good at it that he thought people would get suspicious.'

His difficulties did not prevent him from raising a large family; there were to be eleven children altogether, though not all of them survived. His seventh child was born in 1879, and was christened Nancy Witcher after her mother. About the time of the birth of this daughter, destined to make history, Langhorne's fortunes began to mend. A certain General Douglas, whom he had known during the Civil War, came across him again. Their conversation is one of Lady Astor's favourite reminiscences. 'Douglas enquired how he was doing. My father replied "Not too well", and asked how Douglas was getting on. The general replied that he was a railway contractor, that prospects were good and there were openings. My father saw his chance and said: "I believe I'm just the man you want." "How so?" asked Douglas. "Because I know how to handle Negro labour."' Douglas took him on and he did so well that in a year or two he was able to get contracts himself. In addition to ability, he had charm; his daughter has declared that he never told the same story twice. He was a vivacious, cheerful, friendly fellow, but temperamental and irascible. By no means a teetotaller, his cellar was renowned, his mint juleps widely famous. All accounts agree that he was a personality of exceptional force. He not only recouped the losses sustained in the Civil War but his business acumen and energy were such that in a few years he made a considerable fortune.

In some ways his daughter Nancy was unlike him; she was steadier, more enduring, more master of herself, and much more fastidious. Nevertheless, in courage, humour and vitality she was his true daughter; and, indeed, developed these qualities further than he had, becoming yet more vital than he, more penetrating in her wit, and more courageous. These characteristics were the foundation of her success. But if they had not been augmented by another quality, they could not have carried her so far, a quality she inherited rather from her mother. This, as I have said, was her warmth of heart, a natural goodness, a sort of innocence and charity, a complete lack of pride and personal ambition, which even her bitterest opponents could not deny and which always blunted the attacks of those who sought to decry her.

Her upbringing was free and easy, her education sketchy. At the time of her birth her parents were living at

Danville, a Virginian town on the North Carolina border. When Langhorne had made some money, he moved from Danville to Richmond, the state capital, with his wife and children, among them five daughters; Elizabeth and Irene, the beauty of the family, were some years older than Nancy, Phyllis and Norah a little younger. It was not a strict household. The stories told of this period show Nancy to have been a high spirited tomboy, leading her younger sisters in frolics and escapades. The goat carriage she drove was long remembered in Richmond. One is reminded of a happy-go-lucky Irish family. But the Negro background gave the life a distinctive flavour. The black servants, nurses, retainers, gardeners, were both adoring and familiar, funny and touching. The child Nancy was a great favourite with them. Between her and her nurse, Liza Piatt, always called Aunt Liza, there was a close bond of feeling, which lasted through the years. Aunt Liza smoked a pipe, couldn't read or write, but knew the Bible, though she got the characters mixed. She kept her money in the knee of her stocking. Her stories were very droll and human. It was from her that the future Lady Astor got many of the Negro tales that amused her English guests and which she still tells, mimicking the smiles and accents of her old black friends. A resident of Richmond published some reminiscences in 1920. The following passage successfully evokes the atmosphere in which the Langhorne children were brought up. 'Among the Negroes was old blind Willie, who sold papers up and down the street. He would come tapping his stick and waiting at the crossings for a hand to guide him over. Nancy Langhorne with her friends would shout to him and he would answer, calling each of them by their name. To try him Nancy would sometimes keep silent, but he would turn his sightless face to where she stood and say: "I aint heerd my little mist'ess yit, but I know she thar," and point with his stick. Sometimes we would say: "No, Willie, that's Miss Phyllis." But he would shake his head and show his teeth. "Naw, child, you can't fool Willie. I knows Miss Nancy

13

from here to the Lee monymint." In the yard she gave him his dinner some days, and for thanks he'd sing: "The waters washed Peter to his Lord." Aunt Liza disapproved. "I don't see to save mah life," she would say, "what yo' and Miss Phyllis and dese here young ladies want to be foolin' roun'd dis low-lifeted nigger, gittin' anything fum scarlet fever to fleas, when yo' might be setten up genteel in your mah's parlor.'"

Aunt Liza liked to think she was very superior. There is a story about her which Lady Astor still tells. 'One day she went to Mother and asked for a pair of spectacles. Knowing her eyesight was perfect, Mother enquired why she wanted them. "For my little Liza," said she, for she was married and had a small daughter. "But there's nothing wrong with little Liza's eyes." "No, mam, but she sho' thinks they look stylish."'

The young Nancy Langhorne felt tenderly for these faithful simple people. The memory of rural Virginia remained with her vividly throughout her life. As we shall see, she loved to return there on visits from London with presents for the friends of her youth. Though so busy in the world, she never became worldly and would joke with and tease her old black nurse as she had always done. This attitude towards Virginian Negroes was typical of Virginians of good family.

Chiswell Langhorne continued to make money fast with his contracts. In 1892, when his daughter Nancy was just thirteen he decided to leave Richmond, and bought Mirador, a large estate with a roomy house built about 1820, its pillared porch, marble hall and curling staircase an adaptation of the Georgian. It was not far from Charlottesville, a town of 5,000 inhabitants (nearly half of them Negroes) ninety-six miles north-west of Richmond, and right in the middle of the peach country, a very pretty part of Virginia among the foot-hills of the Blue Ridge Mountains. His plan was, as soon as he had made enough, to give up his railway contracting, retire there and enjoy the life of a country gentleman, administering his estate, which included woods, and riding, shooting and fishing, the kind of life he had been accustomed to before the Civil War. Lady Astor says he declared at this time: 'Only Yanks and niggers work.' Soon after the move he did retire. By now he was quite a rich man. It is said that he was able to allow his daughters, when they came of age, as much as £3,000 a year each, a very handsome income sixty years ago.

The move greatly pleased his daughters, who were delighted to get deep into the countryside, for they were by inclination country girls, very fond of horses, jumping and games. By now they had learned to ride well and could manage difficult mounts, particularly Nancy and her sister Phyllis. But the move to Mirador was likely to limit them to what rural society the place afforded, and cut them off from the larger world, hardly what was wanted for girls nearly grown up. However, they did not think of that nor had their father great ambitions for them. They were happy. Lady Astor now looks back on Mirador as one might look back on the Golden Age. Her father was very hospitable. There was much entertaining. But her schooling remained rather perfunctory. It seems, however, that when she was about sixteen a teacher inspired her with a real respect and liking for books. She began to read privately, a course which for some independent and original minds is more fruitful than class-work. Before she grew up she had at least dipped into many of the English classics, sometimes moved by what she found, and her outlook widened by a glimpse of something beyond the round of tennis, horses, black servants and visits.

By this time her two elder sisters were grown up. An event now occurred which turned out to be the stepping stone between Mirador and the outer world, wherein all the sisters were destined to play a part. The second girl, Irene, was, as has been mentioned, very good-looking; indeed, she was reputed to be the most beautiful girl in Virginia. All five girls were pretty; the handsome Miss Langhornes was how they were generally referred to. But Irene far outshone them. Many suitors proposed and were refused. She was a gentle creature and in no haste to marry. However, in 1895, three years after they had moved to Mirador, she met Charles Dana Gibson, at that time twenty-eight years of age. He was already considered in New York, where he lived, the most brilliant graphic artist in the States. It seems that in Irene he found his ideal of feminine beauty. They were married that year. Inspired by her he created a type of American girl which greatly pleased his contemporaries. With the publication later of several books of drawings, in which his ideal girl, always rather like his wife or her sisters, figured in a variety of situations, amusing or sentimental, he achieved an international reputation. The term 'Gibson Girls' is still remembered today, though taste has changed so much that the modern critic would not allow that Gibson was more than a clever illustrator.

Irene's marriage to so celebrated an artist and her identification with his famous girl type lifted the Langhorne family out of Mirador, which, pleasant though they found it, was obscurity, and introduced them into metropolitan society.

At the time of the marriage Nancy was sixteen. At seventeen she was sent to a New York finishing school, Miss Brown's Academy, probably at her sister's suggestion, who planned to present her a year later in the distinguished circles where her husband moved. Though noted for her vivacity and repartee, quite remarkable for a girl of her age, she was wholly without feminine guile or artifice. To the New York young ladies at Miss Brown's she seemed a country cousin, raw and so lacking in sophistication as to be almost disconcerting. On her side she viewed these city girls with distaste, for she had nothing whatsoever in common with them. They seemed to her pretty and intriguing; they did not understand her humour or appreciate her sterling qualities. She became very unhappy and when her parents visited her asked them to remove her, which they did.

Before going home she stayed a while with her sister,

Mrs Gibson, but after a few months' experience of New York returned to Mirador. Life there moved peacefully and slowly as of old. Content with the affection of her parents, her young sisters and the Negro servants, she felt no urge to plan for a different future; nor had any presentiment that she was soon to plunge into the world and that a disagreeable experience was just under the horizon. On the contrary, she discovered a taste for social work, a taste which she hitherto had hardly shown except in her inclination to be kind to the Negroes, but which in later life was to become a dominant characteristic. She was inspired thereto by Mr Neve, the pastor at Mirador, who afterwards became Archdeacon of Virginia. A friendship developed between them, so deep that for forty years she corresponded with him regularly. Under his influence she began visiting regularly a home for cripples and old people, called the Sheltering Arms, and found that she could talk to them in such a way that her visits greatly enlivened them. Her manner was unlike that of the usual visitor to such institutions. It was both stimulating and from the heart; the cripple or old person found himself rallied and yet warmed with sympathy. While the patients were the better for her visits, she on her part felt the better, too. She was moved by their predicament and has said that she sensed for the first time the mystery of the inner strength or vision which sustained the unfortunate. Charity seemed to her to heal, not only the receiver, but the giver. She was made so very happy by this experience that the idea came to her at moments that she would like to be some sort of missionary.

This aspiration was present with her throughout her life. It is impossible to understand her eventful career without keeping it in mind.

At eighteen she went again to stay with her married sister in New York. Mrs Dana Gibson had by now two years' experience of being a famous artist's wife. She was able to introduce to a wide circle her strangely animated, strangely serious little sister (for Nancy was a tiny little

17

person). One day they went to a polo match. A rather striking young man was playing. When the game was over he came to speak to the Gibsons and was introduced as Robert Gould Shaw. He was a Bostonian of good family and very comfortably off. From the first he did not disguise his admiration for Nancy Langhorne. Speaking of that time, Lady Astor has said: 'I suppose I was flattered by his attentions. He was a popular young man; many women admired him. All of a sudden for him to choose me was an exciting experience for a young girl.' Nevertheless she was not sure that, pleasant though she found his company, she was really in love with him or could ever become so. Her family, however, thought the match a good one. When he proposed, she was persuaded to accept him and they became engaged. Yet, she was not easy in her mind. So much so that she broke off the engagement. But he was not discouraged. He pressed his suit and again they became engaged. His father, for whom she had a regard, for he was a distinguished old man, an amateur of the arts and with one of the best collections of old masters then in the States, begged her to fix a date for the wedding. 'You'll help him to settle down,' he told her. 'He needs somebody like you.' But her uneasiness persisted. What did his father mean by saying that she could help him to settle down? It seems that she half divined that something was being hidden from her. When her own father came to New York she talked it over with him. Sharing her uneasiness he went to old Mr Shaw to ask him frankly whether for any reason the marriage should not go through. Mr Shaw, of course, knew very well his son's weakness, but, believing the girl he loved would be able to steady him, declared there was nothing against the match. Langhorne felt reassured and reassured his daughter. She agreed to marry, persuading herself that she was really in love.

The wedding took place in October 1897. It was at Mirador, in the drawing-room. At that date in Virginia it was not unusual for girls to be married in their own homes. The honeymoon was at Hot Springs in the mountains. At the end of a week she became aware of some sort of incompatibility. She did not feel that she really knew her husband. Young for her age, she felt alarmed and suddenly very homesick. Shaw had to take her back to Mirador. However, she persevered and went with him to stay with his parents. It was there that she discovered what had been withheld: he was a heavy drinker. This was the failing his father hoped she would be able to cure. But she was far too young and inexperienced to grapple with such a situation. She did not know how to go about persuading a toper to reform. On the other hand, pride prevented her from admitting that she had made a grave mistake. She hung on, and lived with Shaw in Boston until a son was born. Then it began to seem past bearing. She went to old Mr Shaw and told him. He tried to reassure her. 'Leave it to me,' he said. 'Go home for six months and then come back. By that time I'll have persuaded him to reform.' But it was no good. At the end of the six months, when she returned, he was drinking as hard as ever. She could not stand it and left him. 'I don't know how I ever had the strength to do such a thing. I was only twenty, but just couldn't bear it.' That is how she once put it to me.

Three years elapsed before she sought a divorce. At first she thought a judicial separation would settle the matter. But she was strongly advised against this course; it would be the height of folly at her age not to be free to marry again. But the idea of a divorce was so distasteful that she would take no action until it was known that Shaw was living with another woman, whom she desired to marry. Then she instructed her lawyers to institute proceedings for a divorce on the plain ground of adultery. This disaster of her youth gave her a horror of drink which she never got over. Not only did she never drink herself ('there was no need to,' she once said to me, 'I was quite cheerful enough without'), but later on in England, as we shall see, she became an ardent temperance reformer, an activity which some people thought an eccentricity for a woman in her position, and others a great nuisance, but which, having its origin in the shock she suffered by the wreck of her marriage, was quite understandable. Indeed, there was no reason to complain, for her tilts at the drink trade, as will appear, gave her wit great scope and much enlivened the House of Commons.

When she left Shaw she had returned home with her baby son, Bobbie. Her mother, thinking a change would do her good, took her to Europe. They visited Paris and went on to London, where the Dana Gibsons were staying at the time. Mrs Gibson introduced her to Mrs J. J. Astor, the wife of one of the Astor millionaires, with another of whom she was destined in the near future to have so much to do. Mrs J. J. Astor took a fancy to her and asked her to stay. This friendship had an influence on the course which her life was to take.

Returning from the London tour at the end of 1901, she went back to Mirador. Of this period she has said: 'I took up the old life as if I had never been away, knocking around in a shabby old riding habit.' It was during 1902 that the divorce was decided on and it went through in February 1903. When her mother died, as happened soon afterwards, she took over all her duties and kept house for her father. This was the quietest and most uneventful period in her life. For all the plans she made, it seemed she might always stay at home. She was in close accord with her father. A passion for all things Virginian grew till she felt that she and Virginia were inseparable. But in 1904 her father said one day: 'How would you like a season's hunting in England?' Hunting was the amusement she liked best of all and she had become a noted rider to hounds. A season with the shires would be an exciting novelty. It was arranged she should go over with one of her sisters, taking with them nurses and children; her father would follow and join them at Christmas. She already had many friends in London, thanks to the stay she had made with Mrs J. J. Astor. Arriving there before the hunting began, she was soon in touch with these friends. They passed her on to other friends in the shires, who helped her find a house at Market Harborough, hire hunters and engage servants. When she rode with her sister to the first meet, she was already acquainted with members of the hunt. For so young and attractive an American woman to come all the way to Market Harborough and set up house without any menfolk attracted a good deal of attention. In this her début in English society she made a vivid impression by the boldness of her riding, her friendliness, the bite in her repartee and something untameable in her personality. She has often said since that she did not care much for the hunting set. She thought their ways fast and was not prepared to accept their familiarities. Nevertheless, in spite of this shrinking from what other girls might have found not disagreeable, she made enduring friends. She relates that she had several proposals of marriage, including one by a Russian Grand Duke, this not as flattering as it might have been, she says, because the gentleman warned her that she would have to take second place in his affections, as his heart was already the property of some woman. Another suitor, it appears, spoiled his chances by asking her to be sure, before accepting his offer, that she would be able to entertain his grand friends among royalty and in the higher nobility. That was not the way to talk to the Langhorne girls who, as Virginians, considered themselves socially superior to most and the equals of any. We should think of her at this time as very gay in manner, her retorts rather sharp, but with something that won you in her smile, and withal a vitality and dash so infectious that your spirits rose. The young Virginian of twenty-five had begun her conquest of Britain, though such an idea never entered her head. When she left for home at the end of the season, she promised to return for the next.

In the autumn of 1905, when on the way back to England, she met Waldorf Astor, who was on the same boat. He was the elder son of William Waldorf Astor, formerly American but now a British subject and reputed to be the richest man in the world. Waldorf Astor seems to have been immediately attracted and to have begun without delay to press his suit. It will make what is to follow easier to understand if we break the main story a moment and explain who the Astors were.

CHAPTER 2

The Astors

The Astors were originally Spaniards and their name then was Astorga. Early in the eighteenth century they emigrated to Germany, where they dropped the final 'ga' and became Astor. The family did not prosper there and by the second half of that century their head was a butcher in Waldorf, a village in Baden. He had three sons. The first left Waldorf for London, where he successfully made his way as a manufacturer of musical instruments, particularly flutes. The second emigrated to America. The third son, whose name was John Jacob Astor, followed the first to London in 1779, when he was sixteen years of age. He remained there for four years, learnt English and helped his brother to make flutes. Being vaguely aware of unusual capabilities, he felt that making flutes did not give him enough scope, and decided to take a gamble. Leaving the security of his brother's business, he boarded an emigrant ship and joined the other brother in America. It was 1783, the year England acknowledged the independence of the States. He had some flutes and other stock with him, which he sold, and used the money to get into the fur trade. It was a buyer's market because during the War of Independence the Indians had been unable to sell and had large stocks. In the course of the next twenty years John Jacob created the American Fur Company, whose agents pushed boldly into unexplored territory. He founded a settlement on the Pacific coast called Astoria, intended to be the emporium for all that region. Between 1805 and 1815 he acquired a fleet of merchant ships and carried his furs for sale to Europe, Russia and China, where prices were far higher than in the home market. Though already very rich, he was only at the beginning of his business career. He now took another gamble. His view was that New York, then a port of only 100,000 inhabitants, was bound to become a great city. He began buying the farm lands immediately outside it, land on which the present metropolis stands. Before his death in 1848, at the age of eighty-five, the value of this real estate had enormously increased. He was said to have acquired a fortune second only to the Rothschilds'.

The entire fortune descended to his son William Backhouse Astor, who was fifty-six years of age and for long had been associated with the business. William Backhouse devoted his life to the nurture and increase of the estate. On his death in 1875 it was five times as large as when he inherited it; he had become a multi-millionaire. An endearing glimpse of this early magnate is preserved in the following quotation from the American press of the 1870's: 'He had no social aspirations and did not plume himself on his wealth. Walking down Broadway one morning to his office, a dingy, ill-furnished and inconvenient counting-house at 85 Prince Street, he stepped into a puddle in the gutter and accidentally bespattered the boots of a man close behind. The man showed he was put out. Whereupon Mr Astor invited him into his office, which was close by, and taking up a blacking brush proceeded to polish the stranger's boots. During the brushing the stranger learned that he was in the Astor counting-house and that his boots were being polished by one of the richest men in the world. He was abashed, and begging Mr Astor to desist, left the premises in confusion.'

William Backhouse had two sons, John Jacob II and William. Two-thirds of his fortune went to the former. John Jacob II modelled himself on his father and with quiet assiduity consolidated the estate, continuing the policy of buying land on the periphery of New York city, and also building houses, said eventually to have numbered thousands. He is declared to have taken no holiday during the last seventeen years of his life. His interests were solely

24

concentrated on the business. He is described as modest, unassuming and unambitious. That 'he bore his prosperity with the utmost meekness' was said. It was not then the fashion for American millionaires to live in a showy way. Their houses were not like those of rich peers in England. They did not have butlers or French chefs; they did not drive out in extravagant equipages.

John Jacob, however, was generally held to be too self-effacing. He was popularly believed to have an income of a hundred million dollars, but only to spend on his household a miserly 750,000 per annum. But, of course, these figures are pure guesswork. His brother, William, who had inherited only the third of William Backhouse's estate, apparently lived in grander style; it was alleged, for instance, that he had a dinner service of solid gold. There is extant a photo of John Jacob II, which shows a big stoutish man with hanging Dundreary whiskers and a drooping moustache. A contemporary writer states: 'He is a very religious old gentleman. Last Sunday in church he wore a closely fitting black Prince Albert coat, black and white English checked trousers and pearl coloured kid gloves stitched in black. His collar stuck up at the sides of his face and his ample scarf was of pale blue silk. His wife was plainly dressed in grey bonnet and velvet wrap. The one evidence of their great wealth was the pair of very heavy ear-rings she wore, in the centre of each a ruby the size of a hazel nut and around it four diamonds of half that size. At the appointed time Mr Astor left his seat and handed round the collection plate.'

This is what the Astors looked like in the third generation of the dynasty, in marked contrast to Chiswell Langhorne at Mirador. In 1883, seven years before his death, John Jacob II handed over the whole of his vast fortune to his only son, William Waldorf, reserving for himself a pension of only 100,000 a year. He took this course because he wanted to avoid a will which would have led to a public disclosure of the exact amount of his money.

William Waldorf, destined to be the first Viscount Astor,

was very unlike his father. He struck out an entirely new line. Had he not done so, there would have been no Astor family in England and Nancy Langhorne's life would have been cast in a different mould.

In 1905, when she first met his son Waldorf Astor, William Waldorf was fifty-seven years of age, had been resident in England for fifteen years and a British subject for six. A book called *Silhouettes*, which he wrote in 1917 and had privately printed, throws some light on why he left America. In 1871, when aged twenty-three, he was taken by his father, John Jacob II, into the family business, the idea being that, as in due course the estate would be handed over to him entire, he should devote his life, as his father and grandfather had done, to increasing it, a sufficient ambition, it was thought, for anyone, as it was a record fortune. Though ready enough to preserve and enlarge his heritage, he was the first Astor with the ambition to use his money so as to live a larger life, both more magnificent and more cultivated than his forebears'. His education had something to do with this resolve. In the sixties his father had taken him on an extended tour through Italy. It awakened his interest in classical art; and what he observed in Europe told him there were many ways in which a rich man could play a part in public affairs that would redound to the reputation of himself and his family. Nevertheless, for several years he worked dutifully in the office, his father deputing to him an increasing share of power, responsibility and income. Not until 1877, when he was twenty-nine years old, did he startle him by saying he wished to stand for election to the New York Assembly. Recording this in *Silhouettes* he says: 'My father made no objection, although regarding this escapade with misgiving as a departure from family usage.' He was elected and was an active promoter of several small measures. His greatest success, he records, was in making it imperative to sell poison only in blue bottles. Next year, when aged thirty, he married Miss Mary Paul of Philadelphia. The year after, 1879, he stood for Congress but though he spent a great deal of money failed to get in. The manner in which he handled the election seems to have offended opinion in some quarters and he was severely criticised in the press for seeking to buy votes. This public disfavour upset him and he began to conceive a distaste for the American scene. In *Silhouettes* he says: 'In September 1880 it occurred to me we should do far better in another land. The idea grew and I suggested it to my father. We occasionally discussed it as the English plan. But he said he was too old for so vast a scheme.'

Two years later, however, an appointment came his way, which took him out of politics and out of America for the time being. The government made him Envoy Extraordinary and Minister Plenipotentiary in Rome. The appointment suited him. The work was not heavy and he had leisure to renew his study of archaeology and art, in which he had remained interested since the Italian visit of his teens. He dazzled the Romans by the lavishness of his entertainments. No previous Minister had ever spent half as much. His residence was in the Palazzo Rospigliosi and comprised a huge ballroom and seven reception rooms. He became, though still only in his thirties, a princely dilettante, filling his house with classical antiquities and even finding time to write *Valentino*, an historical novel about the Borgias. His appointment came to an end in 1886, when he returned home. After the brilliant round of the Eternal City, the New York of the eighties seemed intolerably dull. Nor was he able to impress himself favourably on the public. The press remained hostile. Though his novel went into four editions he was sneered at for having written it. In *Silhouettes* he has: 'We were too prosperous, were a closed corporation, we were exclusive, not hail-fellow-well-met. The English plan became a settled resolve.' His father, however, could not face such an upheaval; and not until he died in 1890 did his son put the plan into operation.

His departure, when it was known to be a permanent move, exposed him again to unfavourable comment. One paper said: 'What are we to suppose Mr Astor wants? Not luxury, not varied pleasures, not ordinary social recognition. More likely he wants distinction. There was no career for him in this country. He would probably not have succeeded in political life. Could he have got into the Senate, could he have been Mayor? Everybody knows he could not.' But though it was understood why he went, the public disliked the idea of 'the landlord of New York, the greatest Nabob, not only in America but probably in the whole world', as the press put it, spending his fortune in England. The younger branch of the family was still in New York. It will be recalled that his grandfather, William Backhouse, had two sons, the second, William, inheriting a third of the estate. This William and William's son, John Jacob III, whose fortune had grown till it approximated to William Waldorf's, were now the American Astors, the real Astors in their opinion. The identity of Mrs J. J. Astor, with whom Nancy Shaw had made friends, will now be clear. She was the wife of John Jacob III, first cousin of William Waldorf. Her mother-in-law, Mrs William Astor, acknowledged leader of New York society, was inclined to sniff at her nephew's abandonment of his native land. She accused him of wanting to hobnob with the English aristocracy. When the news came that soon after his arrival in London he had bought Lansdowne House, she was reported to have said that this was too ostentatious, the Astors had always been a quiet family, and that, if she visited London, she would not call on him there. (It is interesting to remark that even at this early date unfriendly American journalists were surmising that he was after a peerage.)

But the purchase of Lansdowne House was a small thing compared with what followed. In 1893, three years after his arrival, he bought Cliveden, a palatial residence in a great park, a noted beauty spot on the Thames near Maidenhead, paying the Duke of Westminster, as was said, a million and a quarter dollars. Later, he bought a ruined medieval castle, called Hever Castle, near Tonbridge, which he renovated, particularly its gate, draw-bridge and moat, outside which he built a Tudor village, where he quartered his guests. A degree of eccentricity was remarked in his dealings with them, for it was credibly reported that at night he pulled up the drawbridge and secluded himself from them within his moat. In London he had two residences, one at 18 Carlton House Terrace and another on the Victoria Embankment, a Tudor-style building which served him both as a private house and an office. He built it himself at an expense of over a million dollars. It has been described as more a fortress than a house, having the ground-floor windows heavily barred, and only one door, a portal of the kind one sees in Italian renaissance palazzos. The interior was lavishly decorated by the leading English painters and sculptors of the nineties. But the oak beams, mahogany panels, carvings, painted ceilings, frescoes and statues were not the only things which distinguished this gorgeous interior. A writer in a Plymouth newspaper thus describes what he saw: 'I went over the building a couple of years ago and my recollection is of a theatrical sumptuousness. It was excessively grand with stone carvings, ebony pillars, carpets that allowed no sound of a footfall and heavy doors through which no sound could penetrate. By touching an invisible spring on his desk Mr Astor could shut and fasten every door in the building, not only the hall door, but of every room, so that whoever was inside at the moment was shut in a box and unable to get out till the spring was released, a very unpleasant position to be in and one arguing a not very happy condition of mind in the person making use of such an invention, but typical of the whole atmosphere of the building. It was said that Mr Astor was afraid of assassination.'

As this story showed William Waldorf so very eccentric, I asked Mr Lee, who has been butler at Cliveden for over forty years, whether it was true. He said that on the occasions he had been to the house on the embankment he had only been able to observe this much: 'The room doors had no handles inside. If you shut a door, it locked and you could not get out. But guests were told of this and shown a secret panel and how to slide it back. Inside the panel was a button, by pressing which you could open the door. But whether there was an additional mechanism by which, if open, the doors could be shut by a contrivance on Mr Astor's desk, I couldn't say. The house was certainly a queer one. The first Viscount (for so, of course, Mr Lee referred to William Waldorf) seems to have been afraid for his life. Two revolvers always lay by his bedside.'

Mr Lee, however, was at pains to insist that William Waldorf, despite such instances of eccentric depression, was a good-hearted man. He said: 'His butler, Mr Pooley, after being with him for a long time took to drink. At last his lordship could stand it no longer. He sent for Mr Pooley. "Pooley," he said, "you will have to go. But you have served me for thirteen years. Here is something for you," and he handed him a banknote. When Mr Pooley was out of the room and looked at the note, he saw it was for £1,000. That night he went the round of the public houses, showing it with pride, as well he might.' William Waldorf's generosity was widely known; he built and endowed the Children's Clinic at Great Ormond Street Hospital, for instance. But he does not seem to have had the knack of making himself entirely agreeable in society. Had his wife lived, things might have been different, but she died, to his great grief, in 1894, soon after the purchase of Cliveden. He never married again. Lady Astor has told me that he did not receive his guests himself but left that duty to one of his secretaries. 'It has always seemed extraordinary to me', she added, 'that ministers of the Crown and peers of the realm should in such circumstances have accepted his invitations. I suppose it was the lure of his prodigious wealth and the sumptuousness of his entertainments. Inside the family he was kind.' As we shall shortly see, he was very liberal to her. His is a puzzling case. He left the States because he had become unpopular there. He aspired to make a big name in England and was most anxious to gain the friendship of the great families. But he made mistakes which harmed him and may have contributed to his becoming a nervous recluse. As an example of the sort of solecism of which he was guilty I have quoted Lady Astor's testimony. She has also confirmed that two stories, reported with disapproval in the American press, were substantially true. The first was that to celebrate the opening of his extraordinary house on the Victoria Embankment he gave a grand party. But at 11 p.m. when the guests were dancing in expectation of dancing out the night, he suddenly appeared, an imposing figure, for he was six foot four, and saying their carriages were at the door, announced that he was going to bed. As great a *faux pas* occurred at another of his evening receptions. Lord X and his wife brought with them the Commander of the Royal Yacht, who had himself not received an invitation, a liberty on their part more usual now perhaps than then, though considered quite permissible. Informed of the Commander's presence, Mr Astor went up to him and desired him to leave. Lord X and his wife indignantly left with him. That Astor caused to be published next day in the newspapers a statement that the Commander of the Royal Yacht had come to his house without an invitation, made matters worse still. As it was wholly against his policy and interest to be offensive to the English nobility and their friends, one can only suppose him a little unbalanced, and on occasion blind to the impression he was making. Yet, normally, his manner was polite and quiet. He had a great love of music; his collection of objects of art was remarkable.

Such was the gifted but strange character of the father of the young Waldorf Astor whom Nancy Shaw met on board ship in 1905 on her way to a second season's hunting in the shires. But Waldorf was as different a man from William Waldorf, as William Waldorf was from his father, John Jacob II. At the time they met he was twenty-six years of age, exactly the same age as she, for both were born on 19 May 1879. He had been brought up entirely as an Englishman. At Eton he was Captain of the Boats; at Oxford he represented the University at polo. Though very much of an outdoor man, he did not neglect his books and had taken an honours degree in history. He was by nature a person of liberal views and had an earnest strictness of character, which made him a reformer by inclination, though his interest in social problems was slight at this time. Since the age of eleven he had been in England and, growing up the heir of fabulous wealth, was on easy terms with both the British and foreign nobility. He hunted and fished with them and stayed at their country houses, or abroad in their castles. Among his friends on the continent was Princess Marie of Rumania, later Queen of that country, a granddaughter of Queen Victoria. She found his manners charming, for, oddly enough, this wealthy sportsman, beginning to be concerned for the betterment of the working classes, had some of the qualities of a courtier. A genuine and eminently sensible young man, he was the right person for Nancy Shaw to marry. During the hunting season of 1905–6 he continued his addresses and at the end of it she accepted him. For the reason alone that he was the elder son of a multi-millionaire, it was a wonderful match. But that was not what weighed with her. It can most truly be said that she married him for himself, not for his money. There was some doubt at first how his father would view the engagement. William Waldorf had not concealed the hope that his daughter-in-law would belong to the English peerage. That his son had instead chosen a girl from America, the country which he had been glad to leave, was thought unlikely to please him, particularly as her first marriage had ended in divorce. He was wintering at Sorrento on the Bay of Naples, where he had bought a villa. Thither the two went to break the news to him. He was very amiable, however, seemed to take at once to his son's bride, and said: 'If she is good enough for you, Waldorf, she will be good enough for me.'

They were married in May 1906. William Waldorf made splendid provision. To begin with, he gave them Cliveden and several millions to maintain themselves there. As a personal wedding present for his daughter-in-law, he gave her the Sanci diamond. This was a stone with a long history. Though historians are not entirely agreed about it, the first mention of it appears to have been in the fourteenth century when it belonged to Charles the Bold of Burgundy, who got it from Constantinople. In the sixteenth century it was owned by the Baron de Sanci, from whom it took its name. James I and Charles I had it and the latter's Queen sold it in France after her husband's execution. Mazarin owned it and it was worn by Louis XIV at his coronation. Later it passed into the possession of the Demidov family in Russia. How and for what sum William Waldorf bought it, I have not heard. In size and water it has been compared to some of the great diamonds in the regalia. Mr Lee, the butler, has related to me an amusing story of how it was once lost. 'There was a ball one night. Mrs Phipps, her ladyship's sister Nora, was lent the Sanci for the evening. It hung as a pendant from a gold necklace and was as large as the last joint of the thumb. In the early hours of the morning, while dancing was in full swing, word went round that the Sanci was missing. Mrs Phipps could only say that suddenly she was aware it was no longer round her neck. Her ladyship immediately sent for me. "Lee," she said, "the Sanci is lost. Have the staff searched." I thought this high-handed and said: "What use would such a great diamond be to any of us? We could never dispose of it. If anyone has taken it, more likely a guest." "My guests are not thieves," said her ladyship sharply. "Nor are the members of your staff," said I. It was no harm with her ladyship to answer like that. She replied: "Well, look for it, find it." A search was made, as well as we could manage with the ball in progress, but without success. After the guests left at two a.m. the search was renewed with no better luck. We went to bed very depressed. However, at daylight, when the maids were sweeping the rooms, the Sanci, necklace and all, was found below a flap of loose

33

carpet. There was great relief in the household. Each one of us had felt under suspicion.'

Mr Lee has a gift for vivid reminiscence, as the above shows and will others to follow. Though a treasure of a butler, as his mistress has testified, he is not altogether typical of the profession, as it is generally presented in books. As much a countryman as a townsman, he is as handy outdoors as in his pantry. While his manner could not be more correct, he is an independent sort of Englishman with something of the old soldier about him. The parties at Cliveden would not be so enjoyable, were he not there.

The marriage of Nancy Shaw to Waldorf Astor was the decisive event of her life. Allied to him, a social and political career, congenial and suited to her gifts, gradually unfolded before her. The years 1906 to 1919 were her formative period. During those fourteen years she became one of the leading hostesses of England, with a wide acquaintance among the governing class and some devoted friends. Her personality greatly developed. She always had assurance, wit and gaiety; now these qualities won her an increasing admiration. She brought into the world four more sons and one daughter. And, through identifying herself with her husband's career and helping him all she could, she acquired a practical knowledge of English politics and learnt how to speak in public, developing a telling style which was entirely hers. Great though her natural gifts were, she could not in 1919 have launched out successfully on her own career without the experience of these fourteen years.

CHAPTER 3

The Early Cliveden Period (1906–1919)

Cliveden is mid-Victorian; the Duke of Sutherland employed Sir Charles Barry, architect of the Houses of Parliament, to build it in 1850. He modelled it on the Villa Albano in Rome. Two previous houses had stood on the site, a picturesque wooded ridge, some two hundred feet above the Thames on the eastern or Buckinghamshire side before the river reaches Maidenhead bridge. The original house was built in 1666 by George Villiers, second Duke of Buckingham, son of Charles I's favourite. An even more notorious profligate than his father, enormously wealthy and a great patron of the arts, he made Cliveden a place of romance, when he eloped in 1668 with the Countess of Shrewsbury and brought her to live with him there. The Earl had pursued them with fatal consequence to himself, for on catching them up outside London, he fought a rapier duel with the Duke and was run through. (A flowerbed at Cliveden, where plants form a sword and the date, still commemorates the duel, made more thrilling in that the Countess of Shrewsbury, disguised as a page-boy, is said to have held the Duke's horse and seen her husband fall. Incidentally, this flowerbed has misled visitors into thinking that the duel took place at that spot, a misconception, however, which only adds to the romantic aura of the great country seat, inside which hang contemporary portraits of the Duke and the Countess.)

After this dramatic opening the history of Cliveden is less absorbing. The next owner was the Earl of Orkney. It is a coincidence that he was Governor of Virginia from 1714 to 1737. From the latter date to 1751 Frederick, Prince of Wales, son of George II and father of George III, lived there. 'He carried state very high in some respects,' wrote Farington in his famous diary, 'never admitting any person of whatever rank to dine with Him and the Princess at Cliefdon House.' But he came to a sad end. A cricket ball hit him on the chest and so damaged him that he died soon after.

In 1795 this first house was burnt down and remained derelict till 1824 when bought by the Duke of Sutherland, who had it rebuilt. But soon afterwards this second house also was burnt. The mid-Victorian building, which Cliveden now is, was then put up. The only part of the original structure is the terrace and the basement opening off it. After passing through the hands of the Duke of Westminster, the house was bought in 1893, as already stated, by William Waldorf Astor. He redecorated the interior, following his taste for Rome and Italy by laying a mosaic floor in the great hall and having the ceiling of the dining-room painted by an artist imported from Italy with a pseudo-classical banquet of the gods. Some of his decorations were highly felicitous, as for instance the wainscoting in the dining-room, which came from Madame de Pompadour's hunting box at Asnières. He also bought in Paris some tapestries, once the property of the first Duke of Marlborough, which unknown to him at the time had hung in the original house, and been saved from the fire of 1795. Roman sculpture, huge wine jars and other classical antiquities were arranged in the hall. Some excellent sarcophagi of Roman and early Christian date were placed in the grounds; and a balustrade from the Borghese Gardens was erected below the terrace. Altogether he made a much better job of Cliveden than of his Victoria Embankment house.

When Mrs Waldorf Astor, as she should now be called, first saw the Cliveden interior, she was taken aback. A remark which she now often makes is: 'The Astors have no taste.' Cliveden did not look like a place you could call home, she said, and she set to work to brighten it up. She removed the mosaic floor of the hall and the pagan fresco

36

on the dining-room ceiling. She cleared out the statues and the wine jars, bought more French period furniture and put up curtains. But on the whole the interior remained substantially William Waldorf's creation.

The running of so huge a house was no light job and was an immediate test of her capacity. There were twenty indoor servants – six housemaids, two still-room maids, a chef with four scullery maids, a butler, a groom of the chambers, a valet, three footmen and an odd-job man for the fires and coals. 'But,' she has told me, 'though I had never had so large a staff and house before, and so many visitors, I found it easier than managing my father's house, Mirador, with coloured servants, over whom you had to stand for the smallest thing. There was all the difference in the world between them and English trained servants.' This recalled the following anecdote to her mind: 'I remember at Mirador the coloured butler coming in one day with the pancakes. There seemed very few in the dish, and as the butler passed him, my father slapped his pocket. It was full of pancakes.'

Mr Lee did not join the staff at Cliveden until six years later, but some of the amusing anecdotes which he has told me can be cited here, for they illustrate well enough how the house was run. 'At ten o'clock her ladyship would tell us how many guests there would be for luncheon. But that was by no means final, for whoever happened to ring up in the morning would be asked to lunch. We always had to cope with extra guests at the last moment. I remember on one occasion her ladyship saying there would be eight. "And Lee," she said, "don't make the table too big. No luncheon can be a success with the guests too spread out." I made arrangements accordingly. Her ladyship went out for the morning. At one o'clock, not only did the eight guests arrive, but sixteen others. The sixteen were the members of some women's organization and among them were well-known people like Mrs Lyttleton and Miss Tankerville. I phoned the chef: "There are sixteen extra people for lunch. Can you manage?" "How can I manage?"

said he. "The food won't go round." I said: "You've got eggs. Make omelettes. And salads with cold meat." He set to work. Her ladyship did not arrive back till a quarter past one. She was astounded to see so large a party. "I didn't ask you for today," she said to Miss Tankerville. "It was tomorrow you were to come." "No, it wasn't," returned Miss Tankerville, "it was today you said." "No, I didn't," said her ladyship. A set to of this sort always put her ladyship in good spirits. She said to me: "Can the cook do it, Lee?" "Give me ten minutes," I replied. Her ladyship took the twenty-four guests to the drawing-room, where laughing and teasing them she kept them amused. In ten minutes I announced: "Luncheon is served." It was an excellent lunch, with plenty for all. That sort of thing,' concluded Mr Lee, 'often happened.'

To picture the scene on a big occasion one has to remember that up till 1914 the butler and footmen in the great houses wore knee breeches and had powdered heads. The effect of these eighteenth-century costumes was enhanced at Cliveden by the Pompadour dining-room, which was exactly like a room in the Palace of Versailles.

Mr Lee went on to tell me that the luncheons and dinners grew larger and larger. 'Her ladyship,' he said, 'who always thought that spreading out guests interfered with conversation, had now a further reason for keeping them close together; she wanted to fit in greater numbers. The table, with all its extra leaves, would hold in comfort a known maximum. But her ladyship would invite more than that number and tell me to pack them in. "Get those smaller chairs. Eighteen inches per person is ample." I used to protest: "Your ladyship is squashing your guests. They can't enjoy themselves. And what's more, the footmen and I cannot get between them to offer the dishes." I had noticed, too, that sometimes rather than try to help themselves, they would refuse dishes. I remember Mr Winston Churchill saying to me crossly when I tried to offer him the pudding: "Take the damned stuff off. I can't move." But her ladyship was not convinced. At last, however, I persuaded her to send me to Buckingham Palace to make enquiries. There I was told that each guest had two feet six inches. Her ladyship then gave in.'

In case he should have suggested that Lady Astor was in any way difficult to work under, Mr Lee went on to say that her staff was devoted to her, never left, understood her perfectly, knew exactly how to take her and greatly enjoyed her abounding spirit. 'However,' he went on, 'it sometimes happened that her ladyship and I had little tiffs. I had to keep my end up. Indeed, she liked me to. One day, after I had said plainly what I thought, she declared roundly: "Really, Lee, you talk to me more like a husband than a butler!" And he went on: 'It was her spontaneous generosity which won you most. After getting into parliament in 1919, she said that I'd helped a lot at the election and gave me a cheque. I thanked her and said I'd always wanted a gold watch and would now be able to buy one. At that, she snatched the cheque away. "I'll give you a gold watch myself," said she. The watch she gave me had an inscription in it and also a gold chain, and was worth a good deal more than the cheque.'

That Mr Lee was altogether a devoted grateful friend was proved by the way he now took out of his pocket an old and tattered newspaper cutting. I read:

'During a discussion in the Commons last night on the evacuation question, Mr Sorenson (Socialist, Leyton) said one woman, who was sent to a big country house, returned home because she did not like the way the butler looked at her.

Mr Sorenson: I see the Hon. Lady (Lady Astor) laughs. Perhaps she is afraid of her butler, though I don't think she is afraid of anything.

Lady Astor: He is a treasure.'

'For a matter of fact there was one person whom her ladyship was afraid of,' Mr Lee now confided. 'Who was that?' said I. 'Queen Mary,' he said.

One of the first things Waldorf Astor did on moving into Cliveden was to found the Cliveden Stud. He possessed already a thoroughbred mare called Conjure and now purchased another called Popinjay. From these two mares and one other he bought a few years later, all the racehorses in the stud were to descend. It became one of the most famous studs in England. Between 1907 and 1950 his animals won 460½ races to the value of £487,570, and were placed second and third in 547 other races. The wins included such classic races as the Oaks, Two Thousand Guineas, One Thousand Guineas and St Leger. Neither he nor his wife ever betted. She did not greatly care for racing; 'I didn't like the racing set,' she has told me. I remember the head groom once saying to me: 'Her ladyship would have preferred hunters in the stalls.' But she enjoyed such brilliant social occasions as Ascot and the Derby. It was a great disappointment that her husband never won the Derby. 'Five times I have had to watch his horse come in second. After the fifth time, when we were driving home, he said to me: "Never mind. The great thing is the children are well."'

The two had no intention of living like the semi-recluse of Hever Castle and the Victoria Embankment. They began at once to have week-end parties. There were bedrooms for thirty guests. The names of all the people who have stayed at Cliveden from 1906 till today are inscribed, in their own autographs, in the Visitors Books, now piled on the writing table in the great hall. One time when Lady Astor and I were turning over their leaves, she said to me: 'What good company I used to keep in those days! When I first entered the House of Commons somebody said of me: "Is it that she's intelligent or just the company she has kept?" 'Yes, yes,' she went on, 'everyone was here. In my time I have been called the friend of the poor, though as you can see it was more as if I was the friend of the rich! But I was never a lion hunter. Yet the lions came.'

To start with, she invited the friends she already knew in England. She invited them because she liked them. She did not collect people. At this early time there was no thought of politics. She also invited her American friends when they came over. In this way, without planning it, she introduced Englishmen of standing to Americans and was the first English hostess to do so. Later she did it purposely to bring the two nations together. As we shall see, she became a link between England and America, firmly believing that the future peace and happiness of the world depended on the two countries keeping good friends. There were other American wives in great houses, such as May, Duchess of Roxburghe, Consuelo, Duchess of Marlborough, daughter of William Vanderbilt, and Consuelo, Duchess of Manchester. 'These women,' she told me, 'did not know Americans the way I did. They had been educated too much out of America, in Paris or the like. It did not occur to them at first to invite Americans. But every American of any standing who visited England stayed at Cliveden and met my English guests. I remember the Bishop of Virginia coming for a conference at Lambeth. I insisted on him wearing gaiters. "They won't listen to you in this country without gaiters," I told him. He got gaiters, but took them off afterwards.'

Some of the Cliveden visitors were royalty, like Prince Arthur of Connaught and his sister Princess Patricia, who were very close friends. Of him she once said to me: 'Prince Arthur was the greatest gentlemen I have ever met. His manner was quite perfect, so transparent and frank. His tone was exactly the same whomever he was talking to. When dining at Cliveden, which he often did, he would, if it was just a family dinner, offer his arm to Madame Fleury, my husband's old governess, a big stout old person, and take her in. His sister was a very intelligent woman. She asked me to call her Pat, but I never would. Never be rude to servants or familiar with royalty. That has always been one of my rules.'

Mr Lee once recalled for me his impression of royalty at Cliveden. I had asked whether they stayed the night. He said the Kings and Queens of England did not; as Windsor was so close, they lunched or dined. 'They were not

41

accompanied by any staff beyond the chauffeur and one detective. I remember how pleasant was King George V, but Queen Mary was stiff. Her ladyship was always very natural with royalty. She did not put on a special manner, though she paid them the proper deference. On their arrival she met them in the porch and curtsied. But once they were in the house she talked in a relaxed way and seemed just herself. Of course, she was such a wonderful conversationalist, and so lively, that the moment she entered a room all was laughter and fun. With royalty it was just the same; they were soon laughing and happy.'

Some time between 1906 and 1910 King Edward VII paid the Astors a visit. As it was the occasion of one of Nancy Astor's most famous *mots*, it has been described by several journalists of the period, whose accounts vary, though not in the wording of the *mot*, for there is a Nancy Astor folklore, which has grown round some of her doings, a folklore where the story rests on solid fact but the setting is less certain. I have a suspicion that Edward's visit is partly folklore. The story goes that he arrived with a party, which included several women of the set which surrounded him. He found Mrs Astor very amusing and by sitting apart with her in spirited conversation somewhat riled the court ladies, who felt left in the cold. Unable to bear it any longer, they dared murmur something about a game of bridge. The King was not disinclined, for he thought his new friend would partner him. But when he asked her to do so, she said she never played cards, and cried in a rallying tone: 'Why, I don't even know the difference between a king and a knave.'

This *mot* amused the world for years. It was still being repeated in the twenties.

Besides the British royal family, foreign royalty came. One of the more frequently at Cliveden was Princess Marie, wife of the Crown Prince of Rumania, who when her husband succeeded in 1914, became Queen. Her huge scrawl MARIE right across the page often catches the eye in the Visitors Books. An Englishwoman by birth, being the daughter of the Duke of Edinburgh, one of Victoria's sons, she was tall, handsome and strongly built, a good-hearted, affectionate woman, an old friend of Waldorf Astor; before he married he often stayed at the Rumanian court. Lady Astor talks of her in an amusing way. She will tell you: 'Marie of Rumania used to write to Waldorf every day at the time I first met him. I thought this too much on our honeymoon and I said I'd go home if it went on.' Lady Astor's stories are never to be taken *au pied de la lettre*. She tells them for the fun in them; they are not meant to be pressed too far. Actually, she never took Marie of Rumania over-seriously; she was far too clever for that. Though she had not much opinion of her, they became excellent friends.

Mr Lee, the butler, saw Queen Marie from a different angle. He said to me one day of her: 'When she came to Cliveden she was always accompanied by an equerry, who had the rank of Baron and was a very tall man. In the morning he used to station himself in full uniform at the foot of the staircase leading down to the hall and wait for her to descend, standing stiffly to attention, sometimes for as much as an hour. As soon as he saw his queen on the stairs, he bowed very low and as her feet touched the floor advanced and ceremoniously kissed her hand.' Sights such as this vividly brought home to Mr Lee that foreign royalty were treated with greater deference by their own subjects than ever used here. He cited a case which particularly impressed him later in the twenties when the Astors, besides Cliveden, had a London house in St James's Square. 'The Grand Duke Cyril and his Duchess were staying with her ladyship there,' he said, 'and one night, when she was out, were lent the house and the staff to give a dinner to the Russian nobility, refugees from the Bolshevik revolution, who were living in London. I was left in charge. I was much astonished by the servility of the White Russians, particularly as the Grand Duke Cyril, though legal heir to the throne, was only a refugee like themselves.

The Russian nobles cringed to him, only spoke when spoken to, and then to agree.'

I ventured to suggest that perhaps they were dependent on the Grand Duke's bounty, but Mr Lee preferred to think that they had been so drilled in court etiquette under the Tsars that it never occurred to them to moderate it.

The Cliveden Visitors Books show that Winston Churchill was one of the early guests. He first stayed there in May 1907, a year after the Nancy-Waldorf marriage. I asked her once what he was like at thirty-three, his then age. She replied: 'Not unlike what he is now, though he has mellowed. If seated next to a person he did not fancy, he would not utter a word. It is curious that he did not care for Americans at this date. Later they were so kind to him in the States when he was ill, that he became fond of them. His prejudices were very strong.' The fact is that Lady Astor never cared for him personally, though she does not deny him the great title of Saviour of his Country. As we shall see further on, they had many brushes in the Commons. I have heard her repeat with satisfaction an alleged *mot* by Leo Maxse, editor of the *National Review*, where he termed Churchill 'half alien and wholly undesirable'. But one has to insist that in quoting Lady Astor one is always in danger of taking too seriously what was chiefly intended only to amuse. Bores she has always hated, and her resolve has been never to be one, an aim which she has entirely realized.

Another early visitor at Cliveden was Curzon, who stayed there in 1909 after his Viceroyalty of India. Lady Astor once gave me her verdict on his career: 'He was always pompous, yet not always, for suddenly he could be like a boy. Though a big figure, he did not really know what was going on. His grievous disappointment near the end of his life, when the King summoned Baldwin instead of him to succeed Bonar Law as Prime Minister, was due to his being out of touch with realities.'

This view will be thought by many quite sound, for pompous people are seldom realists, but more entertaining, because very droll, will be found a story which Lady Astor often tells in which Curzon delivers a weighty judgment. It goes like this, as I have heard her tell it: 'Among the dinner guests at Cliveden one night were Asquith, Lord X and George Curzon. At the pudding course Lord X said to Curzon: "The Prime Minister's hand is resting on my wife's knee. What would you advise me to do?" Curzon gave the question his careful attention. "How long", he enquired judiciously, "has his hand been resting there?" "Since the soup," replied Lord X. "In that case," said Curzon, "let it rest."'

Personally, I prefer this story to any of hers; it has a drollery, so characteristic of her character, that it brings her more perfectly before you than any description. Her voice has a tone of deep relish for the comical and the absurd as she tells it. One is delighted by the richness of her humanity.

Another guest whose signature in the Visitors Book appears at this time was Dr Jameson, whose Raid was the precursor of the South African War. On my drawing her attention to his name one day a comical story came into her head. He and Hilaire Belloc were invited to dinner one night. Wanting to tease Belloc, she asked Jameson to pretend to be her husband. When Jameson was introduced to him under that name, he was easily taken in, as he had met neither. Lady Astor continues the story thus: 'I said the most dreadful and unkind things to Jameson, contradicting him flatly, correcting his manners and laughing at him. Belloc was deeply shocked that I should treat my husband so.' One feels that it did Belloc no harm to be made fun of.

Lady Astor is fond of this type of pleasantry. I remember her once introducing me to a couple she called by the fictitious title of Duke and Duchess of Brunswick. They were really the Prince and Princess Guirey, cousins of hers.

In point of fact she had been very good to Belloc. When his wife died she invited him to stay for a week with all his numerous children. Yet, on the whole she didn't care for

45

him much. 'He had two manias – against the Jews and against the rich,' she told me. 'I had to give him up in the end.' She admired his brains and held his learning in respect, for she has always been modest in the presence of intellect, being very conscious that she was not intellectual or well read herself. But Belloc lacked the kind of plain sense she liked, and he had not the unworldliness which meant so much to her and which, as we shall see, was the bond between her and some men of great personal qualities, brilliance of mind and even genius, whom she was very fond of, as they were of her. She had a yearning, something very intense, a longing almost desperate, for greatness and goodness; when she found these two qualities in a man, she was his friend. To get that close to Nancy Astor was not easy. You had to be as honest and unselfish as she, and you had to be as clever. A man like F. E. Smith (afterwards the first Lord Birkenhead) was very clever, but too worldly for her. Noticing his name in the 1912 list of visitors, I asked her about him. She made a reply, the substance of which, had it been made directly to that celebrated Lord Chancellor, he would no doubt have parried and returned in kind. 'I met him first at a dinner when I was still Mrs Shaw; it must have been during my 1904 hunting season. At that time he was only a Liverpool lawyer without much *savoir-faire*. His rise to fame and fortune quite rid him of his early diffidence. One day he arrived at a small house in Sandwich where we entertained informally, accompanied by a valet, and demanded champagne.'

Lord Kitchener stayed at Cliveden for Ascot week, 1911, just before being appointed British Agent in Egypt in succession to Cromer. He was already a Viscount and a Field-Marshal, and was aged sixty-two. The Ascot party was as grand as could be, for it included Lords Minto, Kerry, Salisbury, Cecil and the Duke of Roxburghe. Cliveden was at its best when five members of the old nobility and the most famous soldier of the age were the principal guests. I have no documentary evidence, yet feel sure there was nothing stiff or formal in the occasion, for the sufficient reason that Mrs Astor was the hostess and that indubitably her wit was playing over the company. When I asked her what memory remained with her of Kitchener, she said: 'Kitchener was an extraordinary man, grave and austere, but he had a weakness which was really comical. A well-known collector of *objets d'art*, he had picked things up in Africa, India, China. His method was simple and straightforward. When he saw anything he fancied, he praised it and expected the owner to give it to him. I knew this trait of his well, and when I saw him eyeing my things, I just said flatly "I won't give you anything".'

A much greater literary celebrity than Hilaire Belloc was Rudyard Kipling, who stayed two or three times at Cliveden during this period. He had received the Nobel Prize in 1907 when only forty-two. If his prose style was mannered, it was immensely vital and original, and seemed the reflection of an exuberant personality. But, in fact, he was not like that when you met him. Says Lady Astor: 'I found him dour. He was very poor company. He didn't seem able to take things lightly. And there was something laughable about him, though I know I shouldn't say it. He would sit on the sofa with his wife, an American, and before answering a question ask her opinion. As one couldn't get him away from her, it was impossible to do anything with him.'

The fact was that Kipling was too set in his outlook to be able to enjoy the kind of extempore conversational duet in which she excelled.

She attributed her success as a hostess partly to giving her guests a free hand. Her father-in-law, besides his habit of not receiving guests in person, went to the other extreme, she told me, and mapped out their day in detail, a programme which they could no more overstep than a busload of tourists on the continent today. Her method was the opposite. 'There was lots to do at Cliveden. My guests would go off and amuse themselves or talk to people they wanted to, or read, ride, walk, explore the grounds or play tennis. My rule was not to appear before lunch. I never interfered with them. That was how I got clever people like James Arthur Balfour to stay.' She had a great admiration for Balfour's intellect and character. He was the sort of man in whose presence she felt the need to be careful, aware of the deficiencies of her education, though one is bound to say that he is unlikely to have noticed this, for whatever the depth of her respect she did not abate the flow of her badinage.

Besides Kipling and Belloc, other celebrated literary figures of the day came for week-ends, but she does not seem to have cared for them much. Of James Barrie, for instance, she said: 'He got spoiled and lost all his homely Scotch ways after being taken up by the nobs. His cottage charm went and he became ridiculous.' This accusation of snobbery made her recall, what has been mentioned before, that Virginians thought so much of themselves that it never occurred to them to cultivate titles. 'It is impossible to be a snob', she said, 'if your opinion of yourself is as high as ours was. We used even to keep it dark in Boston or New York that we were from Virginia, because we didn't want to embarrass people.' She went on to point out the difference between snobbery and love of tradition. If to admire your ancestors or great figures of the past was snobbery, then John Buchan, a later visitor, was guilty. But 'the Scotch are often that kind of snob,' she summed up. Lytton Strachey seems to have been the only literary celebrity of this early period that she liked. 'He was nervous, but excellent company, so droll and lively.' When I said that his books, too, were excellent company, her expression became respectful. To her snobbery and also self-importance were bogus attitudes, and she detested the bogus. Thus, of a certain nobleman, she said disapprovingly: 'When he drove out, he expected people he passed to take off their hats to him.'

The only artist of reputation whose name appears among her visitors at this period is John Singer Sargent, the Anglo-American. In 1908, when the present Lord Astor was a baby, he painted her portrait, which hangs now in the great hall. A man of fifty-two, he was at the height of his fame and enormously admired. One day when we were looking at the portrait she said: 'His original idea was for me to carry baby Bill pick-a-back, but he couldn't make it fit and left Bill out. A very modest sort of man, there was nothing Bohemian about him but his beard. I remember him saying to me when he first came for the portrait: "You don't want me to paint you in black velvet and diamonds, I suppose?" the way rich hostesses in America like to be painted.' In the event he painted her as a fresh-air girl with her head thrown back as she skipped along, somewhat in the Lady Hamilton tradition. It is an animated impression with bold brushwork, but is not a serious interpretation of her character. She looks gay but insignificant. He did not see that she had qualities which would make her famous. If he had been a greater artist he would have had the intimation.

Of all the signatures in the Visitors Books the most arresting is that of the Archduke Franz Ferdinand of Austria, an extravagant flourish, with twirls like an old-fashioned legal hand, but less controlled. He, his consort and the Duchess of Hohenberg, with their staff of equerries, stayed at Cliveden on 25 May 1912, two years before they were murdered at Sarajevo and triggered off the long tale of wars and massacres and ruin from which the whole world has suffered till now. It seems that these Austrian magnates, though portents of doom, did not impress themselves on her memory, though today their signatures, when suddenly turned up on the page, are startling. She could remark of them only that the Duchess of Hohenberg was another of those royal ladies from abroad who admired her husband.

Many other interesting people stayed at Cliveden, but perhaps enough has been said for the moment to give a sample of them. They were drawn there by the charm of the place, the pleasure of meeting friends, and the opportunity of exchanging ideas, for as time went on the house became more and more a centre where ministers, M.P.s, reformers, and planners met for discussion. The young hostess, however, was the dominant attraction. Her extraordinary power of amusing and enlivening increased as she grew in assurance. Besides her extempore wit and banter, she had a stock of stories, some of them, as mentioned further back, about the Negroes of Virginia, a type of anecdote new in English circles and which she told to perfection, for her imitation of their mannerisms was so true that her face took on a Negro cast. One of her favourites, for she still tells it, and will sometimes ask excuse for its disreputability, has its scene in the kitchen at Mirador. The cook, an elderly stout woman who had once been a slave, saw one of the kitchen maids arrive very gaily dressed up and reprimanded her for coming to work in such clothes. The maid was in a happy and excited state. She smiled broadly. 'I have been ruined,' she explained.

It would be misleading to close this description of the early Cliveden period without emphasizing that celebrities and members of the peerage were by no means the only persons invited. One has to remember that the Astors at this time were young people. Both of them had a host of youthful friends, such as the debonair Grenfell brothers and Lord Winterton. These and cousins and other relatives formed the bulk of the week-end parties, which were lighthearted, gay occasions with fancy-dress dancing and charades of the traditional and family sort. Mixed in with these young friends were men and women whom Nancy Astor admired because of their worth. Lilian Barker, the social worker, was a person of this kind, a woman of superb character who later on became very well known in the sphere of prison reform. Thomas Jones was another, the son of a Welsh mining foreman, who eventually rose to be deputy secretary to the Cabinet. Anonymous American visitors have been already mentioned, people whom no other hostess of Mrs Astor's standing would have invited, and whose presence for that very reason was proof that hospitality at Cliveden was more genuine than at some fashionable gatherings elsewhere. Christian Scientists, who had nothing in common with other guests and were by temperament poor mixers, later were also to be met. And Nancy Astor could make a man as apparently without parts as J. J. Judge her close friend. He was the editor of the country newspaper, the *Western Independent*, in appearance a Victorian figure, modest and scholarly, but greatly valued because of his saintly character. That goodness was what she most valued should always be borne in mind. As her son, David, once said to me: 'She brought us up, not to admire celebrities, but people of worth, and to admire celebrities for their worth only.' In this book, which deals so much with Lady Astor as a wit and a public figure, little is said, and can be said, of her inner self. Yet to be oblivious of it is to risk misinterpreting some of her actions. Underneath her high spirits was a fervent aspiration which looked for support from others of like mind. Allied to this was an extreme fastidiousness, a physical shrinking which made her not a doctrinal but a natural puritan. Yet this severity was so completely transmuted by her humour, in the exercise of which she experienced intense enjoyment, that outside the circle of her close friends it was hardly suspected.

In 1908 Waldorf Astor's heart showed signs of strain. He had to give up polo and other strenuous exercise. The question was what to do instead. His father owned the *Pall Mall Gazette* and suggested that he take over the editorship. But his health was not good enough for office work of the sort. It then occurred to him that he might find a congenial opening in politics. With his thoughts turned that way, he consulted his friends, Balfour and Curzon. Though he was well known to be more of a liberal than the average Conservative M.P., they both thought that he would fit in well on the left wing of that party. In due course he received an invitation to contest Plymouth in the election of January 1910. Though unsuccessful, he won the seat in a second election at the end of the same year.

Nancy Astor took an enthusiastic and very practical interest in his election. With no ambition but the pleasure of helping him and seeing him make a name for himself in parliament, she threw herself into the two election campaigns. 'I loved every minute of them,' she recalls. 'I canvassed from door to door. I must have knocked on thirty thousand doors.' She tried her hand at public speaking, a thing she had never done in her life, and was surprised to find that she had a gift for it. The task was no easy one, because the constituency was working class and the voters had to be brought across. But getting on terms with people was her strong point. She soon became popular and was much admired both for her courage and tireless energy. After they had sampled her repartee, jokes and stories, they fell under her spell, as had her guests at Cliveden. It seemed extraordinary too, that a rich society hostess was able to rough it in the slums of Plymouth; stranger still that she appeared to enjoy it and was perfectly natural with everybody. Yet, it was not so strange when we bear her real character in mind. Striving to get her husband into parliament seemed a cause. It appealed both to the practical and serious side of her nature, and was a stimulating change from receiving guests at the door of her salon. That in working for her husband she was preparing the ground for herself never, of course, entered her head. But, in fact, without the experience she now gained and the friends she won at Plymouth, she could not, when the time came, have got into parliament herself.

In the year following these election campaigns of 1910 she began to feel unwell. Her daughter Phyllis (now the Countess of Ancaster) was born in 1909 and her son David (now editor of the *Observer*) in March 1912. Whether due to child-bearing or not, she had become by the latter date rather an invalid. She was attended by the best doctors, including the future Lord Dawson of Penn. Rest was prescribed; she had been doing too much. Having to lie down for long periods was a penance for a woman of her energy, but she submitted herself to this régime. Mr Lee, who shortly before had joined the Cliveden staff as footman, gave me the following description of her at this time: 'Her ladyship's suite of rooms upstairs consisted of a bedroom, dressing-room and bathroom. The bedroom windows looked towards the river, being over the terrace on the first floor. The furniture was heavy and included a massive four-poster with canopy. While taking the rest-cure prescribed by her doctors, her ladyship used to give dinner parties in her bedroom. Not large, only some six or seven guests. While she sat up in bed, the guests were at a table placed at the foot. We carried the food up on trays. The full courses were served, as if in the dining room. Her ladyship's health did not improve under medical treatment. Some time in 1913 she was attracted to Christian Science, and got in touch with an American woman, who converted her to it completely. She told her doctors that she did not want to see them any more. And sure enough she recovered and it was not long before she was her active self again.' Mr Lee added that henceforth throughout her life her health remained remarkably good. 'She got colds, of course. If she caught a cold, she would stay in that day and do her Christian Science reading, and next day, even if she had had a real running cold, she would be all right.' Her maid, Rose Harrison, confirmed this in her downright and amusing way. She said to me: 'Her ladyship tried to make me take up Christian Science and asked me to read the books. But I didn't. I'm a Protestant, and intend to remain so. In all the thirty years I have been with her, I have never seen anything that would convince me of its truth. I admit that she was never ill after she took it up. The only thing she ever had was a boil, and shingles not very bad, but then she is a very strong woman and Christian Science or not, she would have been well, I expect.'

To dismiss your doctors, and by prayer and meditation cure yourself, requires great strength of mind. As from childhood her strength of mind had always been remarkable, her conversion was in keeping with her character. Like everything she did, she practised Christian Science

53

with enthusiasm. All her children by Waldorf Astor were brought up in the creed, and him she converted some ten years later when, crippled by sciatica, he found that doctors could do nothing for him. The sciatica left him soon afterwards and for twenty years he remained in reasonably good health. 'But,' said Mr Lee, winding up the subject, 'I do not think that he had the same firm belief in Christian Science as had her ladyship.' Nevertheless, Lord Astor tells me, he refused to see a doctor in his last illness.

By 1913 the Astors had increased the number of their residences to four. They built what they called a country cottage a few miles out of Sandwich beside the golf course, a cottage which, in fact, was a large and well appointed house with fifteen bedrooms. It was a place to which they could retire when they wanted a rest or change of air. A town house, however, became a necessity, particularly after Waldorf Astor entered politics. Successfully evading his father's offer to give him his Carlton House Terrace residence, an unwieldy place, he bought No. 4 St James's Square, the house in the north-east corner which the public now knows as the headquarters of the Arts Council. Standing in the centre of the West End, it was well suited for entertaining the government and society. There was a large ballroom and two dining-rooms big enough to seat forty guests. Here the Astors held most of their grander functions. Some of the receptions there will be alluded to later. A house was wanted in Plymouth, too, and a smaller, though still ample, one was bought on the Hoe, where they stayed when visiting their constituency. Cliveden, however, remained the mother house, where close friends came for week-ends and confidential discussions on public affairs could take place in greater privacy than in London. Besides the extensive wooded park, the fruit and flower gardens were a great feature. There were forty gardeners, including the foresters. The head gardener, Mr Camm, noted for his love and knowledge of trees, also grew fruit and flowers with success. 'And,' said Mr Lee to me one day, 'he was very skilful at packing fruit. Quantities had to be sent to the London house and to Sandwich. The grapes when they arrived still had the bloom on them. And every day that her ladyship went to the Commons the spray of flowers she wore had been specially sent down.' None of the other houses could compete with Cliveden. It remained and still remains the family's principal seat.

With Waldorf Astor in the Commons, we find a group of young men, all under forty, coming frequently to stay at Cliveden. One of these was Philip Kerr, heir to the old Scottish title of Marquess of Lothian. He was a man of charm, talent, sound sense and warmth, remarkably unambitious, modest and frank – in short, the sort of person whom Lady Astor has always liked. Though nothing enlivened her more than an exchange of witticisms with clever men, she also enjoyed, perhaps more than the other, a quiet calm talk with men and women of feeling and honesty of purpose. Philip Kerr was such a man. 'He was the greatest influence in her life,' has been said by one who had opportunity over the years of closely observing them both. But he was not primarily a visitor at Cliveden because of such a friendship, but for the reason that he and his companions had ideas how the Empire should develop into a Commonwealth which accorded well with Waldorf Astor's liberalism. Another of the young men was Lionel Curtis, Fellow of All Souls, whose character was more that of scholar and theorist, and whose vision of the Empire, unified as a Commonwealth, leading the world towards universal peace, was the theme of the books he published. The first of them called *The Problem of the Commonwealth*, came out in 1916. Another of the group was Geoffrey Dawson, later editor of *The Times*; and a fourth was Lord Hampden's son, Robert Brand (now Lord Brand), who afterwards married Nancy Astor's sister, Phyllis. These men had served under Lord Milner in the South Africa which the Boer War had added to the Empire, and been inspired by that great Liberal statesman's views. They became experts in Commonwealth affairs. Their influence behind the scenes was personal in part and in part rested

55

on Chatham House, which they founded, and on their other foundation, the *Round Table* quarterly review. Waldorf Astor, as a member of parliament, was the link between them and the Commons. 'Their coming changed all our life,' Lady Astor has said. She herself did not attempt to participate in the frequent discussions which they had at Cliveden, but she was sympathetic and interested in their conclusions. She benefited by living in this atmosphere of debate, which enlarged her outlook and broadened the political education she began at Plymouth. Cliveden, from being a social and sporting centre, was thus acquiring a political status. Its connection with a progressive Commonwealth policy encouraged Waldorf Astor to think that he had something important to contribute to politics.

The work of Kerr and his friends was the germ out of which grew twenty years later the legend of the Cliveden Set, represented as a sinister and secret cabal which controlled the Foreign Office. This will be treated in its place.

M.P. at thirty-two, backed by great wealth and supported by a wife of original talents, who helped him to entertain the leading personalities of both Lords and Commons, Waldorf Astor was exceptionally well placed to rise quickly to ministerial office. The outbreak in 1914 of the First World War put an end for the moment to such hopes. His health disqualified him for active service and until 1917 he held a military staff post, with the rank of Major. In 1918, however, the Prime Minister, Lloyd George, made him his Parliamentary Secretary. The appointment put him right in the centre of affairs at Westminster. But his prospects were not as good as they looked, because two years before an event had occurred which undermined his position. His father, suddenly, without a word to him, accepted from Lloyd George a peerage which in the following year, 1917, was increased to a viscounty. The new Viscount was sixty-nine. He had, perhaps, another ten years of life. In ten years at most

Waldorf would succeed him as second Viscount. Already he was the Honourable Waldorf Astor. His career in the Commons was now bounded, not by his abilities, but by his father's span of life. He could not count on as long as ten years. Could he count even on five? His father's health was not good. Any day he might find himself banished to the Lords, no place for a liberal and a reformer. He was so disappointed that he began an acrimonious correspondence with his father, in which he accused him of ruining his career. His father might at least have consulted him first. But all had been done behind his back. If he did not want a peerage, what point was there in his father buying one in the evening of his life? His father replied that the ennobling of the Astor family was a fitting crown for its achievements in finance. The correspondence in any event was without point, since the creation had been made.

In fact, the first Viscount had only two more years of life. He died in 1919 and was buried at Cliveden in a gazebo by Leoni which he had converted into a chapel. His son, as second Viscount Astor, ceased immediately to be a member of the Commons. His Plymouth constituency had to elect a new representative. In this sudden and unexpected fashion the way was opened for Mrs (now Viscountess) Astor to enter on a public career.

CHAPTER 4

Lady Astor is elected M.P. in November 1919

Another circumstance accidentally favoured Lady Astor at this moment besides the death of the first Viscount and the elevation of her husband to the Lords. These could not have opened the road for her, had it not been that the enfranchisement of women had just taken place. The votes for women campaign dated back many years. It had entered on its violent period just before the war, the very time when she had been ordered to rest. Her sympathies were warmly with these champions of her sex, though she could join in few, if any, of their demonstrations. The heroism of women during the war hastened their enfranchisement. The dauntless stand, for instance, of Nurse Cavell before a German firing squad in October 1915, when she made the classic utterance: 'Patriotism is not enough', was found a stronger reason for granting women all the rights men enjoyed, than any yet put forward. In 1916 Lloyd George, who hitherto had been Minister of Munitions in the coalition government, became Prime Minister in succession to Asquith, who for long had held out against women's demands. The new government sponsored a bill which granted votes to women over thirty, who were householders or the wives of householders. This bill became law in February 1918. That same year a resolution moved by Lord Robert Cecil to permit women to sit in the House of Commons was carried. When therefore in 1919 it was put to Lady Astor that she should take advantage of the new rights granted to her sex and stand for parliament, she was being asked to do what no woman had ever done before and what for most women would still have been extremely difficult, but which by a happy coincidence of time suited her circumstances. A constituency was ready to her hand, Plymouth, which her husband had represented for nine years, and where both of them were very popular. He urged her to stand there if it could be arranged. But would the Conservative party adopt her as their candidate? Was it likely that the electors would agree to such a complete novelty as a woman representative? Certainly most unlikely in the ordinary way. But her case was quite out of the ordinary. Since her husband's election in 1910 she had worked devotedly among the people of Plymouth, establishing, for instance, maternity centres and crèches in the poorer parts of the town. Her private charity had also been unstinting. She had become very fond of Plymouth. It was flattering that she liked to call its citizens the descendants of Drake; that she liked to speak proudly of how the *Mayflower* had sailed thence to America; and she was continually praising the valour of its sailors, who in the late war had lived up to their great traditions. For all these reasons and for her personality, the Conservatives there were ready to break all precedent and adopt her, a woman, as their candidate.

When she knew that she had been accepted for Plymouth (Sutton division) in place of her husband, a rush of energy possessed her. It was as if suddenly she became more than herself. Her nature was not changed, but her powers, which hitherto she had only partly used, were offered free play. She felt the presence of reserves of strength on which she could draw when she fully extended herself. Her husband's horses ran second in the Derby five times; she was to run first the first time at Plymouth. As we follow her through the adventure, her personality emerges with startling clearness.

It has to be borne in mind, however, that her husband was indefatigable in the help he gave her. He acted as the head of her office, her chief-of-staff in the election campaign. She could rely on him for sound advice, for an orderly programme, for drafts of speeches and, when prudence demanded, a restraining hand. He was quite devoted and self-effacing. He focused the light on her, prompted her and then left her free to play the part, confident that she would rise brilliantly to the occasion, as, indeed, she did, for she was one of those pupils who soon surpass their teacher.

Polling day was 17 November 1919. The Astors were in Plymouth some weeks earlier, staying at their house on the Hoe. On 6 November she was asked what she thought of her chances of being elected and she said she thought they were rosy. 'And how do I judge they are rosy?' she cried. 'Why, don't I know the men, women and children of Plymouth and can't I tell whether they are pleased with me or not?' To the same interviewer she said that she was not going to bring her children forward during the election campaign. 'I do not think that they altogether approve,' she said laughing. 'One of my boys[1] wrote to me from his preparatory school today and he said I am really getting rather notorious, "but I don't mean criminal," he hastened to add.'

It was with this kind of breezy manner that she delighted the electors. The press on the same day reported that she was conducting her campaign with all the skill of an experienced electioneer, that her speeches were full of amusing stories and she was never at a loss when heckled. She was well known afterwards for just these qualities and evidently they must have come out at once. At one of her meetings a man asked a question about police arrests of women in the streets, and Lady Astor replied: 'I must tell you something awfully funny that happened to me in London the other day. I saw a young American sailor looking at the outside of the House of Commons. I said to him "Would you like to go in?" and he said "You're the sort of woman my mother warned me against." I went to Admiral Sims that night, and said to him: "Admiral, you

[1] The present Viscount Astor.

have one perfectly upright young man in the American Navy." '

As the days passed her supporters grew the more convinced that she would make an admirable representative. It was seen that she stood for independence and sanity, that she was neither the docile slave of the party machine nor too extreme a champion of women. She would back the government of Lloyd George but would reserve her right to speak her mind frankly on behalf of her constituents; and as the sole representative of women of England would speak for them sensibly.

It was actually on 4 November that she was formally adopted as candidate. Her first set speech was at a meeting at Plymouth's Masonic Hall, and there she immediately defined her position. It was a very unconventional speech: 'Although I am one of the most serious-minded women in England, I have got the sort of mirth of the British Tommy. I can laugh when I am going over the top. I do not believe in sexes or classes. It is the heart that really matters.' This claim was very true. She was always guided by what her feelings told her was right.

In the same speech, she said of her husband: 'I do not believe he has ever had such a shock in his life as when all of a sudden he realized he had to leave Plymouth. Well, I am used to shocks but it knocked me out for a week. Still he thinks I can do it and, as he said, he thinks he knows me better than anyone else, and I hope to goodness he does. Some people find it very difficult to get titles, but my poor husband finds it very difficult to get rid of his title.'

Lord Astor hoped to be able to persuade the Commons to pass a bill enabling peers to resign their titles, but the House threw the bill out.

Lady Astor went on: 'You will not expect long reasoned speeches from me, I hope, because if you expect 'em, you won't get 'em. I can't do it. It is not what I call my style.' Lord Astor provided her, when possible, with prepared speeches but, as will frequently appear, she soon lapsed into extempore talk, which everyone admitted was much more telling.

After repeating that though not a sex candidate, it would be her duty in the Commons to speak up for the unfortunates of her sex and for children, she alluded to the hospital which her husband had built on the Cliveden estate and given to the Canadian army. All through the war she had supervised it and made friends with the soldiers. She said now: 'Twenty-four thousand men passed through the Cliveden Hospital. I was among them all day long, so if my manners are like a sergeant major's you'll know the reason why. I had to say to them – get to work you scallywags and heroes. They like that.'

Many stories are told of her and the Canadian hospital; here is one of the best. Mr Lindsey, an American judge, was staying a weekend at Cliveden during the war and was invited on the Sunday afternoon to give a talk to the wounded. He did so, and when he sat down, the Labour leader, Jimmy Thomas, a man of head and excellent heart, great friend of both the Astors, and who often stayed at Cliveden or in a cottage they lent him on the estate, moved the vote of thanks. Nancy Astor then said: 'Well, boys, while we have Mr Thomas here, let's see if we can't persuade him to talk to us next Sunday.' He agreed and she asked what he would talk about. Thomas replied as a joke: 'How about my telling them what the Labour party, if it gets into power after the war, intends to do with the Cliveden estate?' The soldiers laughed, Nancy Astor laughed. But she wasn't going to let Jimmy Thomas get away with such a joke. 'That will be very interesting,' she said. 'I have always wanted to know that. My own suggestion is that you turn it into a boarding-house and make me the landlady; though in that case, Mr Thomas, you'll have to pay your board, a thing you've never done in the past.' The joke was on Mr Thomas. The meeting broke up in laughter and applause.

Speeches such as Lady Astor's Masonic Hall speech, so fresh and unusual, greatly pleased her audiences. No man soliciting their votes had ever used that tone. As the campaign continued, she maintained the high level of her badinage, yet avoided giving the impression that it was all a joke. In a character sketch of her in the press of this date, the writer says: 'Full credit may not be given to her deeper feelings by those who judge her superficially. Everyone knows her vivacity and sharp wit but with all her banter and superlatives she has a keen mind and a behind-the-scenes knowledge of politics. And if she rallies others, she will laugh at herself too, and has been heard, for instance, to tell the story of how one day at Cliveden, when showing a soldier her youthful portrait by Sargent, he said: "It must have been painted a long time ago, ma'am." ' The writer then cites another example of her humour. In a back street she took in her arms a crying baby, which immediately reached for her necklace. 'You see, the way to keep your children happy is to let 'em play with a rope of pearls,' she said to the working-class crowd.

There has been allusion further back to her aversion to wine and spirits, an aversion dating from her teens and which was much increased by her sad experiences with her first husband. As time went on her ardent nature drove her, not only to abstain herself, but to become an advocate of temperance for all. This was one of the convictions she shared with Waldorf Astor when she married him in 1906. Among the reforms he desired was greater control of the sale of drink. During the war the matter came up in a practical form. In 1915 Lloyd George, then Minister of Munitions, asked a committee to report how far making it more difficult to buy drink would increase factory output. Waldorf Astor was associated with that committee. Its report resulted in the Liquor Control Board. There was great indignation in the country at this interference with a man's right to his glass. But in face of the national danger the Board was reluctantly accepted as a part of the war effort. The temperance reformers however, saw it less as a war measure than as a step towards a permanently sober Britain. Total prohibition was in the air. In January 1919, ten months before Lady Astor contested Plymouth, it was adopted in the United States.

In view of her connection with liquor control, she was now obliged to state her policy in regard to it. If she identified herself at all closely with prohibition she would spoil her chances at the poll, for public opinion was against any such policy. On the other hand, she was too honest to try to conceal that she favoured some control of the liquor trade. The matter was brought to a head by a newspaper announcement that she was a prohibitionist. This produced a telegram from her to the chairman of the Plymouth Conservative party: 'I have neither been asked to stand as a pussyfoot candidate nor have I any intention of doing so. It seems to me I detect the claws of some other sort of envious cat in this misleading suggestion.' During the campaign she declared more explicitly that she wanted to see curbed the power of the drink trade. With sailor audiences, whose strong dislike of liquor regulations was notorious, she was courageously frank, saying bluntly that if they wanted more rum they shouldn't vote for her. But knowing that she was no narrow kill-joy, they didn't seem to mind. They liked her so much they couldn't believe she would do them any harm. The Trade itself remained calm; the distillers and brewers knew very well that she would not have the parliamentary support to be dangerous.

It was also necessary for her to define to the electors her general policy. A reporter managed to get this statement from her during the first day or so: 'What an alarming twist of fate to find oneself a candidate here! It's not the fight I'm afraid of, but the responsibility afterwards if you elect me. I can tell you this, though. There is not going to be any screaming in the House. Not that I'll be silent. But I'll be sensible. I'll plod along and stand up for British men and women.'

No one believed she was going to plod along. 'The House of Commons will be a vastly more interesting place if she enters it; she promises to impart new life into dead bones,' declared the *Ladies' Field*.

The feelings she aroused in Plymouth were sometimes those which only an idol of the populace can awaken. During some procession, it is reported, women and girls broke through the police cordon and surrounded her carriage to press her hands. Others in third-storey windows cheered and threw down flowers. She herself became as demonstrative as any, and, evidently in her element, waved and called up to the women above. She was in her forty-first year, a small trim woman, very neatly turned out, agile, with quick movements, sudden gestures, her expression mobile, now laughing, now admonishing, and all the time her wit flashing out. She had two opponents, Isaac Foot, the Liberal candidate, and W. T. Gay, a Labour party man, reputed to have been a pacifist in the war. 'Mr Gay represents the shirking classes, I represent the working classes,' she told an audience. 'If you can't get a fighting man, get a fighting woman.' Her *bons mots*, always impromptu and tossed off at random, now began to be called Astorisms. They made good copy and wherever she went she was dogged by the press. 'The reporters simply do for me. I can't enjoy myself,' she complained. One of the news-hounds wrote: 'I set out with her this morning, when she toured the constituency in a gaily decorated carriage and pair. Pressmen and photographers awaited her at every turn. When she came on them, she would cry: "Spare me!" or in mock distress: "To the rescue, men of Devon!" ' In the poorest quarters she had most applause. Her coachman was a picturesque countryman called Churchward, with a red face and the look of a Dickens character. He wore a rosette the size of a soup-plate in his buttonhole. 'He had appointed himself her master of ceremonies. On seeing a likely crowd at a corner, he pulls up the horses.' She used to speak from the carriage. Once when the heckling grew very hot, Churchward started remonstrating, 'Hush up, Churchward,' she called out, 'I'm making this speech, not you.'

Sometimes she feared that she was becoming too much of a joke. She is recorded as protesting: 'I promise you here and now that I will behave at Westminster in the most dignified way and not pull members' legs more often than necessary.' But it was her fun that was the great attraction. The *Evening Standard* has: 'Lady Astor is laughing her way into parliament.' Her meetings were crammed, even in the afternoon, and crammed with women, most unusual for political meetings. Her voice carried to the furthest corners. (I remember her once saying to me: 'My voice is not beautiful, but everyone can hear it. If your audience hears distinctly what you say, you'll convince them better than the best arguments they can't hear.')

The Astorisms came thick and fast: 'I'm no orator and don't want to be – I've heard too many fine phrases from the emptiest heads in Europe.' And when they said to her: 'You're too rich to get the working men's vote,' her reply was: 'You'll see. It won't be the 17,000 millionaires living on the Hoe who will elect me.'

At the end of the first week she was known throughout the constituency as Our Nancy. She told people that she thought this very impertinent. But they continued to call her Nancy to her face. It could not be otherwise, for they had taken her to their hearts, as she had taken them to hers. She had a wonderful flair for what would go. On 12 November a coal-heaver, his face as black as his hands, challenged her, yelling: 'What has your husband ever done for us?' 'Charlie, you old liar, you know quite well what he has done,' she said. Immediately afterwards she posed for a photograph with Charlie. On the 13th, when in the poorest part of the town, she stopped her carriage to speak to a group of women. One of them shouted: 'Why did you call me a virago once at a meeting?' 'I'll go down on my knees and apologize if I did,' said Lady Astor. 'Well, you did,' insisted the woman. (It was obvious to all that she was a virago.) 'Come, let's forgive each other,' said Lady A. 'You forgive me my sins and I'll forgive you yours.' 'I have got none,' said the woman. 'Got no sins!' cried Lady A. all astonishment. 'You are a lucky devil.' This verbal quip raised a merry laugh against the woman. But sometimes there would be a knockout punch. A young woman who had been asking question after question to try to catch her, enquired whether she favoured a reform of the divorce laws, evidently intending a sneering reference to Lady Astor's divorce of sixteen years before. This was too much. With a wonderfully simulated air of concern, Lady Astor replied: 'Madam, I am sorry to hear you are in trouble.' There was a great roar of derisive merriment. The paper recording the exchange adds: 'The woman paled and left the building, shocked and silent.'

But her wit was more often playful. She loved teasing her audience and somehow they got to like being teased; her drolleries were so much to their taste. One speech she wound up by saying: 'And now, my dears, I'm going back to one of my beautiful palaces to sit down in my tiara and do nothing and when I roll out in my car I will splash you all with mud and look the other way.' The applause was deafening, as it was when she said: 'Today I heard a thing they are saying about me and must tell you. "We know Lady Astor. She comes among us all smiles and then goes back to her big house and calls her maid: 'Have my gloves cleaned, I've shaken hands with a Tommy.'" '

Canvassing as gay as this was a great treat. Plymouth was not the only place amused by her. Her anecdotes and repartees were repeated in every newspaper in the United Kingdom and gave her a sudden and extraordinary celebrity. As a general rule the result of a by-election is the only fact reported. In this case everything she said and did was carefully gathered up. Americans, remembering she was one of them, followed her campaign with intense interest. Even the continental newspapers had articles.

Long before she was due to make a speech in a hall a long queue of men and women formed up, in contrast to the meagre crowd at the Liberal and Labour meetings. She became fond of her Liberal opponent, Isaac Foot, but never stopped ragging him. One day she said to him kindly: 'You really oughtn't to risk forfeiting your deposit and impoverishing your wife and children. Far better withdraw straight away.' There was the other occasion, too, when Foot intended to address his constituents in the market and arrived there a few minutes before she drove up with a similar intention. 'How dare you come here,' she cried when she saw him. He gave up all idea of making a speech and sat down contentedly to listen to hers.

Sometimes, far from dreading hecklers, she would incite the audience to ask questions. 'Come along now. Who'll take me on? I'm ready for you.' And she would explain to her supporters in an aside: 'It takes opponents to get me gingered up.' It was 'as good as a theatre', wrote the *Daily Chronicle*. Her energy was unbelievable. She spoke each day at three meetings in halls, generally visited a couple of institutions and held impromptu talks in the streets. Sometimes she was reported 'in a tart mood', when her sallies were more devastating than usual. On such days she amused herself by delivering admonitions, as, when passing a man driving a petrol tanker, she called out: 'Going to vote for me?' and then severely: 'If you don't put out that cigarette, you won't vote for anybody.'

She had a wonderful power of getting the crowd on her side. In what was headed 'A fiery passage', there is a description of how a man in her street audience began to abuse her. She turned her back on him and addressed herself to a group of women. 'I want every woman in this street to see that this man doesn't vote for me. I don't want the vote of a man who curses a woman when he is sober.' The unexpectedness of the last word was very telling.

She had a habit, when deploring the ills of the world, of pointing out that men could not escape blame for them, for hitherto they had been in sole charge of affairs. You could blame men for most things. Once when a large audience of women demanded irritably to know why they were packed into so small a room, her answer was: 'Because the meeting was arranged by men.' The way she stood up to men made people say: 'If she can do it here, she can do it in parliament.'

Many explanations were put forward to account for the

impression she made on all who saw and heard her. Some said it was because she looked so wholesome and genuine. 'She is just the same, whether in a ducal drawing-room or a Plymouth cottage.' It was not supposed that she thought a working man the equal of a duke, but she liked him just as much. Nor did she think a working man her social equal. She was not a Socialist. What was far more important, her heart warmed to any man, whatever his class, if he had qualities such as bravery, honesty, kindness and humanity. (In thinking of Lady Astor I am often reminded of Confucius as he is revealed in the Analects; to be a gentleman, he thought, was the greatest thing and anyone whose behaviour was determined by a love of goodness was a gentleman.)

On 9 November she entered on the second week of her campaign, and despite her prodigious activity was reported still to be as fresh as paint. The pressmen, though continually battered by her wit, were greatly enjoying themselves. Even when she declared, apparently enraged with them: 'I have a very good case, but the papers make fun of it; they would make fun of anything; they would make fun of the dead; they would do anything for fivepence,' they found it so much less boring than listening to Mr Gay. It is true that they did make fun of her. 'To judge by some newspaper reports,' said *The Times* reprovingly, 'she is treating the whole affair as a huge joke,' but admits that her natural vivacity may have misled the reporters. In point of fact, however, she had an excellent press. As soon as people got the hang of her humour, she was well understood, not only by the press, but, more important, by the people, as the event proved.

The Astorisms showed no signs of drying up. As they were always prompted by the occasion, they were always fresh. She did not repeat herself. 'Any man who has ever saved anything,' she told the socialists, 'is a capitalist.' People, who twitted her about palatial Cliveden, were asked: 'What is the use of a palace to me, if I haven't any time to sit in it?' Pointing her finger at Mr Gay's supporters, she pronounced: 'I don't say we are very civilized, because I don't think we are, but I am not prepared to hand over what civilization we have to the Labour party.' To a Mrs Simson, who told her that her face was pretty but that was all one could say for her, she gave this nice little slap: 'I'm sorry I can't return the compliment as an honest woman. Perhaps if I had been in politics a bit longer I could have managed it.' And the heckler who accused her of snobbery because she was a Viscountess, got this: 'I have noticed that snobbishness is not confined to dukes.'

While her discourse sparkled with these terse *mots*, her plain humour was no less appreciated. At a meeting in the sergeants' mess of the garrison artillery, she said: 'Where are the drummer boys? The first time I came here I gave fifty of them toothbrushes. When I saw some of them the next time, I said: 'You haven't used those toothbrushes. Look at your teeth!' They said: "Yes, we have. We polished our buttons with them." When I asked why they did this, they replied: "Because the sergeant looks at our buttons, but he doesn't look at our teeth." '

This bit of humour secured her the sergeants' votes.

She did not neglect the babies, though it is not on record that she went round kissing them. She always relied more on fun than sentiment. Her advice to working mothers to soothe their babies with ropes of pearls has been cited. There is also the anecdote that, finding a family of six small children waiting to welcome her, with their dog asleep in a bath, she tickled the youngest under the chin and called on him to state his political views.

It may have helped that dogs liked her. In one quarter of the town she made the acquaintance of a bulldog pup, which sat in a puddle under her carriage while she was addressing a crowd. The pup met her again in another part. He was now wearing round his neck the ribbon of the Conservative party. Recognizing her in the carriage, for the horses were walking, the pup followed and when she stopped crept under again, and again sat in a puddle. Its evident devotion was observed and convinced the crowd that she was a good woman.

As already remarked, the Americans followed her Plymouth campaign with excitement. How extraordinary that the girl they had known long ago as one of the beautiful Miss Langhornes of Virginia was standing for the British parliament! They were immensely proud that she was one of them and saw no reason to conceal their pride. Their press of November 1919 is full of such headings as: LADY ASTOR HAS VOTERS GASPING BY THE PEPNESS OF HER CAMPAIGN. LADY ASTOR BLASTS CRITICS WITH VOLLEY OF EPIGRAMS. The following description of her is typical: 'This brilliant woman, dressed all in black, driving through the streets behind the dashing team of sorrels, with silk-hatted coachman, his whip and the bridles of the horses adorned with red, white and blue ribands.' The spectacle of a rich peeress, not satisfied to enjoy her money and position, whose programme was to improve the condition of the lower classes, held all their attention. The Astorisms, described as 'cryptic punchy epigrams', were repeated from one end of the States to the other. An anecdote which particularly appealed to American taste had to do with an Irish heckler. At a lively meeting a man shouted at her: 'Go back to America.' 'Go back to Lancashire,' she retorted. 'You don't belong to Plymouth.' 'I'm an Irishman,' said he. 'I knew it,' she said. 'I knew you were an imported interrupter.' 'If I'd imported you,' said he, 'I'd drown myself in the sea.' 'More likely in drink,' said she. He replied that he was a teetotaller. Her reply silenced him: 'Well, go and have a drink today, it might sweeten you.'

But though the Americans were richly entertained by such stories of her ready wit, the force of her personality did not escape them. Her power of handling every sort of audience greatly impressed them. They observed that she did not set about convincing her hearers by a reasoned argument of the usual sort. She just said out what ought to be done. Her presence sufficed to entrance the crowd, which at her mere appearance underwent a change. Yet, conscious of her power, as she must have been, and surrounded by adulation, she kept her head and remained simple and direct (as indeed she remains to this day, for she had never assumed the air of an important person). Some of her American fans went further than this and credited her with power to influence Cabinet decisions. Had she not frequently entertained all the leading ministers of the Crown? The Prime Minister, Lloyd George, was on such close terms with her that it must be supposed he sought her advice. And the story was told how he would sit by the fire in the great hall at Cliveden and sing Welsh songs, while her sister, Nora Phipps, accompanied him on her ukukele. With such friends in high places, a brilliant career awaited her in the Commons. They saw her in due course a member of the Cabinet. If she was to be the first woman in parliament, might she not one day be the first Prime Minister? An American woman ruling England! Such were the delightful fancies that danced before some American eyes.

Fancies they were, total misconceptions. She was, as has been said, simple and unambitious. There was not a trace of the intriguer in her nature. She was far too independent to pull strings. Her nature was to blurt out what she thought right, whether what she said was in line with this policy or that. She herself had only one policy – to right wrongs. *Fiat justitia, ruat coelum!* She didn't care what anyone thought. It was a true saying that she was just the same with a duke or a cottager. She didn't bother what either said. She only really cared for what her conscience told her.

This was the sort of person whom the good people of Plymouth on 17 November 1919 decided should represent them at Westminster.

Let us take a last peep at her still canvassing on the morning of the election. Outside a polling booth she saw a woman holding a baby in long clothes. 'What shall I do with him, when I go in?' the woman asks the official at the door. 'I can't vote and hold him.' The official declined firmly to hold the baby. At this moment Lady Astor arrived. 'Give him to me,' she instantly directed. 'I've had six of my own.' The woman entered the booth and recorded her vote. That she voted against the lady who was holding her son and letting him pull at her rope of pearls, doesn't seem to me at all likely.

When the result of the poll was declared, Lady Astor's name was at the top. She received 14,495 votes. Mr Gay 9,292 and Mr Foot 4,139.

The Plymouth by-election was over. It was hard to remember that it was only a by-election. For an historical event had occurred. An agitation which had lasted for decades had been crowned with success. A woman had at last got into parliament. And so pleasantly, with laughter and fun.

CHAPTER 5

Lady Astor Takes Her Seat

After the results had been declared at the Town Hall, bluejackets and women dragged Lady Astor's carriage to the Conservative Club, from the balcony of which she made a brief speech, in which she pledged herself to the cause of women and children. And ended: 'I ought to feel sorry for Mr Foot and Mr Gay but I don't. The only man I feel sorry for is the poor old Viscount here.' He was standing with her on the balcony and certainly looked very tired, for it had been exhausting for him, particularly as he was beginning to suffer from sciatica. On the balcony, too, was their son and heir Bill (now the third Viscount), who was twelve years of age. Called on for a speech, he managed a few words. He was heard to say: 'I have seen you elect Daddy and now I have seen you elect Mother. I have to thank you very much for it.'

On the way home to Cliveden, they had to change trains at the London terminus. A big crowd of women was waiting on Paddington platform. Some of them were old fighters in the movement for women's rights, who ten years before had suffered arrest, been thrown into prison, gone on hunger strike and been forcibly fed. One of them, grim enough looking, it was said, came forward with some badge she had, and presented it, saying: 'It is the beginning of our era. I am glad I have suffered for this.' Anything genuine and deeply felt always touched Nancy Astor. She clasped the hands of the old creature, who with her companions felt the mysterious glow whose warmth so many men and women had felt, wounded in hospitals, poor in back streets, lords in great houses, Negroes among the Virginian fields. Yet, Lady Astor was so different from what they had thought the first woman to sit in parliament would be like. She was so rich, so elegant, petite and smiling, unmarked by struggle, nor hardened nor narrowed by it. Strange that such a woman should turn out to be their champion! Yet, having seen her face to face, they were satisfied that it was so. With Lady Astor, moments of tension or emotion were not infrequently relieved by comedy. At this moment, a man further back was heard shouting: '*I* never voted for you.' His appearance was so very unprepossessing, that when she replied: 'Thank Heaven for that,' everyone took the point and laughed heartily.

During this scene young Bill Astor got mixed up in the crowd. However, he was extracted in time to catch a train which took him back to his preparatory school, for it was the middle of term. His parents then made for Cliveden. As they drove up to the park, they could see bonfires blazing. At the gate was waiting a crowd of tenants and gardeners, who begged them to get out of the car and sit in an old victoria. To this vehicle the men yoked themselves and dragged it down the broad avenue to the house. It took a lot to tire Lady Astor, but she was dead tired now and immediately went to bed.

December 1st was the date fixed for her introduction in the Commons. She and the Viscount moved to their London house some days beforehand. The introduction of a new member was a ceremony with whose procedure she had to acquaint herself. Two sponsors also were required. It was pleasant when her friends, Lloyd George and Arthur Balfour, volunteered for this duty. Apart from friendship, the Premier was moved by the historic nature of the occasion. Lady Astor was not the first woman elected to Westminster, because the previous year an Irish constituency had returned the Countess Markiewicz (*née* Gore-Booth). But she refused to take the Oath of Allegiance. Lady Astor was to be the first woman actually to sit.

A minor matter to be settled, but one which intensely interested all women, was whether she should wear a hat.

The rule in the Commons was that an M.P. brought his hat with him, could wear it when he sat down, must wear it when he rose to catch the Speaker's eye, but could take it off if he liked when making his speech. Obviously a woman could not be continually putting on or taking off her hat. It would have to be ruled that while in the Chamber she either wore or did not wear one. The Speaker on being asked for a ruling, sensibly decided that Lady Astor could either wear a hat throughout the sitting or be bareheaded, as she pleased. She as sensibly elected to wear a hat.

On the afternoon of 1 December the Chamber was packed, as were all the galleries. When she arrived at the bar of the House shortly after 3 p.m., question time was in progress; Mr Devlin, the Irish member, was on his feet. She waited, chatting with her brother-in-law, Colonel Spender-Clay, in the ante-chamber below the bar. She was plainly dressed in black with a white fichu, white cuffs and white gloves, and wore a smallish black hat, somewhat Tudor in shape as was thought. Ten minutes passed in this way. The House is described as impatient to see the end of questions and the entry of the first lady member. When told they were nearly over, she took her stand at the bar again, with Lloyd George on her right and Balfour on her left. In a moment the Speaker, Mr Lowther, would signal to them to advance into the Chamber. Lloyd George was watching and as soon as the sign was given, stepped briskly forward, too briskly because the two others had not noticed and were left behind. Finding himself alone, he had to go back. All contemporary observers declare that he blushed. I find it hard to believe this of a man of his experience. Nevertheless, he must have shown some confusion, for members began to laugh, a laugh prophetic of the twenty-five years' laughter which Lady Astor was bringing to the House.

The three were now again in line, and stepped over the bar. Even so, the two men tended to go too fast and Lady Astor, with astonishing sang-froid, was seen at one point to stretch out her hands and draw them back level with her. Half-way up the floor she made her first bow to the Speaker, as by rule all three were bound to do. But Lloyd George did not, perhaps still confused by his false start. She was distinctly heard to prompt him: 'George, you forgot to bow.' At which Will Crooks, the Labour leader, shouted out in his cockney accent: 'George, you will be losing your job.' On reaching the Speaker's chair, the sponsors withdrew to their seats, their task of introduction at an end. It was now for the Speaker to carry on. Custom was that he remain seated. So, even though in this case the new member was a woman and a Viscountess, he did not get up to shake hands with her. There was some artificiality here, for he had often dined at her table and been flattered by the invitation. No doubt, however, he was right. To have scrambled to his feet, as if in a drawing-room, would have been comical. But Lady Astor was incapable of keeping up a masquerade for long. She had waited, advanced, made bows, shaken hands. Surely she could be natural again? We find her then pleasantly chatting to him. Among the hundreds whose eyes were glued on the scene, some afterwards testified that he seemed embarrassed, since the etiquette was for a new member, after shaking hands, to depart humbly to a seat. But if he was embarrassed, she chose not to notice it; her manner was easy, her eye bright. The Serjeant-at-Arms now showed her to a seat in the second row below the gangway on the Speaker's left, where she sat down, thereby completing the ceremony.

Beside her was Mr William Young, the Liberal member for Perth. He looked at her coldly, but she at once began to talk to him and soon gathered that he was a dyed-in-the-wool anti-feminist. 'When canvassing at Perth,' he said, 'I told them plainly that women had no business in parliament. Yet nine out of ten women on the register voted for me.' 'Ah,' she said sympathetically, 'but you were honest.'

This Astorism fits the American definition by being

77

cryptic and punchy. One perceives roughly what it means. Lady Astor pretends to make out a case for Mr Young, a stupid fellow, who had one quality only, his honesty. It was the same with the Perth women. Because of his one merit, they overlooked his being so dense. But one should not try to dissect Astorisms. When pronounced by Lady Astor they struck right in. People realized something had been done to them, but were not quite sure what it was.

The debate happened to be on a motion by Horatio Bottomley, the editor of *John Bull*, then the most widely read of the weeklies. Bottomley was very popular during the war. A mass meeting with him as speaker was a greater attraction than anyone except Lloyd George could stage. He had just lost £40,000 in the Manchester Cup, but was planning to make a fortune by a Victory Bond Scheme, which he was launching in *John Bull* and which a couple of years later landed him in jail for seven years. This swindler, the last of the demagogues, as he has been called, was shortly to make a disgraceful attack on Lady Astor. There he was now on her first day, a gross specious rascal haranguing the House.

During the debate she got up from her seat and moved about the chamber, exchanging a few words with this friend and that, with an ease and self-confidence which those who did not know her thought extraordinary for a newcomer. Presently she went over to speak to T. P. O'Connor, called the Father of the House. With him was Mr Devlin, the Irish member, the person who had been asking questions when she arrived, and was not personally known to her. On his being introduced, she said to O'Connor: 'I want to tell Mr Devlin what I think of him for keeping me waiting ten minutes at the bar.' Mr Devlin was taken aback. Her banter was evidently a little too abrupt for him. Though she was smiling, he thought some sort of rebuke was intended. He muttered an apology, excusing himself as having been bound by duty to his constituents. He was evidently a trifle put out, not seeing that she was only teasing him. Still teasing, she said: 'Don't

78

do it again,' and left to speak to someone else. Later in the day he ran into her in a lobby. She stopped him. Her conscience had been worrying her a little. 'You don't think I was in earnest this afternoon?' she said. Immediately mollified, 'Of course not,' he assured her. 'Well,' she said, 'will you do me the pleasure of coming to a dinner which I'm giving shortly in my St James's Square house?' Quite won over, he accepted with pleasure. On the appointed evening he came to her door. A footman conducted him to where she was standing in conversation with her guests. On the footman announcing his name, she came quickly forward, took him by the two hands, and humming a tune waltzed him round the room.[1]

The mention of T. P. O'Connor above reminds me that he used to relate how in the course of the afternoon he came on the second Astor boy, David, aged seven, staring down from his seat in a gallery. 'Exciting, isn't it?' he said to the child. To which yound David replied, 'Yes, and Mother told me if I got too excited to recite poetry to myself.'

Reciting was to soothe him, though poetry is generally supposed to rouse. One feels, however, that in her cryptic way Lady Astor was right in associating the idea of poetry with her inauguration, certainly not a prose occasion, like the thousands of former installations of new members. There was something elfin about it; this woman flitting about the chamber and already casting her spell upon it. In the weeklies and monthlies writer after writer sought to sum up the impression she had made. The attempt in *Nash's Illustrated Weekly* of 13 December is worth citing: 'A certain great man was asked for an adjective which would describe Lady Astor. Said he: 'Well, you can always fall back on vivacious.' I shall try to go a little further. No one who ever knew her doubts that she is a genius. Her charm is a thing quite incredible to those who have never

[1] This account is founded on a statement made soon afterwards by Mr Devlin himself, to another Irish member, Michael Macdonagh, who on 28 February 1938 published the story in *The Irish Independent*.

met her.' And he goes on to say that the House of Commons has a character of its own; it is unlike a dinner table, unlike the hustings, to which Lady Astor came and saw and conquered. With its parties, division bells, lobbies, whips, it is a regimented assembly, whose discipline members must accept if they are to make their mark. Lady Astor, he feels, has not the makings of a party politician. Her character is too marked, she is too independent. Is there any future for her there? Is there scope for her genius? Will she not be blocked by the machinery? To these questions he has no answer. He feels that she will do something, which is sure to be unique, but has no idea what.

To wind up the great day she gave a dinner party in the House of Commons, to which came Lloyd George and his ministers, the leaders of the opposition and what other members she elected to ask. That she had the knowledge, the aplomb and the means to give such a party on her first day in the House set her apart from all former new members and particularly from all women afterwards to be elected. She was a *persona grata* from the beginning. Already a great figure in society, she had stepped from that limited circle on to the stage of the world. Yet she was not to change; had never changed. In Virginia was foreshadowed the hostess of Cliveden; at Westminster she gained further experience, but it was the qualities which had made her so far that carried her on. It would be paradoxical to say that she never learnt anything. Nevertheless, persons born with gifts sufficient to lift them out of the ranks, need not learn in the ordinary way. For them to try to model themselves on this or that, look up to a leader or subscribe to a programme, is to damage the freshness of their natural abilities. But, indeed, they are in no danger of making that mistake, for they have not the capacity to copy. Their intelligence is of a different order. Lady Astor tried at times to accommodate herself to the humdrum routine of parliament. She even attempted to be useful on committees, to scrutinize bills.

But she was not good at such things; they were too contrary to her inclinations. Her proper course was to trust to her natural intelligence. Prompted by it, she formed judgments which were generally right.

CHAPTER 6

Lady Astor's First Speech in the House of Commons

Lady Astor is fond of recalling an expression which the great Anglo-American, Henry James, once used in conversation with her – 'the dauntless decency of the English'. And she will add: 'That was how I was received by the Commons. Very few M.P.s were really pleased to see a woman in such a man's sanctum, but nothing could have been kinder than the way they treated me.' She may go on, however, to say that forbearance would be a better word than kindness. They bore with her presence; they put up with her. There was Winston Churchill, for instance, who ignored her, though they had known each other for so long. One day she confronted him and asked the reason. He replied that he found a woman's intrusion into the House of Commons as embarrassing as if she burst into his bathroom when he had nothing to defend himself with but a sponge. Her reply was: 'You are not handsome enough to have worries of that kind.'

Nevertheless, as will appear, members for the most part found her a great attraction. She was careful not to trespass on their privacy. She did not go into the smoke rooms or the bar nor did she eat in the dining-room except very occasionally. A private room had been placed at her disposal, to be shared with any future women members, where she could sit with her secretaries and attend to her correspondence. The result was that she rarely met members except in the Chamber itself or the lobbies. They were able to enjoy unmolested the amenities of their exclusive political club.

At the time of her taking her seat, she was represented in Madame Tussaud's, that permanent side-show of the London scene, by an effigy placed beside the figure of Pussyfoot Johnson, whose recent triumph in America had put him in the news. You had to be much in the public eye to have an effigy there, and that Lady Astor was such a draw is as good proof as any of her celebrity. But to be stationed beside Pussyfoot Johnson was less agreeable, as at Plymouth she had dissociated herself from prohibition. A day or so later, when opening a bazaar, she thought it necessary to clear this up and repeated that prohibition would not suit England: 'The moment you say to an Anglo-Saxon, "I prohibit you from doing this," he just goes and does it. I am like that myself.' It was on this occasion that she said to a press photographer: 'I'd do anything to stop looking like the mummy of Rameses as I generally look in the newspapers.' This remark was telegraphed all over the world under the ridiculous misapprehension that what she had said was 'I'd do anything to stop looking like Rameses' granny.'

She was soon involved in a round of immense activity. Wherever she was, a speech was demanded. When distributing presents to patients at Great Ormond Street Hospital, she also distributed some lively dicta: 'We are worse than publicans; we are hypocrites'; 'Avoid bunkum and just try to be decent.' When thanked for visiting the hospital, she retorted: 'Don't flatter me. The moment people believe they are of use, they cease to be of any use to the state.' In another such little speech, she came out with an Astorism to describe the Irish nationalists: 'They always go forwards looking backwards,' and begged the Irish to stop hating the English. 'Men's hearts must be changed' was the root of all her political thought. At a big meeting at the Albert Hall in support of the League of Nations, she was optimistic that this change was possible. But, said she: 'Don't expect to clear the moon in your first jump. Begin with a footstool and then go on to the sofa.' Founding the League was a good start. 'It may still be only half a League, but it is half a league onward.'

But how best to be of practical use in parliament? That was the big question. Could an individual member do more, in fact, than join in debates, ask questions on behalf of constituents and vote for the party? So humdrum an existence was too alien to her nature. She must try to steer a middle course, not so independent as to be obnoxious, yet leaving her free enough to act in such a way as to get things done. There were plenty of things that wanted doing, mass of things that women wanted. She would have to feel her way. As the first woman in parliament and the only woman there, the eyes of thousands were fixed on her. The *Pall Mall Gazette* of 10 January 1920 has this remark: 'Her postbag is enormous and it has been absolutely impossible for her to cope with a quarter of the letters from women with a grievance, suggestions and desires from all over the world.' They regarded her as the representative of the women of Britain of all classes and views. Many were the reforms which they had long hoped for – such as votes at the same age as men, pensions, improvement of their labour conditions, reform of the property and marriage laws, legislation to protect young children more adequately. Now they had someone to present their claims. With the weight of more than half the population behind her, it was thought that directly or indirectly she could exert much pressure. She gladly accepted this duty. It was to be her principal role for twenty-five years. But she was no methodical reformer; she had her own ways of doing things, methods which women without her wit, her wide acquaintance, her daring, her overwhelming high spirits could not adopt nor could even imagine. Her unconventionality was such that no one could foresee what she would say or do, the more so because her interests extended beyond social reform in the ordinary sense. That is why we may be sure, as we follow her career, that we shall find it full of variety and the unexpected, of crises and predicaments, which keep the story alive.

In January 1920 everybody was speculating what her first speech in the House would deal with and when she would make it. While waiting for it, the press was obliged to chronicle the smallest things she said, such as 'Hear, hear!' or 'Yes, he is', when a speaker demanded to be told whether the Prime Minister, Lloyd George, was an honest man or not. At last it became known she would speak on drink. 'I was warned not to touch the temperance question,' she said later, 'but I was not anxious about *my* future. I knew I was stirring up adders, and I remembered that St Paul handled snakes and was bitten by one, but I found the courage.' The occasion was a debate on the Liquor Control Board, the wartime measure already mentioned. Now that the war was over, the time had come to abolish it; such was the opinion of many people. Accordingly, a motion to that effect was put down for 24 February 1920. The government decided to oppose the motion, not that they wished to maintain indefinitely the war restrictions on the sale and consumption of liquor, but because they planned in due course to introduce a bill of their own which would embody the experience gained by the Control Board in the form of a certain degree of regulation. Lady Astor's name was on the government list of those opposing the motion.

The House of Commons could never approach a liquor debate with a grave face. It was generally an occasion for a great deal of facetiousness. Lady Astor was expected to add to the entertainment. Though she had not yet spoken in the House, her reputation as a wit had preceded her. The benches were filled to capacity. Those unable to find seats crowded the floor and overflowed into the galleries. It was like a night when some important pronouncement was to be made by the Prime Minister on foreign policy, though members were joking instead of waiting with gravity. The motion to abolish the Control Board was moved, and Sir John Rees rose to support it. He adopted a jocular tone, expatiated on the convivial associations of drink and suggested that teetotalism was synonymous with Bolshevism, a teetotaller a variety of crazy theorist. Though the government was not for the motion, his sallies were greeted all round with laughter. He had a good joke to wind up with. Looking at Lady Astor, who was down to follow him, he said archly: 'I know what is coming to me from the next speaker. Not only shall I accept the chastisement with resignation, but I shall be ready to kiss the rod.' This made her raise her eyebrows and say 'Oh!', but she quickly joined in the laughter.

In this atmosphere of hilarity, far from conducive to serious argument, Lady Astor got up to make her maiden speech. But she was not at a loss; she knew what to do, knew that she must first answer Sir John Rees's witticism with another, if she was to hold the House. Looking at him with that mixture of hardihood and hesitation which people found irresistibly droll, she said: 'I shall consider the Honourable Member's offer – after his conversion.' The retort served, the joke was on Rees. His attempt to laugh her out of court had failed. She opened her remarks by saying that she would not ask the House's indulgence, for it had already granted her that in full measure by the courtesy extended to her on her first appearance. 'I know it was very difficult for some honourable members to receive a woman, but I assure you it was as difficult for a woman to come in. To address you now on the vexed question of drink is harder still. It takes a bit of courage to dare to do it. But I do dare.' It was observed that her voice was a little hoarse, as if she felt the strain. But as she continued her nervousness went and her voice became clear. 'It was the clearest I ever heard in the House,' wrote one correspondent. Her argument was that liquor control during the war had greatly reduced drunkenness, an enormous boon for women and children. As a woman to whom many women looked, she begged the House not to expose her sex again to the miseries so many women

86

of the working class had endured when there was no control. 'I could talk for five hours on the benefit to women the Board has been,' she exclaimed, at which there was a loud roar of protest. 'Do not think I am urging prohibition. I am not so stupid as that, though I admit I hope England will come to it one day and I am not afraid to say so.' Though members were listening kindly, this was too much for those who had been inclined from the start to treat her as a romp. But undeterred by their merriment she continued to her conclusion with what one hearer described as 'the almost child-like bonhomie which had stood her in such good stead at Plymouth'. This was a very true observation, for it was her easy good-nature which made it impossible for any honest person, even if he disagreed with her, to dismiss her as a joke. When she wished to joke, no one could do it better. But even persons who disliked her had not the face to declare that she was no more than a joke. Her speech had a flattering press. The *Evening Standard* saw truly that its success was due 'to her evident human sympathy, sincerity and earnestness, combined with her humour and vivid phrasing'. The motion to abolish the Board was defeated. This did not mean that the government agreed with her temperance views but only, as explained, that it would be dealing with the subject later in its own way. She could feel satisfaction, however, that the loss of the motion prevented an immediate return to the position before the war, whose evils her speech was designed to expose. The liquor trade journals, of course, were not as kind as the *Evening Standard*. In them she was accused of confusing alcohol with alcoholism, of imagining she was convicting drink when she was only denouncing drunkenness. They summed up her speech as rather an earnest plea than an ordered argument. These criticisms were reasonable debating points. That nothing less mild was said is proof of how bravely she, a single woman, was thought to have faced an audience of five hundred men. She has told me that afterwards Lloyd George congratulated her. 'Your voice is your fortune,' he said. And when she expressed doubts about the cogency of her argument, he declared: 'It's not what you say that matters, but whether you hold your audience. That you did from start to finish.'

CHAPTER 7

Adventures and Misadventures of First Two Years in Commons

There are plenty of stories about Lady Astor which belong to the period between her maiden speech in February 1920 and her visit to the United States in 1922. The following, which may perhaps rest more on folklore than on fact, concerns a question she is said to have asked Sir Auckland Geddes at a dinner party just before he left London for Washington as ambassador. 'Sir Auckland,' said she in her teasing way, 'I am told that anatomy is one of your subjects. Well then, answer me this. Why is it that my eyes being beautiful, my nose good, my mouth the right shape, my hair lovely – so people say – and yet I am not a pretty woman?' 'Because,' replied Sir Auckland, 'they don't fit.'

The curious thing about this story is that Lady Astor's retort is not extant. Such stories are very rare, as are stories where she gets the worst of the exchange. The present one, circulated in the States, was considered tasteless by the many who remembered her as one of the beautiful Miss Langhornes of Virginia. The Americans had been following her recent adventures with intense interest. To show her gratitude for the kind things they were saying, she wrote to the editor of the *Evening Journal*: 'I am overwhelmed by the way Virginia is backing me up. I had no notion that anyone outside Plymouth would really care. I don't like the limelight, but I do like the friendship of my friends. The joke is, I am the most ordinary person you ever met.' She had more than personal reasons for being pleased. If their friendship for her inclined them to be more friendly with the British, it would forward the greatest desire of her life.

In March 1920 the Hon. Mrs Alfred Lyttleton, wife of a former Colonial Secretary, and a leading feminist of the day, published her view of Lady Astor's character. It supports much of what has already been said, but coming from so reliable a source a few at least of its sentences will bear quotation: 'A woman of many gifts, who can be mordant, even a little cruel, in her laughter, but never so by intention, for above everything else she has a heart. No one is old, dull or dim to her. I have seen her change the whole atmosphere of a hospital ward in a few minutes. She can, and often has done it, sit for long stretches by the sick and dying.' Of similar sense is the touching remark attributed to one of the wounded Canadians in the Cliveden Hospital: 'Her scoldings don't mean anything.'

Testimony such as this appealed very much to Americans, but human nature being what it is, the most popular tales of her were humorous. In 1920 a bill was introduced into parliament to give women the vote at the same age as men. It was becoming ridiculous to suppose that the modern young woman between twenty-one and thirty was less competent than men of that age to record a vote. The failure of the bill to pass made Lady Astor very sarcastic. Her anecdote about a certain Mr Boggs, told in London in November 1920, reflects her feelings. 'I was canvassing once for signatures to a petition about a certain Viceroy of India, when I called on Mr Boggs, a grocer. He read the petition carefully and then said: "Who is this 'ere man?" "Our Indian Viceroy," said I. "What is a Viceroy?" asked Mr Boggs. I explained as best I could. Mr Boggs, satisfied, dipped his pen in the ink, and then looked up anxiously. "You're not letting the women sign this?" he asked. "No, indeed," said I, eager for him to get on. "That's right," said he, slowly tracing his signature, "that's right, ma'm. Women don't know anything about these things."'

As can be imagined, Lady Astor had difficulty in accommodating herself easily to the rules of debate. One such rule was that a member must not wrangle directly with another member, but, referring to him in the third person, address his remarks to the Speaker. She was too impetuous to remember this always. Not infrequently the Speaker (or, if the House was in committee, the chairman) would say to her: 'I must ask the hon. member to bear in mind that in this House it is not in order to say you, you, across the floor of the House.'

Generally she bore the rebuke meekly, but she was known to try to justify herself by urging that to address the chair took too long when you had lots to say. She was developing a technique of interruptions and interpolations, which later she used with such skill that in the view of many she was more effective in making her points that way than in a set speech. Examples of her method will be given later on. Suffice it to say here that just as in Plymouth she was on the top of her form when duelling with a heckler, so a match with a single member of the Commons suited her to perfection. The issue was in little doubt; she almost always won. It was her excitement when delivering light-ning repartee that sometimes led to her kicking over the traces and to the Speaker, portentous in his wig, calling her to order in solemn tones, while members tittered with delight. That there was something schoolboyish about some members was an impression she formed, as also that there was something old-womanish. On another occasion she relieved her feelings by this *mot*: 'I will not express an opinion about women in parliament, but looking round the House of Commons I sometimes wonder why men are there.'

She has told me that one fine day when Lloyd George was standing with her on the terrace at Cliveden, looking across the formal garden and down to where the Thames flowed at the foot of the woods, a very lovely view, he said: 'If I owned Cliveden nothing would induce me to leave it for Westminster,' and he spoke of the disappointments of political life, the ridicule one was exposed to, the under-hand attacks. Why had she deserted ease and home for parliament? She did not tell me how she answered him, but we know that her reason was not ambition. Now in the spring of 1920 she was to have her first experience of how hateful public life could be. In April a private bill was introduced to give legal effect to the recommendations for easier divorce made by a recent commission. Desertion for more than three years, insanity or life imprisonment were to be made grounds. Most people thought it likely that she would speak for the bill, as it favoured the deserted wife, and the wife tied to a criminal. But she did not support it. Women, she said, did not want easier divorce; the preservation of the family was fundamental to their nature. Only men would take advantage of the proposed facilities, to the detriment of women. The unexpectedness of her speech and the earnestness with which it was delivered made a great impression. But it was unpopular in some quarters. Women wrote in to say she had no mandate to speak for women as a whole. At a Labour party women's conference, held that week, a resolution to that effect was passed. Some disagreeable things were said about her – that she was just a very rich woman, out of touch with the working class. Seeing the way opinion in some quarters was veering against her, Horatio Bottomley thought an article in *John Bull* attacking her would be a popular move, and published a very nasty one, accusing her of hypocrisy and cant, and of fooling the House. Had she not herself taken advantage of the easier divorce law of Virginia to obtain a divorce from her former husband, Shaw? To draw attention to the article he advertised it by placarding London with 'Lady Astor's Divorce' in huge letters. The public, naturally supposing that she was divorcing, or being divorced by, Viscount Astor, rushed to buy *John Bull*, eager to read of the scandal. True, when they read the article, they saw they had been duped; the divorce in question had happened seventeen years before. They had to content themselves with the charges of hypocrisy and cant. But the many who did not read the article remained under the impression that she would soon figure in a divorce case. It so happened that on the day the article appeared, she was in France, visiting the battlefields. On her return, when she entered the Chamber, she received an ovation, for members wanted to show that, though Bottomley was one of their number, they dissociated themselves from his attack on her, considering it a mean and tricky way of besmirching a woman. Those who knew the true facts of her divorce, as they have been set out earlier in this book, were aware that the charges of hypocrisy, et cetera, were without any foundation whatever, as she had not taken advantage of any concessions, if they existed, easing divorce under Virginian law, but had brought an ordinary case of misconduct, as she might have in London. The harm, however, was done, for few could know exactly what had happened in a foreign country so long ago. For the time being many people believed that her action in opposing the divorce bill was irreconcilable with what she herself had done. To be suspected in this way was exceedingly unpleasant. The ovation in the House did not mean more than that members thought Bottomley a cad. She felt that she must do something to clear her name. Action for libel against him might well have succeeded. But she shrank from the horrible publicity of such a course. Yet something must be done. She decided to speak to those who had sent her to parliament, the people of Plymouth, who were fond of her, and of whom she was fond, and who deserved to be told the exact truth. Accordingly, in July, she took her constituents into her confidence at a meeting of the Conservative Association. Some of her audience wanted to assure her that they considered it quite unnecessary for her to defend herself against charges made by a man like Bottomley. There were cries of 'We don't want to hear it', and 'Tear it up'. But she persisted, rightly feeling that a public statement was essential, and addressed them with considerable emotion. 'I have waited,' she said, 'for this meeting to deal with charges which if true would affect my position as your representative. However unpleasant it is to deal with a period of great unhappiness I went through seventeen years ago, I prefer to tell you all about it.' And she went on to speak of the placards in the London streets, how the

93

public generally was misled, of the article which accused her of collusive conduct, insincerity and hypocrisy, and then gave the true facts about her divorce. She concluded: 'This is the history of these painful occurrences. I have told you fully of the sorrows of my early life. I knew that when I set out from Plymouth I would encounter foul weather and be tossed by storms.' She had returned to her home port of Plymouth to refit.

This heart to heart talk profoundly moved the faithful people of Plymouth, who found their affection for her increased. A resolution of complete confidence in her was passed. At the end Lord Astor, who was present, said that he had never felt so grateful to a Plymouth audience as he was that evening. It had, indeed, been a very upsetting affair. Bottomley was not yet known to be a swindler; he and his paper were still popular. He might have succeeded in throwing doubt on Lady Astor's integrity. But the line she took of a public refutation, made in person before the audience most concerned, and which the audience publicly accepted, stultified his malice. His decline and fall, which followed rapidly on these events, was in part attributed at the time, whether rightly or wrongly, to his rout at Lady Astor's hands.

Attending regularly at the debates and occasionally serving on committees, she learned a great deal more about parliamentary practice than she had been able to do when an onlooker in the gallery. Some of the things she saw, she disliked and was bold enough to say so. On 19 June of this same year, 1920, she had a view of how private bills were smothered. The bill in question was designed to reduce shop hours and benefit women. Rule required that, as a private bill, it must pass by 4 p.m. or fail. After various amendments were considered she asked for the closure of the debate so that the bill could be put to the vote before four o'clock. When the Speaker refused her request, Sir Frederick Banbury, a Conservative of the right, began to speak. He was known for his inexhaustible flow of chat; if he got up at twenty minutes to the hour a private bill was doomed. Sure enough on this occasion he talked it out. This made her angry. Obstruction revolted her. In an article she wrote immediately afterwards for a paper called the *Women's Supplement*, she said: 'One thing which must strike newcomers to the House of Commons is the appalling congestion of business. The number of grievances that remain unremedied causes perpetual irritation. There is not enough time for discussing big subjects and too much opportunity for obstructing small bills by talking.' This was her first experience of Sir Frederick Banbury. As will appear, she was to come to blows with him, literally to blows as some alleged, when he talked out a bill of hers.

One of her objections to men like Banbury was that they were idle, worse than idle, for their idleness took the form of preventing others from doing anything. For an industrious person idleness is very irritating. How industrious she was may be seen from a list of her parliamentary activities during her first six months, to which must be added looking after her house and children, entertaining high and low, answering thousands of letters and attending to her numerous charities. In the Commons she spoke in the following debates: the bill to give women equal votes with men, on the naval estimates where they touched Plymouth, on early closing, drink, marriage, welfare of the blind. She served on four committees, including those concerned with a plumage bill and women police. Bills concerned with milk for children and pensions for widows with children also received her support. She was not the first nor the only person to press for these reforms, but she pressed for them with might and main. 'There is too much dislike of enthusiasm,' she said of the government. 'There is a lack of initiative and enterprise.' She felt there was so much to do for the people of England by whose sacrifices the war had been won. She was in a hurry. Delay was anathema to her. One is astonished how she maintained the pace. During the six months she also addressed large audiences at Birmingham, Liverpool, Leeds, Portsmouth and Cardiff, as well as in London at the Albert Hall,

Mansion House, Queen's Hall and elsewhere on a variety of subjects from the League of Nations to infant welfare. She was now forty-one years of age, in the prime of life; her health was wonderful. She owed it, in her opinion, to Christian Science. 'But had I not been able to afford three first-class secretaries, I could not have kept up the level required of me,' she said recently when speaking of this time. Even so, her enemies declared that often she did not know what she was talking about. But they could not deny that she knew how to hold her audiences and that was what counted. If she did so more often by her impromptus than by keeping to the solid presentation of a case which her secretaries had prepared, it suggests that, however necessary they were, they were less essential than her wit and intuition. Those were the gifts which gave her more news value than any other living woman. Whatever she said was immediately telegraphed to the four quarters of the world. When she spoke against drink it was great news, though few agreed with her contentions. The way she put it was so original. Thus in November 1920 she said at Wolverhampton: 'Whether they take it well or not, I can't leave the drink question alone. At home they say to me – where are you off this evening? My reply is – I'm off on the drink. I have been asked by the House – why don't you leave that drink alone? You'll be so popular if you do. I said – I could no more drop it than drop a baby.' This was certainly not drafted for her by her secretaries; it came out of her fresh – and still sounds fresh. A press account of this meeting happens to confirm this: 'She began her speech by reading. Then there was a flutter of leaves. "I have got my notes mixed," she cried. Having escaped from her notes, she said many witty things.' Some of them must have made the anti-drink fanatics stare, as: 'I know a great many publicans I like far better than some of those preaching temperance.' Her life was so much broader than such people's. The Sunday after the Wolverhampton speech she was playing golf with Lloyd George at Sandwich. When the Free Church heard that she and the Premier had been breaking the Sabbath, they wrote in a stiff protest. The various worlds impinged on her, but she did not exactly fit into any of them. Though Philip Kerr was her greatest friend, she liked and admired Lloyd George very much. She made no secret that she thought him a genius. Later on she was to meet and find most congenial two other men to whom that term could be applied. That men endowed beyond the ordinary saw in her a kindred spirit answered the question sometimes asked – what can they see in her? What they saw was something resembling themselves. It may be that one of the attractions she had for great men was her humility, for humility is a characteristic of greatness. That under her sparkling exterior she was essentially humble has hardly been suggested so far. Her intimates knew it well and sometimes it showed itself on a public occasion. In the spring of 1921 she was invited to address the Bloomsbury Central Church from the pulpit. Her staff had written her out a speech, but when she stood in the pulpit she felt that she could not use it; it contained what, in the sudden mood which had overtaken her, seemed to show her too pleased with herself. But she had prepared nothing else. Late though it was to disappoint her audience, she must tell them so. She said: 'I feel that I cannot say what I want to say; I cannot make a speech.' There was a murmur in the sea of faces. 'Oh, do, do,' people begged. She found that she could not refuse them. 'Oh, all right, then I will,' she said, and gathering herself together spoke extempore, a speech very different from that in her hand. It contained these sentences: 'I cannot stand humbug, yet know that I myself am self-righteous, for which I am sorry. It is really a terrible temptation for people who are trying to do right. Every now and then I find myself saying – Thank God, I am not like other politicians.' And she continued in this touching way, saying: 'I am not highly educated, I am not brilliantly clever. I have just got a little knowledge. Sometimes I wish I could understand things better; I wish I could understand the Budget.' At this sudden turn there was laughter, and

97

relief that she was her amusing self again. But they treasured the other glimpse.

During 1921 the House began to regard her more and more as its privileged jester. A French-Canadian newspaper put it this way: 'Les députés et ministres de Londres ont l'air de la laisser parler et agir comme si il s'agissait d'une enfant gâtée.' An English paper has: 'Members laughed and cheered, expressing their greatest appreciation perhaps when her ladyship sent her sly shafts at their own heads.' One of such shafts was: 'Members are not losing their idealism. They never had any.' And she is stated to have urged women's societies to send postcards to M.P.s who opposed reforms with the words: 'All right, my man, your time's up,' a threat to oust them at the next election by means of the women's vote. Her rôle was to keep the Commons up to the mark. She shot at them from all directions. When invited to a fête where the setting was to be eighteenth century in the style of Wheatley's *Cries of London*, she said: 'I won't come as a London cry, but I might come as a parliamentary nuisance.' She also gave the receipt for keeping the Commons in order: 'Don't hit them on the head, but pull their legs.' And speaking of the plumage bill, she said with her droll smile: 'I made myself disagreeable, but in a very cheerful way.' Another Astorism of this period was: 'It is true that some M.P.s are more ladylike than I am, but I went to parliament to try and get things done.'

For over a year now her wax effigy in Madame Tussaud's had drawn crowds. The management, having made their money, decided to melt it down, as was their custom, and make an effigy of somebody else. This gave A. P. Herbert, M.P., the famous humorist, a chance. In a caricature of her she is shown as objecting: 'You can't boil down the women of England.' A. P. Herbert, though most amusing on paper, had nothing like her reputation for spoken wit. But she had one rival (though a bad second) in the House, a Scotch member called Macquisten. He was helped by a delightful Scotch accent. One of his jokes (directed against sobriety) once made her whistle. His joke is forgotten, but her whistle is part of history. News of it was telegraphed immediately over the earth under such headings as LADY ASTOR'S WHISTLE, WHY DID SHE WHISTLE? It was, of course, the first time a woman had ever whistled in the House of Commons.

It should not be forgotten that in spite of her enormously busy life indoors, she remained an out-of-door woman. We find her during the tea hour practising with a golf-club on the terrace of the House for a competition called the Parliamentary Handicap. The sporting correspondent of a paper wrote: 'Only lack of practice has so far prevented her from proving a first-class player in her sex.' In the Handicap, playing with eighteen strokes against bogey, she sliced badly and came in six down. But she persevered and we shall meet her again on the golf course.

In 1921 Lord Astor's sciatica got much worse till he was quite crippled by it. On the advice of his doctors a tour in North Africa was prescribed, where the dryness would do him good. Accompanied by his wife, he set out. The press followed the tour, hoping for news. There was nothing to report at first except that she won a silver cup in a golf tournament at Algiers. Later, stories began to be put out that both she and the Viscount had been kidnapped in the desert and were being held for ransom, the figure fixed being a million. This was shown to be a *canard*. In its place was substituted a story that they had a narrow escape from being crushed by a rock which an ill-disposed Arab rolled down on their car. One feels this also is an apocryphal story and belongs rather to the Astor folklore. But certain it was that the trip did not cure Lord Astor. He was bedridden after his return and, yielding to his wife's entreaties, now turned, as has been mentioned, to Christian Science. Some months later he was able to go fishing in Bimini, Bahamas. A photograph shows him with a catch, including a barracuda or something huge of the sort.

If Lady Astor was not kidnapped or nearly crushed by a rock, she had on her return from Africa an authentic adventure in her adopted town of Plymouth, when a man threatened to kill her. The episode is curious, and important for the light it throws on her character. She was standing, it appears, by the hall-door of her house, 3 Elliott Terrace, on the Hoe, when a man came up to her and said: 'I intend before the week ends to return to prison on your account.' The words were said with menace. Was he a lunatic? His face was very odd. She came straight to the point: 'Are you threatening to kill me?' 'Yes,' said he, as directly. Most women would have screamed for help. Not so Lady Astor. She wanted to manage this affair herself. She had had experience with half-demented soldiers in Cliveden hospital; in visiting sufferers she had met some strange people, and had known how to calm them. One essential was to keep cool, like a lion-tamer with a lion. She spoke quietly to the man; he listened, was soothed, coaxed, and went away. Any woman one can think of, had she dared so far, would now have summoned the police. But that was not her way. No other woman would have done what she now did. She followed the man. The adventure excited her; she wanted to see it out. The man turned into a lane. She went down it after him. He now saw that she was following him. The sight frightened him and he quickened his pace. She did the same, and he broke into a run. In an account given afterwards she said: 'I gathered up my skirts, ran after him and caught him in the yard of a mews. "What is your name?" I said. "I will not tell my name," he answered. There was nobody in the yard. I thought – if he wants to kill me, now is his chance. But when he looked at me, he became dismayed, and took to his heels again. Again I followed. He now ran into a public house. I do not go into public houses but did on this occasion. He bolted out through the back door. I continued the pursuit.' The man shortly afterwards was stopped by a policeman, as he looked like a runaway thief. When Lady Astor came up, the policeman asked what the matter was. 'I want his name,' was all she said. The policeman demanded his name and he gave it. 'That is all,' said Lady

Astor. 'You are not charging him with anything?' the policeman asked. 'No,' said she, 'but you should keep an eye on him.' With that, she went back to her house.

A story recorded of her when she was Nancy Langhorne is relevant here. A horse ran away with a man, who thought himself lucky to get back uninjured. 'Let me ride that horse,' said Nancy Langhorne. 'You're mad, he'll kill you,' said the man. She threw herself on the saddle, struck the horse and let it go at a furious gallop. When it was tired, she brought it in. 'What made you do that?' asked the man. 'I wanted to see if I could do it,' she said.

In twenty years she had not changed. It intrigued her to see whether she could handle a half-witted man who wanted to kill her. She found that she could and was satisfied. She no more wanted the man punished than she had the horse.

This episode, which was great news in all the world's press, was found very odd, very difficult to understand. The Commons could make little of it, but had to admit that she was an even more intrepid woman than they supposed. But they were able to resist her efforts to subdue them in the matter of drink. In the second half of 1921 the government introduced, as it had promised, its own liquor bill. The kind of bill which she had advocated would have included state purchase of the whole trade, public houses and all, and authority for local bodies to opt for total or partial prohibition in the area they controlled. The government bill contained nothing of this sort. It abolished the Liquor Control Board and eased the restrictions, not quite to the point where they were before the war, but near enough to prevent any outcry. As Lady Astor's minimum demand was that no facilities beyond wartime restriction be given, she was very disappointed. No doubt, however, her friend the Prime Minister had told her privately that a temperance bill of the scope she desired would inevitably be thrown out and probably the government along with it. But she did not give up all hope and, as we shall see, managed some time later to induce the House to pass a small liquor bill of her own, which dealt only with juveniles. For the moment she came in for some carping criticism and jibes, but did not take them seriously and maintained her high spirits. Two months later (November 1921) we find her addressing her constituents in Plymouth: 'I do not know if I have become a force in the House of Commons as much as a nuisance. Perhaps you regret sending me. But I'll sit until you get somebody better.' And she told this little story against herself: 'I saw today an old lady of over a hundred. Another lady, introducing her to me, remarked: "This is Lady Astor, my dear. Some people likes her and some don't."'

That her chin was well up is also shown by an Astorism which belongs to this time. 'The toast used to be – The Ladies, God bless 'em. Now that women have the vote it should be – The Gentlemen, God help 'em.'

At the end of 1921 she received an invitation to attend the Women's Pan American Conference to be held in the States in April 1922. She accepted it. She was longing to see her native Virginia again. Some ten years had elapsed since her last visit.

CHAPTER 8

Lady Astor's Visit to the States in 1922

Anglo-American relations at the time of Lady Astor's visit were not cordial. The events of great historical importance which shortly preceded it explain the reason. In June 1919 President Woodrow Wilson signed the Treaty of Versailles, a document which contained the allied peace terms with Germany and also incorporated the Covenant of the League of Nations, his own creation and on which he pinned his hopes for a better world. In November 1919, however, Congress repudiated what he had done and refused to ratify the treaty, mainly on the ground that American opinion could not countenance a European settlement which might involve the sending of American soldiers and sailors to fight in foreign lands at the bidding of the League, a body over which America had insufficient control. She must remain isolated and avoid all entanglement in European affairs. Wilson suffered a nervous breakdown at finding himself repudiated, and during the remainder of his term of office he was an invalid. In 1921 Harding became President and in October of that year a separate treaty was made with Germany, which contained no reference to the Covenant of the League, outside which America remained. She did not, however, cease altogether to associate herself with world affairs and in November 1921 called a conference at Washington to discuss world disarmament. The conference, however, could effect nothing in the face of French determination to remain armed unless guaranteed against a possible German revenge. Isolationist America would not bind herself in this way. In April 1922, when Lady Astor set out for America, the members of the League of Nations were discussing the problems of Europe at a Geneva conference as best they could by themselves.

Whether America was justified or not in withdrawing from the League of Nations was the burning question. It was also a delicate question for a woman coming from England to discuss, because in the States it was generally considered as settled in America's favour. This was not Lady Astor's opinion. In her view the peace of the world depended upon America and the British Commonwealth working closely together. Ever since she left the States she had been convinced of the paramount importance of an irrefragable understanding between the two English-speaking nations. It will be recalled how, long before the war, she strove to bring Americans and English together under her roof. A deep and enduring friendship seemed to her now in 1922 even more essential than before. She determined to do what she could during her visit to cement it. Her visit, of course, was entirely unofficial, though the British government could only applaud her intention. The most convenient forum, she thought, for arguing her case, would be the conference to which she was invited. If she could win over all American women to her view, she would have half the population with her, a very practical first step. In her speech to them she would have to advocate America's return to the League of Nations at the risk of being written down as no more than a purveyor of British propaganda. Friends in England warned her – keep off the League. The subject, however, could not be avoided, if she was to speak on Anglo-American friendship. She hoped, however, if presented as part of a woman's campaign to lay the foundations of universal peace, that it would appear in a fresh light. One sees here the influence of Lord Lothian, whom she will certainly have consulted and without whose backing she would hardly have contemplated so bold a line as to advise the Americans to reverse their foreign policy.

Her tour was arranged accordingly. There was first Baltimore, where the conference was to be held. If all went well, she would then go to Washington. The tour would end by her visiting Virginia. Her father had died in 1918 and Mirador had been sold. But many old friends there and at Richmond and Danville were eager to see her.

She planned to be away about six weeks, since she could not absent herself longer from parliament. The coalition government under Lloyd George, hitherto immensely strong, was showing signs of cracking. The Conservative party, led by Bonar Law, was becoming restive and might any day desert the coalition, when a general election would follow. She must be back in good time for that.

Accompanied by her husband and her close friend Mrs Lyttelton, she left England by the *Olympic* on 12 April 1922. The Americans were showing much interest in the visit. Her career had been astonishing for an American woman. Moreover, by being the first woman to enter the House of Commons she became the outstanding leader of the feminist movement. Besides her feat of getting into parliament, her reputation as a wit made them long to hear her talk. Her origin, achievements and original gifts assured her of a great welcome from a people, who, more than any other in the world, adore receiving notabilities from without. Nevertheless criticisms and sarcastic comment were inevitable. There were those who disapproved of Americans abandoning their country and becoming British subjects. This feeling had shown itself in the case of the first Viscount. Some also professed to dislike the idea of a Viscountess coming over to tell them what to do. Others again, who regarded her witty sayings as merely disagreeable, saw no reason why Americans should be plagued with her. But the wind was taken out of these criticisms by the fact of her having been invited by the women's associations. It was pointed out, however, that when invited, it was not known that she intended to raise the question of the League. This was now known, for some ten days before embarking she had given the united press a statement: 'On my visit I wish to try to persuade American women to take a constructive interest in world affairs. Through their efforts I hope the United States will abandon its theory of isolation and take a responsible share in the work of reconstruction of the world, which is necessary if Europe is to be rescued.' These words left it in no doubt that she intended to mingle high politics with such purely women's subjects as the conference had on its agenda. But if some people considered it great presumption for a woman from Westminster to intrude and tell American statesmen that their foreign policy was wrong, Virginia heard of her coming with nothing but delight. It was reported: 'Nancy Langhorne is coming home, coming back to Mirador. Even though it is to be just a short visit, her county of Albermarle rejoices. All the old folk of hereabouts who remember the tomboy girl are getting out their best bib and tucker. Virginia's welcome awaits, not the woman leader of Great Britain, but Nancy Langhorne of Mirador.' Her old Negro servants and friends were also very excited at the prospect.

The conference at Baltimore began on 20 April and was to last ten days. The International League of Women Voters was the promoter. Three thousand women from all over the Western Hemisphere had come. Its main object was to create solidarity between the women in the two Americas. It was the most comprehensive women's conference ever attempted. Lady Astor made her address on 26 April at a mass meeting after a dinner given by the State president. The pith of it is in the following quotation: 'We thank God for the Washington Conference of last year. But we had better pray God for the Geneva Conference now sitting. I wish from the bottom of my heart that America was at Geneva. I think that America will go to Europe yet, because I think that she will see that she has got to go.'

The speech won the support of the conference. Next day the delegates passed a resolution urging the United States to take prompt action in entering a federation of nations. (It was evidently thought safer not to use the term 'league of nations', which was in such disrepute.)

Lady Astor was next booked to address a mass meeting in Washington. The occasion revealed her at the top of her form. She had the seat of honour on the platform. The Viscount settled himself modestly on the edge of the stage, half hidden by the American flag. Reporters said that she kept her eye on him and when she lost the thread of her argument, as she often did after an excursion into chaff, would turn to him and demand: 'Waldorf, what was I talking about?' Her sallies, as usual, came off well, particularly the one where she told the vast audience that House of Commons men were a lot of grown-up school-boys. The following pleasantry was also liked: 'I have one favour to ask. Don't make too much fun of women in politics. I know it's a tremendous temptation. We are funny, but so are you. Make fun of me if you like, I'm used to it, and have got a sense of humour. But some of these women are sensitive and it will scare them off.' When she came to the question of the League, she said, looking at Mr Hughes, the Secretary of State, who had spoken first: 'You men talk about conferences, but not leagues. You don't realize that there's a league of peace in the world today and that is in the hearts of women. I tell you, no matter what policy prevails, America will not want to progress alone. I have been told not to mention the League of Nations, so I shall call it the League of Peace.'

She had an invitation next day to go to the Senate. After a call on President Harding in the White House, whom she found nearly as enlightened as herself (so she told reporters grateful for the good copy), she was escorted onto the floor of the Senate, a very signal privilege. The visit was informal, and made extremely so by the freedom of her manner. When introduced to Senator Overman of North Carolina, she exclaimed: 'Why don't you fix yourself up?' and grasping his tie, put it straight, a liberty thought permissible since he was a Southerner like herself. Before leaving she insisted on shaking hands with the coloured messengers and servants, exclaiming: 'This makes me feel like I was back home.' To the photographers waiting at the exit, she said: 'Mind you make this picture like me!' and made the joke about the mummy of Rameses. When this was wired back to London (as was everything she said and did), she was accused of repeating herself and of running dry, for an unending flow of fresh humour was expected of her. In this case, however, as she had been misquoted, some argued she was right to make the joke a second time. The question was debated throughout the world. The final verdict I do not know.

So much for the more political aspect of her tour. Before leaving Washington she had a shopping spree, and bought herself nine pairs of shoes. She also lunched with General Pershing, then Chief of Staff. That the President received her kindly, that she was made much of by the Senators, and that General Pershing, the greatest military figure in the States, gave a luncheon in her honour, shows that far from offending the government by her frank criticisms, she had endeared herself to everybody.

The Virginian tour, starting on 2 May, began by a visit to Richmond, where, as will be recalled, she lived for some years as a young girl. Of this it will suffice to say that five thousand people were waiting at the station to welcome her as she stepped off the night train from New York at 7.30 a.m., a welcome so warm that though her spirits were very high she could not help crying as well. A procession was formed outside the station and with the band playing 'Dixie' and 'Carry me back to old Virginia', she was brought in triumph to the house where she was to stay. The way she entered into the fun of the thing made her appear to them, not as Lady Astor, wealthy, titled, famous, successful, but as Nancy Langhorne, an unspoiled Virginian girl genuinely pleased to be home again. The demonstration, as was said at the time, was unprecedented for Richmond, a quiet conservative town, never known to indulge in such an outburst of enthusiasm.

Her next stop was Danville, her birthplace, where she stayed on 5 May. Here the scenes of enthusiasm were repeated. Business was practically suspended; the entire populace made a holiday of it. She was received by the city council, given the freedom of the little town, a gold key and an illuminated address containing the text of a resolution renaming a street after her. At the conclusion of this ceremony, which included a speech by her, she was escorted to her old house at the junction of Main and Broad Streets (the latter the one renamed Nancy Astor Street), where she addressed the waiting crowd. The public's insatiable appetite for speeches was exhausting for her. When leaving Richmond and asked for a parting speech, she had said in expostulation: 'Nobody knows but just so much, and nobody should say more than that. I've said everything I know and you've printed it. Speeches don't just come out of the air. You have to think them out first. I don't believe people realize what speaking means.' And she added: 'You've been kind enough to say that I haven't made an ass of myself.' At Danville she was expected to make speech after speech. As she could not prepare so many beforehand, she had to depend on her natural fluency. ('It is all very well to be natural, but the thing should not be overdone,' she once said.) As we have seen, when she spoke extempore her real genius came out. She was more amusing, and also more penetrating, that way. At Danville she said some delightful things. But alas! there is no room to record them. The witty sayings of her life, if all gathered up, would fill many volumes. One amusing remark, however, made by somebody else, cannot be omitted. It amused her so much that even now, thirty-seven years later, it is one of her favourite anecdotes. Her father's old cook was still alive at Danville, a Negress called Becky. Becky came to call. Spick and span in new store clothes she announced who she was and was warmly welcomed. To interest her, Lady Astor showed her photographs of Cliveden. 'That's my husband's house where I live, Becky.' Becky rolled up her eyes and exclaimed: 'Good lawd, Miss Nannie, yo' sho' outmarried yo'self.'

Lady Astor was not going to leave Virginia without paying a visit to Mirador, the place she loved best. She had more old friends there, particularly among the Negroes, than at Danville and Richmond. A stay of three days was made, not in the house itself but with friends in the vicinity. By this time she was very tired, but found it restful to wander in the garden of Mirador and walk round the estate, visiting the Negroes, some of whom had been there when she was a girl. Under the heading 'Visit cheers old Darkies' a reporter has this: 'Many poor hearts have been cheered by this visit of Lady Astor, for in her ramblings about the old home place she has stopped at shack after shack to ask how about Aunt Sarah, Uncle Mose and all the rest. To all she is the same. "Lawd, Miss Nan, you ain't changed one bit, honey," they said.' Her fondness for the Negroes was very genuine. Their humour and humanity, the way high spirits and sadness were mingled in their characters, their warmth and humble constancy, greatly appealed to her. Their music and singing also moved her. At Richmond on 2 May, as soon as she took her seat on the platform, she had been surprised and delighted when the Lorillard coloured chorus began singing. The voices, rising and falling in melancholy cadence, chanted the famous spiritual, 'Swing low, sweet chariot'. It was noticed how rapt she became. When the last mournful notes died away she sat silent a moment and then leaned over to the mayor and whispered the name of another song. Word was passed to the vicar 'In a moment,' wrote an eye witness 'a thunderous volume of sound burst out as the splendid old Negro hymn "Roll, Jordan, roll" filled the building. A tremulous smile played on her lips and she swayed with the sighing hymn the Negroes sang.'

To have omitted this episode from the book would be to give an incomplete impression of Lady Astor. That she was so deeply affected by this African music, so truly religious, reveals what was perhaps the most essential element in her being.

Towards the end of May, after a flying visit to Canada, she was on her way home to England. Before she left, the people responsible for inviting her wrote to say that her visit had been 'of inestimable value to American women'. The *New York Telegraph* of 26 May delivered this balanced verdict: 'Lady Astor has sailed away. It is no exaggeration to say that she has left a grateful memory. We did not take her very seriously up to the time of her arrival a few weeks ago; that is to say, we did not look upon her as a really great person. But she took us seriously and in discussing us and our affairs, always within the limits of good taste and courtesy, she revealed those qualities which have made her Great Britain's foremost woman. Her gifts are remarkable; her faculty for saying the right thing at the right time amounts to genius.' Such acrimonious criticism as there had been died away. It was a very reassuring send-off. She had certainly improved Anglo-American relations, as far as it was possible for one person to do so. On her, the effect of the visit was to give her henceforth an international position. It was said she had made over forty set speeches. Some of these are included in a book called *My Two Countries* which she published in 1923. Observers recorded that she was more nervous when addressing a large audience than was immediately apparent; only those very close up could see the strain she was under. But she kept going, her courage held, she got through, never gave way. Of all her talents, it was her spontaneous wit which made the greatest impression, for wit of that nature is a pure gift which cannot be acquired and pertains to the marvellous. This chapter contains no example of the many Astorisms which she scattered about the States, but may end with one I like very much, which she is known to have come out with there, though in what connection is not recorded: 'Between the spiritualists who see what the dead think, and the psycho-analysts, who see what we don't think, one has to be up and doing.'

CHAPTER 9

Lady Astor and the Drink Trade

During her visit to the States, Lady Astor was, as we may well suppose, eager to find out how prohibition was faring. The amendment to the constitution which its enactment entailed was passed in January 1919 and took effect in January 1920. It had, thus, been in operation just over two years. The evasions which were later to bring it into contempt had already started, but were not yet so notorious as they were to become. She and her husband, it would seem, prosecuted their enquiries more among temperance reformers than opponents of the measure and were told that all was going well, that prohibition would never be repealed, and that, when America had been dry for a decade and in consequence was a healthier and wealthier country, other countries would be constrained to follow or be outdistanced, and prohibition would spread over the world. People with plans for the betterment of mankind incline to be over-optimistic. Nevertheless, Lady Astor was careful during her visit to say that though she thought prohibition well suited to America, it was not practical in England; a general measure of prohibition could not be passed through parliament. But a greater control of the sale of liquor than at present was possible, she believed. As mentioned further back, she thought that a bill buying out the trade and giving local bodies, such as municipalities and county councils, the power to opt for partial or total prohibition, might get through. But she knew very well that no government would sponsor such an enactment; the only way it could come before the Commons would be by a bill presented by an individual M.P. She felt it her duty to bring forward such a private bill. For a matter of fact, just before going to America, she had had drafted, printed and circulated a local option bill. It did not include state purchase of the industry. That would follow, she hoped. Her main reason for wishing to buy out the trade was that as long as the sale of liquor was a private business, the firms concerned would press drink on the public, like any other commodity which it is desired to sell, by advertisements and the like. But as she did not feel strong enough to join in such a battle *à l'outrance* with the trade, her bill was confined to local option. Now, on her return from America, she found that it had had a poor press. It was backed by her friend Jimmy Thomas, the Labour leader, and by Mrs Wintringham, who recently had been elected to parliament at a by-election and so was the second woman to sit there. It was depressing to find that some of the women's organizations were against it. Even the non-conformist weeklies treated it with frigid silence. Support was so small that it was clear that it would never pass. As the bill's chances had been correctly assessed by the trade, distillers and brewers were not unduly alarmed, but they considered Lady Astor a nuisance and hoped she would lose her seat in the coming election. The bill, in fact, was doing her no good at Plymouth, where it caused a split in the Conservative electorate. In September 1922 a doctor called Wansey Bayley was talked of as likely to oppose her there. An appeal to the country was expected very soon, as Lloyd George's coalition seemed about to break up. Of this bill, suffice it to say that it did not reach a second reading, the first real step in the progress of a bill.

At a meeting in the Carlton Club on 19 October 1922 the Conservatives under Bonar Law finally decided to leave the coalition. This obliged Lloyd George to go to the country. The date for the general election was given as mid-November.

As had happened before, Lady Astor's unpopularity was momentary and passed. The Conservatives nominated her again as their candidate for Plymouth (Sutton division) though Dr Wansey Bayley remained as a rival Conservative, supported by the trade and people of like views. Her position, however, was far stronger than his. The people of Plymouth liked her so much that most of them were willing to overlook her liquor bill. The strength of her position is shown by the attitude taken up by the Countess of Selborne. This lady was the president of the National Council of Women. Dr Bayley asked her to speak on his behalf, because he knew that she was opposed to Lady Astor on liquor control. Her reply requires to be quoted: 'Dear Sir, I certainly could not speak for you at Plymouth because if I had a vote in that borough I should certainly give it to Lady Astor. It is true that I disagree with her about the amount of control which should be applied to the liquor trade, but she has done such yeoman service in matters in which I and many other women take the deepest interest that I should be very sorry to see her out of parliament.' Even stronger testimony to women's trust in and admiration for Lady Astor is shown in a statement to the press by the Labour leader's wife, Mrs Philip Snowden, who was invited to oppose her at Plymouth as Labour candidate. 'I would not in any circumstances stand against Lady Astor. I am a Labour woman, but the work which Lady Astor is doing for women and children both in parliament and the country makes her services invaluable.' It is impossible to imagine a greater compliment than this, coming as it did from a woman of importance in the opposing camp. With backing and trust of this sort behind her, Lady Astor had little cause for anxiety. If she had gone too far in her temperance crusade, the excess was ascribed to her good heart and an honest conviction that she was doing right and ought to persevere whatever the consequences to her career.

The election campaign opened on 10 November 1922. It was rather fierce and less amusing than the by-election of 1919. Dr Bayley, the Independent Conservative, was said to have plenty of funds behind him supplied by the liquor trade. A big sum was publicly mentioned. Lady Astor was not alarmed. 'All the better,' she said. 'Let them spend it in Plymouth.' The Labour candidate was a man called Captain Brennan. The *Daily Chronicle* said: 'The blazing glowing personality of Lady Astor reduces to drab insignificance the other two candidates.' Nevertheless, she thought it prudent to pipe down about temperance and prohibition. In her manifesto, after a summary of what she had striven to do during the last three years for all sections of the community, she declared: 'I refuse to be the mouthpiece of the brewers. You may be told I want to impose prohibition. This is not true. All I want is to give voters freedom to control the drink trade, instead of being controlled by it.' She was referring to her belief that the trade was battening on the public. Her strongest cards were her undiminished popularity and the fact that Bayley and Brennan were undistinguished. The result of the poll was that 14,000 persons voted for her, giving her a majority of three thousand over Brennan and ten thousand over Bayley. It was a personal triumph. Her success may be compared with the failure of the thirty-two other women who contested seats throughout the country. Only one of them, Mrs Wintringham, got in, for it was still a very difficult feat for a woman to accomplish. In thanking her supporters she said with engaging modesty: 'I have made mistakes and very likely shall make more, but I don't think I have ever done anything of which Plymouth need be ashamed.'

The election resulted in Bonar Law and the Conservatives coming in with an overall majority of seventy-four. Lloyd George, instead of being the powerful leader of the coalition, was left with a small following of sixty-four National Liberals. Those who thought that Lady Astor, as close friend of the late Premier, had been able to influence Cabinet policy, saw in his defeat a curtailment of her power. But this was to misread her character. As has been made clear, she had never aspired to a position of power behind the scenes. The suave and tactful qualities which give success in that rôle were not hers. Independent and outspoken, she had no fixed line of policy but said out plainly what she thought a particular occasion demanded, whether it pleased or displeased her own party and friends. The change from Lloyd George to Bonar Law made no difference to her politically, though a friend had been displaced by an acquaintance.

Where the election results did have some bearing on her life was the totally unexpected defeat of Winston Churchill at Dundee by a Mr Scrymgeour, a man quite unknown outside that town and who was only notable there as an out and out prohibitionist. So extreme an exponent of temperance could only be an embarrassment to her. His excessive zeal would harm the cause she had at heart, though at least his views would make hers seem moderate. Indeed, he thought her very lukewarm. There was something a little comic in the situation, a comedy which she enjoyed as a humorist, but knew she must keep clear of, if the ridicule he invited were not also to damage her. The curious thing was that Mr Scrymgeour, though a fanatic on the drink question, was a really good-hearted man, whom it was very difficult to dislike. Nevertheless, when he declared after his election that his defeat of Mr Churchill – evidently a miracle – was explained by God's desire for prohibition, and that England would therefore go dry within the year, it seemed to members there was a lunatic in their midst.

When Lady Astor's liquor control bill failed to reach a second hearing, she drafted a new bill, small in scope and very moderate. Its sole object was to exclude boys and girls under eighteen from drinking in public houses. It became evident that she would have support, for many people considered the measure sensible. But a private bill, even when the government supports it, as in this case seemed likely, takes a long time to get started. There are so many private bills that only those which win a place in a ballot come up for discussion.

While waiting for a favourable ballot, Lady Astor resumed her active round. Her self confidence seems to have been increased by her return a second time for Plymouth. She felt assured enough to look critically at her own party and to aspire to liberalize its views. Her objection to the Conservative extreme right was as strong as to the Labour extreme left. Of the extreme right she remarked: 'We have some Conservatives who belong to the days of Noah. Not only have they not come out of the ark, but to hear them talk one would say that they had never *looked* out of it.' We find her in this critical mood a month after the election at the annual conference of a Conservative organization. In the course of her speech she said: 'People who live in two houses do not realize what it is like to live in two rooms. That's what is wrong with the Conservatives.' The words were spoken with more acerbity than was usual for her. The audience was shocked. There were cries of 'shame' and 'withdraw'. Not in the least intimidated she retorted: 'Why, you're worse than a Labour audience.' The shouting increased. She rebuked them: 'It is not very comfortable to be howled down at one's own party meeting. I would remind you that there is a danger to this country as great as Bolshevism and that is reaction.' This observation was followed, in the words of the press, by 'disorder, uproar and pandemonium'. When the turmoil was at its height, Mr Bonar Law appeared on the scene. The shouting died down at sight of the Prime Minister. The press was inclined to take her side. The ferocity shown by her own party puzzled the *Evening Standard*, which remarked: 'After all, she was only saying what she thought,' as if one could always say what one thought with impunity. That she had that licence was not everyone's opinion. A month or so earlier, an M.P. by the name of Charles Edwardes had called her at a public meeting at Newport 'the cheekiest little sparrow that ever sat on a doorstep', and another had said that 'she hadn't the manners of a street corner cat'. Of this remark the *Catholic Herald* said reprovingly: 'She brings these not inaccurate descriptions upon herself.' But she never minded criticisms of this kind; the hurly-burly of public life, though sometimes she declared it insupportable, really suited her. She said what she thought because she conceived it her duty to say it, and so was never sorry afterwards. In her view no man was ever the worse for hearing the truth. She applied this principle both outside and inside the House. In many a debate she roused a storm by her running comments on a member's speech. 'Mind your manners,' the exasperated man would exclaim. 'I won't,' she would reply. Of such an occasion it was recorded: 'The Speaker gave her a homily on the evils of interruption and her ladyship with exclamations, a wave of white gloved hands and jerks of the chin, enthusiastically agreed with him.' Irritation vanished in laughter. The fact was that after three years she was thoroughly at home in the Commons. When a member let fly at her, she was not disturbed. She herself to this day likes to recall such brushes. What Mr Kirkwood, a Scotch Labour member, said to her at this time is one of her favourite anecdotes. She relates it thus: 'One night I was leaving the House of Commons, when I heard such a row in the Chamber that I rushed back to see what was up. There was Kirkwood waving his arms and denouncing capitalists in broad Scotch. I sat down opposite and laughed. He called out to the Speaker: "Mister Speaker, look at that woman! She's come to irritate me. I canna abide women or Jews." An M.P. doesn't have to go to the theatre for amusement.'

On 16 February 1923 it was announced that in the ballot for private bills her bill, officially called The Intoxicating Liquor (Sale to persons under eighteen) Bill, had won third place. Mr Scrymgeour had drafted a total prohibition bill and by chance it too was lucky that same day in the ballot and secured seventh place. On hearing this Lady Astor exclaimed: 'Fancy old Scrymgeour and me in the first seven places! It really looks as if what he said was true and God is on the side of temperance.'

On 9 March the bill was discussed at its second reading, the first being merely its formal presentation. Lady Astor made a lively speech, describing the various organizations behind it. 'It is in no way my bill. I am only its godmother, I hope its fairy godmother.' It did no more than prevent, she explained, juveniles under eighteen from going into a public house, ordering a drink and drinking it there. It did not stop a man from standing such a juvenile a drink, nor a juvenile buying a bottle or a jug of beer and taking it away.

As usual with liquor bills, the House found it difficult to be serious. There were many jokes made, which repeated now would seem insipid. The best of them perhaps was Sir George Hamilton's, who said that the bill was not godmotherly but grandmotherly legislation. Mr Scrymgeour, of course, was bitterly opposed to it, as entirely inadequate. Again and again he strove to catch the Speaker's eye, as he was bursting to denounce it. At last, at the end of his patience, he exclaimed: 'Am I not to be allowed to express my views?' The Speaker did not vouchsafe a reply. The debate continued. Despite criticisms that the bill could not be worked (for how could a publican tell the age of clients?), it passed the second reading and was referred to a committee for closer examination. The government had supported it because to have opposed so very moderate a piece of social reform would have seemed reactionary. It would be a sop to the temperance enthusiasts in their constituencies and make it easier to reject more far-reaching measures. No upheaval would be caused, for not many juveniles drank in pubs and the liquor trade stood to lose but a negligible sum.

Mr Scrymgeour's bill did not find a place for second reading on the same day as Lady Astor's, and came up on 20 April. He spoke for eighty minutes; it was a comical harangue. Rumour went that students had tried to kidnap him on the way to the Commons. The House itself, it was reported, presented a forlorn appearance. There were more vacant than occupied seats. The Home Secretary was the only member of the government present. A handful of visitors listened from the gallery. Lady Astor was conspicuous by her absence. But the cheerless atmosphere did not damp the eloquence of Mr Scrymgeour. He said drink was a greater enemy than was Germany at the height of the war. 'I have a divine mission to wipe out drink in the kingdom,' he exclaimed. He is described as benevolent looking, with a big head, kind eyes, a Scotch accent and a grey moustache. He was so deadly in earnest that his voice shook with emotion. His peroration contained this sentence: 'God has taken possession of me and brought me here in the most marvellous fashion against all the forces of the press and all political organizations.' Only hushed laughter, it was said, greeted this final absurdity; it was so heartfelt.

When he sat down at last the House filled, eager to hear the ridicule that was coming. There was plenty of that. Admiral Gaunt's speech was held the most amusing. He described his experiences under prohibition in the States. Americans were so hospitable, he said, that they would pursue you down the street and drag you to where you could get a drink. The ability to make illicit liquor was the chief recommendation for a gardener or handyman. He also entertained the House with descriptions of the utensils in which liquor was secreted, a favourite one being hollow brush-handles. 'This is the prohibition,' he concluded, 'which the hon. member for Dundee seeks to bring into England.' Sir Arthur Holbrook, who followed the admiral, produced an anecdote which was the *coup de grâce*. He said with a solemn face: 'In the States if a man has a snake bite he is permitted to have alcohol as an antidote. When I was there one American went into a queue outside a place where a snake was kept for the purpose. Although he arrived there early it was midday before he got in and the snake was then too tired to bite him.'

On being put to the vote the bill was defeated by 236 votes to 14. One can well understand why Lady Astor kept clear of the debate; the members would have teased her mercilessly. And to have watched the whole temperance movement being turned into a farce would have been too disagreeable.

Such was the first and last attempt to make England dry.

Lady Astor's own bill was amended in the committee

stage more than she liked. As she had drafted it, both the juvenile who bought the drink and the barman who sold it were liable to fine. The committee felt this was unfair on the barman. If misled by a juvenile's mature appearance or false statement of age, how could he be blamed? Only if proved to know that the drinker was under eighteen should he be liable. The word 'knowingly' was therefore inserted after a debate lasting over two hours. Those who disliked the bill were delighted, being convinced that, as you could never prove a barman knew, the bill was as good as torpedoed. Lady Astor had been becoming more and more irritated. When Mr Remmer, a Conservative, moved a further amendment that beer, porter, cider and perry be excluded from the operation of the bill, she broke out and called him the village donkey. This remark was greeted with indignant cries. It was shockingly out of order to call an hon. member a donkey and to suggest that the House was the village where he brayed. Her old friend, Jimmy Thomas, was the Chairman. But friend or not, he was obliged to admonish her. 'The noble lady,' he said as severely as he could, 'has no right to apply that phrase to any member of the House.' 'Well, I'll do it outside,' she replied. The committee demanded she withdraw the expression. Whereupon she did so, though she added that there was evidently intent to make a fool of her bill. Mr Remmer's amendment was then amended. It was resolved that persons between fourteen and eighteen could order beer, wine and cider, provided that they drank them, not at the public bar, but in that part of the public house used for serving meals, and at a meal. Amended thus, the bill, now so mild that it could offend nobody, was sent back for its third reading in the Commons.

This took place two months later. As a government sponsored bill, it was not exposed to the full danger of being talked out, like ordinary private bills. If by 4 p.m., the closing time for private bills, members were still debating, it was not out for good, but could come up again, though perhaps after a delay of months. Lady Astor not unreasonably hoped that, after the gruelling her bill had received in committee, there was no more to be said and it would be voted on promptly. But she forgot Sir Frederick Banbury.

The first private bill of the day was an agricultural one. She expected it to be through in plenty of time to allow hers to pass. At a certain stage Banbury got up. This was an ominous sign. Did he intend to talk out the agricultural bill and so exclude hers also? As he rambled on and on, she became agitated. At 3.45 p.m., when it seemed certain that he would occupy the remaining quarter of an hour, he sat down. The vote was then taken. Little time was left, though perhaps sufficient for a bill which a committee had so carefully amended. But to her consternation she heard the Speaker call upon Banbury to move an amendment to her bill of which he had given notice. While he was rising to do so, she went quickly to him and tugged his coat-tails in an effort to hold him down. 'I'll hold on,' she said. 'You shan't get up.' 'You're not strong enough,' he replied, and resisting the pull with a bland smile and a show of manners, but with malice in his eyes, began to speak. After he had been talking for some five minutes on a minor detail already discussed in committee, she asked the Speaker to close the debate. But the rules did not permit so precipitate a closure and she was refused. Banbury continued to dawdle on until 4 o'clock. The Intoxicating Liquor (Sale to persons under eighteen) Bill was talked out for the time being.

The reporters in the gallery, who had already got a Lady Astor story out of the pulling of Banbury's coat-tails, were now to be rewarded by a scene which they exaggerated into a fracas. They reported that she lost her self control, went up to Banbury, pummelled him in the ribs with her fists and then left the House in tears. What actually happened was less dramatic and more in keeping with her character, for in all her career she never lost control of herself in public nor put herself so far in the wrong that she could not recover with a joke. In this case, though certainly vexed, all she did was to threaten to pummel Banbury in a jocular way, saying as she did so – I'll get even with you yet – which in fact she did. For she had only to wait a fortnight for her bill to be given room again. On 13 July 1923 it passed its third reading by the big majority of 247. Banbury again moved amendments, but failed to obstruct it long enough. In this debate Mr Scrymgeour denounced Lady Astor as a traitor to the cause of temperance and condemned her bill as a mere licensing measure, wholly inadequate to avert the doom towards which a drunken England was heading. But extravagances of that sort only amused. What she found less amusing was the enormous amount of time and trouble involved in getting a private bill through. It was now July and she had been hard at work on hers since the ballot in February. Indeed, it might have taken very much longer, or fallen by the way, as had her first drink bill, had not the government starred it. This was not very encouraging for a social reformer. Her experience of parliament already told her that she could achieve little by herself, and to get the reforms she wanted should direct her energies to persuading her party to adopt them. She was to have a try with other private bills, but the bill which she had steered through now was the only bill in her long parliamentary career where she was successful. Not that she could reasonably have expected otherwise. Very few members managed to get even one private bill passed.

In this chapter we have seen her buffeted about and rather disappointed, a contrast to the enthusiastic plaudits of America the previous year. But she saw the humorous side. Politics were an up and down career. Fame was precarious, all right when you have it, but not worth regretting when you hadn't. An anecdote which belongs to this time gives us a glimpse of her as such a laughing philosopher.

From pure good nature she had promised to go and talk to the girls of the Tottenham High School. In the midst of so much else of importance, she neglected to prepare her talk and when the day came had no subject in mind. However, she set out for the school. How a subject occurred to her, she told the girls in her speech. 'When I left home I was wondering what to talk to you about. On my way here I came by Madame Tussaud's, and I remembered how the last time I passed that way, there was a large placard outside – Lady Astor M.P. – and how, thinking it was rather nice to be famous, I said to myself: "Go in and have a look at the old gal." What I saw was a grim hard-faced old gal. Well, today there was no notice, but I went in. In the place where my waxwork had been was Bluebeard Landru, the brides-in-the-bath fellow. So I am wondering whether fame is really such a nice thing after all, girls.'

CHAPTER 10

Lady Astor Retains Her Seat

In May 1923, while Lady Astor was busy with her private
bill, Bonar Law fell ill and resigned the Premiership to
Baldwin, this being the occasion when Curzon was passed
over, much to his surprise. As Baldwin was no more
congenial to her than Bonar Law, the change made no
difference. After the passage of her bill, she and Lord
Astor went abroad for the summer. On her return in
October she published an article in the *Pall Mall Gazette*,
a newspaper owned by Lord Astor, again warning the
Conservatives about the danger of reaction and outlining
what she thought should be the party's forward policy, if
it was to stay in office; for it seemed to her that opinion in
the country was veering in favour of the Labour party.
The matters to which in particular she drew attention were
town planning by the state and the provision of more
houses; a revision of the Poor Law, including allowances
for widows with young children dependent on them; state
care of public health with special reference to maternity
and infant welfare; in education the school age to be raised
from fourteen to sixteen; a reform of the penal system, the
lunacy laws and prison administration. In advocating a
social policy along these lines, she was voicing the views of
the more intelligent Conservatives and of Lloyd George's
National Liberals. As all these proposals have since been
declared sound the been adopted in one shape or another,
one is bound to say that she and the friends who advised
her had a clear grasp of the tendencies of the age. Such
views gave offence among the extreme right. Even in her
own constituency she was attacked. Ten days after the *Pall
Mall* article a body of Plymouth Conservatives issued a

circular which contained the following: 'For some time loyal Conservatives have been placed in an intolerable position owing to the support given by Lady Astor to principles opposed to true conservatism.' The circular went on to say that a genuine Conservative should be selected to stand at Plymouth next time. The authors did not foresee that the Conservatives were more likely to retain the seat if their candidate had a social reform programme agreeable to Labour.

In following Lady Astor's political career, one has not to forget that out of the Commons she moved in circles where members of the House of Lords, their families and relations, were the chief figures. Thus, at the very time when she was putting forward views upsetting to the right, we find that she lent the Crown Prince Gustav of Sweden (now King Gustav) and his bride, Lady Louise Mountbatten, her house in Sandwich for their honeymoon. It is true that in this particular case she was lending her house to a Royal Highness with views as advanced as her own. Nevertheless, that she was in a position to oblige persons of that rank gave her so influential a standing in the Conservative party that she could smile at the efforts of a diehard section to discredit her.

In November 1923 Baldwin decided on an appeal to the country for support in his protectionist policy, as his majority in the Commons was too small. The general election was fixed for December. In consequence Lady Astor had to seek re-election at Plymouth at the very moment when her popularity there was said to be threatened. But, in fact, the diehard section was on no more solid ground than had been Dr Wansey Bayley in the election of the year before. There was little likelihood of her losing her seat. The *Evening Standard* of 22 November has: 'Apparently it is possible for a candidate to be too popular. That, at any rate, has been the uncomfortable, if flattering, experience of Lady Astor, whose meeting in Plymouth last night was so densely crowded that she could not enter by the door and had to climb in through a window, an aperture more usually associated with the escape of an unpopular speaker.'

It was not, however, quite so easy as that. For the first time she was having a straight fight with Labour without a Liberal candidate in between, and at a moment of reaction in favour of Labour. It was reported that 'an organized gang of Labour and Communist agitators follows her to all her meetings to heckle and interrupt. But Lady Astor's pet hobby is tearing hecklers to pieces'. One of her most famous retorts belongs to this election. Somebody, sure this would catch her out, asked in the accents of a country yokel: 'Say, Missus, how many toes are there on a pig's foot?' Quick as a flash came the answer: 'Take off your boot, man, and count for yourself.'

Another quick repartee is also recorded. While Lord Astor was speaking at one of his wife's meetings, there was a loud snapping noise, as of breaking wood. 'What's happened?' exclaimed Lord Astor. 'It's only a seat,' shouted a voice from the back of the hall, 'but I don't know whether it's Lady Astor's seat or not.' 'Oh, no,' said she, 'it is not mine. Mine is a safe seat.' On the Sunday following the *Observer* agreed that it was a safe seat. 'The tide is turning for Lady Astor and her vigorous social policy. It seems certain that she will hold and more than hold her seat, though the chances of a candidate with less progressive views would be small against so strong a socialist attack.' That was the point. Her progressive views were turning out an asset for the Conservatives. But, as on former occasions, her amusing way of talking helped most, as when she said to the crowd: 'If you vote for me, you will be getting tuppence for a penny, because you will be getting me and my husband as your representative. No other candidate can offer you as much. I belong to the tried old firm of Astor & Co.'

On 8 December the poll was declared. She was in with a majority of 3,000. But the Conservative party did badly. Baldwin found himself with only 259 supporters, a bit more than Labour, but not more than Labour and Liberals combined, a very precarious position. In a letter to *The Times* on 12 December Lady Astor rubbed in the moral: Conservative losses were due to the diehard attitude they had adopted towards social reform. If Baldwin could have counted on Liberal support, he would have been secure, but the Liberals at once decided that they would rather have a Labour government and, joining with Labour, turned him out. In January 1924 Ramsay MacDonald was summoned by King George and asked to form a government, the first Labour government in English history.

This turn of events did not disturb Lady Astor. She had never had much regard for labels; nor had any *a priori* objection to the Labour party. They would have her support where she judged support was due. She would continue her independent line and intervene in the debate from any angle she thought proper. Eight women had been returned to parliament on this occasion and, whatever their party, they looked up to her as the woman who had led the way in, had won three elections and had four years' experience. Her attitude to them was generous and friendly. Mrs Wintringham, again elected, she had liked very much from the start. Two of the others were the Duchess of Atholl, whom she already knew socially, and Miss Margaret Bondfield, a Labour member, a clever, hardworking, conscientious woman, a secretarial type very different from her. When Ramsay MacDonald gave Miss Bondfield the junior ministerial post of Under Secretary to the Ministry of Labour, Lady Astor declared at a reception she gave for the new women M.P.s, that Miss Bondfield should have had a place in the Cabinet. 'Some people say that she was not admitted because she had had no parliamentary experience. I know the Cabinet pretty well and there are some men in it whose parliamentary experience is not to their credit.' Thus without a trace of jealousy she congratulated the newcomer on her immediate promotion, though she herself in her four years as an M.P. had not been offered anything.

Her standing at this date in the opinion of her sex is

reflected in an article published in a woman's paper. 'Lady Astor always seemed to do the right thing, though she often did the unexpected thing. She was openly and fiercely at war with all the more degraded and retrograde elements in the House, the former headed by Sir Horatio Bottomley and the latter by Sir Frederick Banbury. When women wanted anything done (and we wanted an unending multitude of things done) she was always the one to undertake to do it.' The article goes on to say again how extraordinary it was and how unforeseen that a brilliant and witty hostess should turn out to be the woman destined to blaze the way for her sex.

It was proposed at this time that a portrait of her be commissioned, depicting her introduction in the Commons by Lloyd George and Balfour, and that it be hung in the House, for she was beginning to be seen as an historical personage. Charles Sims R.A. was given the commission. As will appear, the idea was not as good as it seemed.

Thus, with enhanced dignity, a more established reputation, she took her seat in the new parliament. There was one person she was very happy not to see there. Sir Frederick Banbury had been made a peer in the New Year's Honours. She was rid of him; her husband had him now. We have to think of the Viscount during these years doing his best in an uncongenial atmosphere to support his wife's efforts for social reform. The arrival of Banbury was not going to help him. In recording Banbury's translation to the House of Lords, the *Daily News* summarized his qualifications for that honour: 'M.P. for the City of London for 17 years. Hates social reform legislation. Has talked out many bills in his day. A Tory of Tories, but fond of dogs.'

CHAPTER 11

American Comment on
Lady Astor's Doings

It is not to be thought that the Americans ceased to interest themselves in Lady Astor after her return to England in the spring of 1922. On the contrary, her tour of the States had made her such an international figure that everything she did was closely followed. A few of the things they found striking or which particularly amused them are given in this chapter. Admiring her as they did, they thought some of the abuse levelled at her in the election following the break-up of the coalition quite shocking. 'We never treat a lady like that over here,' they said. But others were sure she could look after herself: 'Britishers who attempt to howl down Lady Astor ought to know it is impossible.' Winston Churchill's defeat by Mr Scrymgeour at Dundee seemed so extraordinary as hardly to be credible. 'What sort of freak tide of electoral humour had washed that street corner dry orator into the House of Commons?' they asked. How could the English prefer a man, 'whose voice, from howling on soap boxes that prohibition was his religion, had become hoarse', to the statesman who had been First Lord of the Admiralty, and War Minister? Was England about to adopt prohibition? But Lady Astor had told them that could not be. Scrymgeour must be just a joke, a joke which, they hoped, amused her as much as it did them, despite her temperance views. As at the moment they were short of new amusing stories about her, they published an anecdote which she was alleged to have narrated at a banquet in Baltimore the previous May. 'Old-fashioned people like Mr Rudyard Kipling', said the

Viscountess, 'still object to women in the House of Commons. According to them every voting woman is – is – is – is a – Well, I will tell you a story. Two men, a fat man and a thin one, burst into the pullman carriage of an express train. The fat man, who was heavily armed, yelled: "Throw up your hands. We are going to rob all the gents and kiss all the gals." But the thin man said gallantly: "No, no, pard; we rob the gents of course, but the ladies, God bless them, we won't harm a hair of their dear little heads." At this a severe looking female shook her finger in the thin man's face. "You mind your business, young fellow," she hissed. "Your partner is robbing this train, not you."' This story, delivered with all Lady Astor's brio, must have been just right at a banquet after a heavy day listening to serious speeches at the women's conference, but it was considered too flippant to report at the time.

The Americans also showed great interest in a dinner party which she gave in March 1923 at her address in St James's Square. At that date, it will be recalled, the Conservatives under Bonar Law were in power with a safe majority, but, aware of a growing popular support for Labour, she had warned her party to be less reactionary. Labour's attitude to the Crown was then somewhat revolutionary. If she could get its leaders to dine with King George V and Queen Mary at her house, she might effect the reconciliation which common sense required. The King and Queen, when approached, were willing to try the experiment, though none of the Labour leaders had ever been invited to the Palace, a state of affairs which seemed odd to the Americans, considering that the Labour party numbered 140 and was the second party in the state. The dinner took place on 9 March. The chief Labour guest was Ramsay MacDonald, fated to be Prime Minister in nine months, though no one expected this to happen so soon. As court costume was considered *de rigueur*, he and his followers had to dress up in knee breeches and silk stockings. It is said that an exception was made in the case of Philip Snowden, afterwards Chancellor of the Exchequer, who had a game leg. The Americans read with satisfaction how the hostess, the Virginian who had broken all Virginian records, entered the dining-room on the arm of the King, and were glad to be told that she knew how to hit the right mean, being neither over-impressed nor less correct than required. There were touches which greatly entertained them, as when she said to Jimmy Thomas: 'Pull up your stockings,' for he had allowed them to sag. Under such headings as LABOUR IN KNEE PANTS, the story went all over the States. But as well as its comedy, the dinner's importance was understood. The King made himself very agreeable and invited Ramsay MacDonald, Jimmy Thomas, Snowden and others to dine at Buckingham Palace. Indeed, the dinner was such a success, that the Labour left wing grew suspicious and denounced it later as a conspiracy. It was stories such as these which gave some of the American public the impression that an American woman was governing England, a fantasy, certainly, yet not lacking some truth, for it was undeniable that Lady Astor was doing what no other woman in England could do.

The Banbury affair was, of course, a great treat for the Americans, whose relish for the ludicrous, I think, exceeds, our own, certainly when the joke is not on them. Thus, from the Astor-Banbury debate, the following gave much pleasure:

Banbury: You can hardly see any drunkenness among the upper classes.

Mr Sexton (Labour): You don't see it.

Labour voices: They go home in cabs.

Teetotal debates in America were notoriously dull, but in England, with their Lady Astor in charge, everything went with a lively swing.

The expression about the village donkey, as a very English expression, gave the Americans food for thought. It was debated from several angles. Some argued that it showed Lady Astor to be now wholly English, for the term went with thatched roofs and hedged lanes; it conveyed nothing in America. Others expressed satisfaction at learning that all the donkeys in the world were not in Congress.

Entangled as they were in the toils of prohibition, a monster which somehow or other they had invited in, the Americans liked a drink joke better than any other. The rather poor story told by Mr Morrison, M.P., a former teacher, in the Astor bill debate, was voted a good one. Said Mr Morrison: 'Once a boy in my class brought to school a petition in favour of total prohibition. His mother had sent it and she hoped I would sign it and get all the boys in the class to sign. I told the boy I could not do this. Next day I asked him what his mother had said. "Please, sir," he replied, "she said she was sorry to hear you were a drunkard."'

But it was to the rich spectacle of Scrymgeour, 'the blue ribbon bulldog', that they returned again and again. 'In this amusing maniac's bill,' wrote one correspondent, 'there is a clause that alcoholic liquor should be sold only in octagonal bottles of a blue colour with a label containing the word Poison in capitals surmounted by a death's head and bones. A Scotch M.P., one of the sponsors of the bill, gave me these details between two whiskies and sodas.'

The Americans found Lady Astor's doings more absorbing than those of any woman in the States. In the matters here reported, they were deeply grateful to her, for her humour helped them to bear their ordeal, the ordeal of living in a dry continent.

CHAPTER 12

Lady Astor Continues Her Independent Course

Lady Astor never let an opportunity slip of reminding the Americans that the English desired their friendship and were ready to return it with a friendship as warm. It was not enough to entertain their notabilities at official receptions, where measured courtesies were extended to them. Something more spontaneous than the formal speech of welcome was required, if they were to feel among friends. When called upon to make such a speech, hers was always unconventional and playful. A good example of her method was how she addressed Mrs Kellogg, wife of the newly arrived American ambassador, at a luncheon given in her honour in January 1924. 'I am getting an old hand at welcoming ambassadresses and ambassadors. They come and go, but I seem to go on for ever. I want to warn Mrs Kellogg about one thing, and that is the climate. Someone said to me today that the climate was all right but the weather was bad. I have never seen an American ambassadress or ambassador arrive here who did not immediately say: "I don't know how we are going to face this English weather." But I have never known one of them go away without saying: "I don't know how I'm going to face the climate at home."' No one else in England could manage so skilfully this tone of cordial informality. The possessor of so valuable a diplomatic gift, she was well fitted, it was thought, for an ambassadorial appointment. Why not send her to represent Britain at Washington? But she was not cut out for anything so regimented as a diplomatic post. She knew well that she could never face up to office routine in an embassy nor, for that matter, in a ministry at home. That she was never offered any such appointment and so was not tempted to abandon her freelance career, was, I feel sure, all for the best.

She could afford to be a freelance, for she and her husband were rich enough to finance in part what they advocated; they had the money to give a lead and set the government an example. In this year of 1924 they made the handsome gift of £10,000 to provide workmen's dwellings in Plymouth. The houses were built from this sum and it was arranged that all rents, after the upkeep of the property was paid for, should go to a fund for the erection of new houses. One can well understand that, with a fairy godmother of this kind (the building of these workmen's houses was only a fraction of her charities), the citizens of Plymouth were in no hurry to elect another representative.

Little has been said here about her charities because they were for the most part unknown. In fact, every day she tried to help people and was ready to listen to anyone who sought her aid. When the House was sitting, she would go out to the lobby if an applicant sent in a note. 'One observed,' writes a reporter at this time, 'that Lady Astor was constantly appearing in the central lobby to grant interviews and receive petitions for help.' As an example of her kindness and disinclination to turn anyone away, we find the following in the *Daily Express* of 24 June 1924: 'A Cardiff man turned up at the House of Commons and sent in his name to Lady Astor. She came out into the lobby and found him carrying a four-year-old child, who was not well. He said that since his wife's death there was no one to look after it. He was out of work and had difficulty in going out to search for a job because of the child. Lady Astor at once undertook entire responsibility for its care for the time being.'

But she was sometimes approached in the lobby by people who wanted to get a rise out of her. On one occasion a man approached, saying he had a request to make. On her inviting him to tell her what she could do for him, he said: 'I want you to become a member of the ancient order of frothblowers.' The press has this comment: 'Her ladyship was unable to conceal her annoyance.'

Her reputation for charity being so widely known, she was the prey of impostors and rogues. 'Her ladyship,' said Mr Lee, her butler, to me one day, 'was much pestered by beggars at her house in St James's Square, for at first she handed out money without making enquiry and all sorts of frauds came flocking to get some. There was a man called Cook, I remember. He called, wanting this and that, and would put his foot in the door and frighten the housemaids. The maids sent to Cliveden, where I was, asking me to come and drive him off. When he next knocked I opened and on my threatening him, he left in a hurry. I remember another bogus case. I was footman at the time and one day was sitting by the chauffeur in her ladyship's new Lanchester car, when he was driving her back to the house. On arrival we saw a dirty old beggar woman seated on the steps. "What do you want?" asked her ladyship as she got out of the car. "I want a roof over my head and some place where I can look after myself," replied the old woman. "Well," said her ladyship in her prompt way, "get into the car and I'll drive you to a good place I know." The woman got into the back seat with her ladyship. As we drove off, the taxi-drivers in St James's Square laughed and called out: "What have you got in there?" They knew the beggar woman well. The place her ladyship had in mind was a church house. She arranged for the woman to stay there. But when I called next day to enquire, I was told that she had gone. Evidently that was not the sort of charity she wanted.' Mr Lee went on to say that frequent experiences of this sort made Lady Astor more wary. At last orders had to be given that money was not to be handed out. Applicants for charity were to have their cases investigated by one of the secretaries and only deserving persons were to be helped.

Nevertheless, Lady Astor held herself free to deal

directly if she felt inclined. She had a taste for dramatic acts of charity. David Astor has told me the following: 'One day when we were all out riding at Cliveden we came on a woman tramp on the road a short distance outside the park gates. She had a remarkable face with clear cut features, an impressive air of dignity, like a very duchess of the road. Mother drew rein at once, struck by her appearance, and asked her where she was going. The woman maintained an absolute reserve, replying in some laconic monosyllables. Mother could get nothing out of her; she gave no information about her means of livelihood nor whether she was in want of anything. Her farouche independence delighted Mother, who suddenly said: "Come and live at Cliveden. I'll give you a cottage and a nice job." The woman put the offer aside with indifference. "You're afraid to come!" said Mother. "I dare you to come." The woman averted her hawk-like face and without further word passed on down the road. Mother remained watching from her horse. When the woman came to Cliveden park gate she stopped a moment and then turned in at the gate. Mother was overjoyed. The woman's name was Mrs King. She was given a cottage and light work. She remained at Cliveden for thirty years. We got very fond of her.'

Lady Astor, as we have seen, has had little luck so far with her temperance crusade, except for the small private bill. She put this down to the influence of the liquor trade among Conservatives and hoped there would be a better chance now that the Labour party was in power. Early in 1924 a bill was introduced to restrain drinking in Wales, where it was said to be very bad. She supported this bill, in a speech described as her best for wit and spirit. 'There is a vital spark in her that will make it very difficult for anybody quite to eclipse her; she will continue an inimitable personality.' Such were some of the press tributes. But though the House was greatly entertained, they were not moved by her arguments. It was evident that Labour was no more a temperance party than the Conservatives.

Temperance, she declared, was in their election manifestos, but not in their hearts, and the many women who had voted for them had been deceived. But these diatribes only raised smiles. It became evident that there was no support for temperance in any quarter. 'I am left alone to cry for it, like John the Baptist in the wilderness,' she ended. The bill was rejected for all her plain speaking.

But though chagrined by Labour's indifference to sobriety, she strongly supported Ramsay MacDonald's policy abroad during 1924, which resulted in the return of the Ruhr to Germany and an agreed reparations treaty, a peace policy which strengthened the League of Nations. It was thought that Germany had turned over a new leaf and, now that some of the asperities of the Treaty of Versailles had been softened, would settle down in the comity of nations. Most people believed this, in spite of the Hitler-Ludendorff *putsch* at Munich the previous year which, though it did not come off, was a straw in the wind. Yet a *Daily News* reporter, sent to enquire into the nascent Hitler movement early in 1924, wrote: 'Hitler, the tub-thumping patriot, may be heard from again some day,' and added: 'After recovering from his war wounds he had a vision and stated that he had been summoned as saviour of Germany.' It is notable that this was said fifteen years before the Second World War. As will appear, Lady Astor's sanguine temperament landed her in trouble in the late thirties when it inclined her to believe that negotiations were still possible with Hitler. She was blamed for this belief and suspected of being a pro-Nazi, when, in fact, she was only an optimist, like a great number of other people who could not believe that Hitler was a paranoiac.

As the year 1924 went on the Labour party's position became less secure. From the first it depended on the Liberals' vote, but there were signs that their goodwill was cooling. Lady Astor, however, pleased with MacDonald's foreign policy, was in no hurry to see the last of him. She put in a good word for him when addressing the Conservatives of Plymouth. 'We must give the devil his due,' she advised them. In the House at times she lectured his party but declared that she was not one who wanted to turn it out. In this debate her description of the Labour M.P. Tom Shaw as having 'a heart paved with good intentions' showed her indulgence, as it also declared her confidence that a middle policy of reasonable give and take was the way to solve all problems. Not that she was ever accepted as an arbiter or even thought of herself as arbitrating between parties. Nevertheless, her actions took that form.

While steering her intuitive course, she was embarrassed in the middle of this year by a happening which was trivial yet unpleasant. Charles Sims completed the large canvas of her introduction as M.P. by Balfour and Lloyd George, the painting which Lord Astor had commissioned, acting on suggestions made to him the previous year. The Commissioner of Works, whose department dealt with such matters, was asked whether the Commons would accept it as a gift. He replied that they would, after he had made some informal enquiry. Accordingly, Lord Astor handed it over to him and he hung it in a good position outside the Chamber. The sight of it there was a surprise to those members not in the know, some of whom raised the objection that the House should have been formally consulted before it was hung. Was a painting of living M.P.s desirable? There was no precedent for such a thing. Questions were asked at a sitting. The unpleasant suggestion was made that the whole was a little plot to push Lady Astor, engineered by her husband and with her consent. Lord Astor, who was the last person on earth to engage in anything underhand, attempted to explain in a statement published in the *Morning Post* that he thought everyone knew of the picture from the beginning. Balfour and Lloyd George had posed for Sims, as had the several other M.P.s depicted in the background, and all of them had talked freely of what was going on. There was no secret about the matter. He had not tried to foist the picture on parliament. As for his wife, when told of the proposal to hang it in the House of Commons, she had, he said, been against the

139

idea, until assured that members really wanted it. In spite of this, a petition was presented to Ramsay MacDonald claiming that the Commissioner of Works had exceeded his authority and protesting against the picture's permanent exhibition. To avoid further unpleasantness, Lord Astor at once asked leave to remove it. This was granted, but before it was taken down, somebody had scribbled on it in pencil. It was a humiliating episode and would not have happened if the Astors had been more worldly. However, the last word rested with Lady Astor. After the picture had been removed and hung in the Bedford College for Women in Regent's Park, she said: 'They missed the whole point. It was not a picture of Lady Astor; it was never intended to be a picture of Lady Astor. It is a picture of an historical event. The people who kicked up the row thought they were hitting at me. But what they were hitting at was an idea, the idea of women in parliament. But the idea is still in the House of Commons and they will never get it out.' The Americans summed it up neatly: 'Lady Astor's picture has passed out of the House of Commons. But that does not mean that Lady Astor has passed out of the picture.'

In the autumn of 1924 Ramsay MacDonald, extending his efforts for European peace, sought a treaty with Russia. The Bolshevist régime had already been recognized but nothing more had been done to ease relations. Such, however, was the horror felt for the Bolshevist revolution that the Liberals deserted Labour. Outvoted, MacDonald had to appeal to the country. During the election campaign in October 1924, the publication of an alleged letter from Zinoviev, president of the Communist International, calling on Communists in England to tamper with the army to facilitate a revolution, so terrified electors that they identified the Labour party with Bolshevism and gave the Conservatives under Baldwin a huge majority. The swing over favoured Lady Astor at Plymouth. She won her fourth election with ease, her majority being double that on the previous occasion. Out of the other forty women who stood, only three got in, the Duchess of Atholl again and two new names. Miss Bondfield, who had held the under-secretaryship, and Mrs Wintringham who had been elected twice, failed. These results demonstrate the strong position which Lady Astor, now a parliamentarian of six years' standing, had acquired in England. In spite of her independence in the Commons, where she voted for her party or against it according to her judgment, and where she never tried to make up to anyone, she survived better than the solid Mrs Wintringham and the industrious and efficient Miss Bondfield, both of them obedient and amenable to party discipline. Many people thought that she would now be offered a ministerial post. Instead, the Duchess of Atholl, though much her junior in the Commons, was given the minor appointment of parliamentary secretary to the Board of Education. But to conclude that Lady Astor was passed over would be incorrect. In an interview to the press some days before Baldwin's list of office-holders was published, she said: 'I very much hope that they will give the Duchess of Atholl an under-secretaryship.' The same week Lady Rhondda wrote in *Time and Tide*: 'I trust that Lady Astor will not under any circumstance allow herself to be persuaded into committing the blunder of accepting minor office.' In point of fact, Baldwin had no intention of appointing any woman to the Cabinet or high ministerial office, but thought it prudent to make the small concession of the Duchess of Atholl's appointment. Lady Astor was too celebrated a figure for him to have offered her such a minor post. It was a disappointment for her and she felt it. Because the top posts were out of reach and the minor posts unsuitable, she was left with nothing.

During the first three months of 1925, she continued her charities, her work for women, her duties as hostess and mother, and was little in the news, so unusually little that some people were stupid enough to think that she had lost heart or her bite or something. That this was a false alarm, her altercation in April with the Labour member,

Mr Hayday, conclusively proved. She was speaking, when he interrupted to ask whether there was a working mother on a certain committee to which she was referring. The question irritated her, for her view was that a mother was first and foremost a mother, whether Conservative or Labour, a rich or a working mother. That there was a mother on the committee insured that women's interests would be taken care of. She therefore replied crossly to Mr Hayday: 'I hate that assumption that a working mother is different from any other mother. A mother is the same in all walks of life.'

Mr Hayday: 'In society gatherings puppy dogs take the place of children.'

This personal remark enraged Lady Astor and she retorted: 'If I told all I knew about the hon. member, I would give the House something to think of today. I would go into some of the company that the hon. member has kept that would not reflect credit on him nor on his party.'

This onslaught seems to have knocked the wind out of him for the moment. However, he rose and protested to the chair: 'I really think this is going beyond the bounds.'

The Speaker: 'I think so too, and the noble lady ought to withdraw.'

Lady A: 'He asked for it.'

Commander Kenworthy: 'The noble lady has made innuendos against the hon. member. The House ought to have an explanation or else a withdrawal.'

Lady A: 'I am quite willing to withdraw. But the hon. member's reference to toy dogs was also insulting.'

The Speaker: 'If the noble lady will accept my advice, often given to her, she will not entangle herself in such discussions. She should address me personally and avoid all this.'

Lady A: 'I quite agree. (Laughter.) I wish I could accept your advice, but I do not suppose that any member speaks under more provocation than I do.'

The Speaker: 'I cannot agree that the noble lady is not herself sometimes provocative.'

Lady A: 'I agree to that, too.'

In this fashion, by a mixture of charm, humour and contrition, she retreated in good order from an untenable position. There was a bit of comedy to help her also. Mr Hayday had no less than eighteen children. To accuse him of disreputableness was more a joke than an insult. But he seems to have been a silly man, for that night he brooded over what she had said and came to the conclusion that though she had withdrawn she had done so in so light a way that it did not amount to a serious withdrawal. He wrote and asked her for an apology. This false move exposed him to ridicule. He received a letter from her secretary to say a full withdrawal had been made, but of course if he was dissatisfied it was open to him to raise the matter again at the next sitting. He had not the sense to perceive the danger of this course and sure enough got up in the House three days later and declared that the insult to him had not completely withdrawn. But the House was no longer in the mood to take his insult seriously. By this time his extreme respectability and the insinuation against it seemed equally ludicrous. When Lady Astor immediately said: 'I thought I had made a complete withdrawal of the words used, but if the hon. member thinks I did not, I will do so now most unreservedly,' there was some laughter. The words were irreproachable, but their tone was somehow or other a little droll. Too late, Mr Hayday recalled that it was dangerous to engage in a verbal duel with Lady Astor. Men much cleverer than he had failed to get the better of her.

The encounter, as was usual with such brushes, had an enlivening effect on her. She entertained a London audience a few days later with this reference to Mr Hayday: 'I got a little nettled last Friday, but I am going to change. I am changing. I am really very much better than I used to be, and I am going to be better every day and in every way.' This sally was greeted with merriment. Poor Mr Hayday was still being laughed at. The *Daily News* next day continued the joke: 'It would be a mistake,' it said roguishly, 'to take Lady Astor's good intentions too seriously. The temperance pledge is the most difficult of all pledges to keep. Lady Astor will almost certainly be nettled again. Members will see to it that she is by deliberately provoking her. She will be tempted and she will fall. If she did not, the House of Commons would become unbearably dull.'

The new Commons, with its overlarge Conservative majority, was undeniably stuffy. They no longer had Mr Scrymgeour, for instance, to amuse them, for he had not been re-elected. But we have a glimpse of him at the very moment of the Hayday affair among the stump orators at Marble Arch. An anti-prohibitionist speaker on a pulpit labelled LADY ASTOR AT IT AGAIN was challenging the 'Virginian creeper', as he called her, to come there and answer him face to face. Next to him was Mr Scrymgeour on a soap box, no better disposed towards Lady Astor, though for opposite reasons, trying to smother his rival's harangue with his own.

What an addition Lady Astor was to the Commons is also the theme of the journalist Mr A. G. Gardiner, who knew her well, in a lively article in the *Daily News*. After describing her as 'an embodied emotion bursting into the sobrieties and decorums of the world with the same impulsive gaiety with which as one of the Langhorne sisters she careered in youth over the Virginian pastures', he goes on to declare that 'it is not her opinions that make her so unprecedented a figure in the English public scene, but the gallop of the spirit with which she enters the lists, her terrific pugnacity and her gay indifference to the formal respectabilities of behaviour. The House of Commons, said Bolingbroke, loves the man who shows it sport. And wherever Lady Astor's "View halloo!" is heard, there is the assurance of sport. She is as ready to back Mr Baldwin or Mr MacDonald as she was to pull the coat-tails of Sir Frederick Banbury, and she has declared that she would go to Timbuctoo for the joy of fighting a brewer.' Several other well known writers of the twenties, among them

Philip Guedalla, attempted impressions of her, but none of them with more relish than A. G. Gardiner.

It has already been remarked that one of the reasons why she did not resemble the politician *de carrière* was the largeness of her life, so much wider than most M.P.s', which gave her a perspective and aplomb they could not have. She had the knack, not only of getting to know, but of becoming close friends with, the notable personalities of the moment. In 1925 she grew to like the heir to the throne, Edward Prince of Wales, who was then thirty-one years of age. She was attracted to him on account of his modern democratic outlook. In 1923–24 he had toured the English industrial cities in an effort to get to understand the working man and his wants. As she in her various ways had long been trying to do the same, they had much in common to discuss. When in London he often dined at her St James's Square house. There he would sometimes meet Labour members of parliament and talk freely to them. Lady Astor found him much more congenial than his parents. George V was so old-fashioned, Queen Mary could be so crushing, as on the occasion when the Queen and she were visiting a home for the blind. Lady Astor, after chatting in her vivacious non-stop way to the inmates, asked the Queen to come and speak to a particular man. 'Have you talked to him?' enquired Queen Mary. 'Yes, indeed,' replied Lady Astor. 'Then I think', said the Queen, 'that will suffice.' The Prince never made this sort of dry remark. But as a matter of fact, he sometimes did, but his manner was not like his mother's. One night Lady Astor and he were at a public dinner in the Savoy, where she had to thank him for coming. In her speech she complimented him on his readiness to make personal sacrifices for public duty. 'For instance,' she said, 'on this occasion he might easily have stayed at his delightful home in Sunningdale and played golf.' 'Not after dark,' interjected the Prince.

The Americans had already begun to follow the doings of the Prince. When he dined with Lady Astor, it was double news. At one such dinner Will Thorn, the Labour M.P., was a guest. A remark which he made to the Prince got into the press. 'I told the Prince I would get some dirty bouquets sent along to me for putting my feet under the table with royalty'; for the extreme left still remained very cool in its attitude to the Crown. Indeed, Ramsay Mac-Donald during his nine months as Prime Minister was said by some of his followers to have 'consorted too closely with the nobs'. The democratic young Prince was trying to break down this prejudice. He replied to Will Thorn that he did not want the word royalty to be used about him. Couldn't people just call him the Prince of Wales, which, after all, was his name. His amiable endeavours not to be stand-offish led some Americans to exaggerate his liking for equality. He was given the nickname of Red Willie and as early as May 1923, thirteen years before the abdication, was reported to have said to his brother, the Duke of York: 'You had better learn to be King of England, for I never shall be.' He was represented as a sort of daredevil, and said at one function to have appeared with a black eye and bandaged finger, after a fall in the hunting field. 'With no regard for matrimony, the sceptre or his life, he is astounding old England,' the New York *Evening Journal* declared. As such an exciting picture of him prevailed, it was no wonder that his friendship with their own Lady Astor thrilled the Americans. The truth of the matter was less dramatic. Lady Astor felt that he had the makings of a popular king. Some of his associates, however, would do him no good. Though an indefatigable traveller, he wasted too much time with frivolities. She genuinely liked him as a person and thought that she could help him to cultivate his good qualities, to the benefit of both himself and the state.

In 1926 Will Thorn published his autobiography, *My Life's Battles*, which contains an account of the dinner in Lady Astor's town house at which he made the above-quoted remark: 'One evening in the House of Commons Lady Astor asked me if I would like to dine with her to meet the Prince. I agreed on one condition, that I should be allowed to wear my everyday clothes. Her reply was that I could wear any clothes that I liked. I decided to go. When I reached the house in St James's Square several magnificent motor cars were lined up outside and crowds of people were waiting to see the guests arrive. Finally, I plucked up courage and pushed through the crowd, marched up to the door, conscious all the time that I was a little out of place. The door was opened by servants in gorgeous livery. They looked at me with amazement and I am sure they wondered who I was. My hat, stick and coat were taken and I was escorted to the grand staircase, at the top of which was Lady Astor, beautifully dressed and crowned with a glittering diamond tiara. She gave me a hearty welcome and introduced me to some of her friends. The silvery notes of an oriental gong summoned us to dinner. At the time I was speaking to Lady Astor's sister. I offered her my arm and escorted her to the table, where Lady Astor had seated me near the Prince of Wales. The general atmosphere of luxury gave me a rosy glow. I looked at the beautiful women around me and turning to Lady Astor's sister remarked that the beauty of it all reminded me of a song I had often heard in the East End. She was curious to know what it was and finally persuaded me to hum the song.'

This story of Mr Thorn's is quite characteristic of Lady Astor's dinners. People who hadn't got evening clothes didn't have to wear them and if you felt like singing that was all right. She herself had a freedom of manner at the dinner table which astonished people who saw it for the first time.

In Will Thorn's tale of the dinner there is also this sentence: 'Lord and Lady Astor are teetotallers, but there was an abundance of wines and spirits.' The reader may have wondered how Lady Astor could have become a famous hostess if her parties were teetotal. How did she get people to come if there was nothing to drink? Mr Thorn gives the answer – there was drink, an abundance of it. One day I asked Mr Lee (as butler for so many years he was the best authority on the subject) what actually was the rule. Was there, for instance, any substance in the story of somebody being asked one day at St James's Square whether he would have lemonade or lime squash and that he replied: 'Lime squash, there's more kick in it'?

'Well,' said Mr Lee, 'there was always a jug of lemonade in the hall. Day or night, you could get lemonade in the hall.'

'In the hall, yes,' I said, 'but what about those big luncheons, those grand dinner parties, when even royalty might be present, and the house parties at Cliveden?'

Mr Lee replied: 'My orders were that no cocktails should be served before lunch or dinner, and no drinks between meals for those staying in the house. But at meals sherry was offered first, then a white wine, followed by a red or champagne, and, after dessert, port, brandy and liqueurs. His lordship was very particular about the quality of his wines. "Only the very best, Lee," he would say to me. I am not a drinker, but it was my duty to taste the wines. I can say that they were good, the most expensive vintages.'

This reminded Mr Lee of a story and he said: 'I remember the first time the Prince of Wales came to dinner. That was before he knew the ways of the house. His equerry, Major "Fruity" Metcalfe, rang up first. He said to me: "His Royal Highness knows Lady Astor's principles. I am sending a bottle of his favourite brandy along with him. He hopes that you will be able to let him have a glass or so of it at the end of dinner." I replied "It is not necessary, sir, to go to such lengths. While it is true that her ladyship dislikes liquor and neither she nor his lordship takes any, their guests are always served with the best. I have been ordered to offer His Royal Highness some 1828 brandy." On learning of the famous brandy, Major Metcalfe immediately withdrew his suggestion. I rather think the Prince was told what to expect, for after dinner when I asked in the usual way: "Will your Royal Highness have port, liqueurs or brandy?" he looked up at me with such an amusing face. "*Your* brandy," he said.'

Lady Astor has always insisted that from the twenties onwards she did not entertain for the sole pleasure of it (though she certainly enjoyed having people about her and was at her best in brilliant company), but because she thought it important to bring people together, Americans and English, Conservatives and Labour, and let talk in pleasant surroundings smooth out differences to the advantage of all sides. Part of the pleasant surroundings had to be drinks. She accepted them as inevitable. But that was no reason for abating her efforts in the cause of temperance.

Her way of advocating sobriety could be hilarious. A temperance meeting, when she was there, was never depressing. She was just as amusing on a blue ribbon platform as on any other. Thus at Glasgow in 1927 she showed how to make a temperance bazaar a success. She began by telling her audience to be intemperate: 'Buy intemperately at the bazaar,' she begged them. There followed hits at the House of Lords: 'The difficulty about the drink trade in England is that it is so respectable. When a man gets on in the world through selling drink he becomes a peer. There are three subjects that really bring the Lords to their feet – beer, land or women. The day one of these is for debate, the old fellows roll up in their hundreds. They know about drink, land and women! That's the way to fetch 'em.' And she mimicked to perfection an old lord hurrying into the House. These witticisms were as good as a pick-me-up. The Glasgow reformers bought recklessly at the stalls, repeating her latest Astorism: 'It is hard enough to be a Christian when you are sober. It is absolutely impossible when you are drunk.' Seven thousand pounds was raised that afternoon.

Some of the papers described her speech as 'a sparkling temperance bouquet.' But it was only Lady Astor not being dull. She was not boring at a temperance meeting because she was not boring anywhere. But she knew that in letting her humour have full play, a creative act, which for her was the breath of life, she gave people a handle against her. If she made fun of them, they would make fun of her. This may have been in her mind when, a few days after the Glasgow speech, she heard that A. G. Gardiner, the man whose article on her has been quoted, was shortly to broadcast on her character. For she sent him the following telegram: 'Go slow, comrade. I tremble to think what you might say with all truth. Don't be just. Be merciful. Nancy Astor.'

About now the following story was going the round. A friend of hers is related as saying: 'You are so very illogical, Lady Astor, and you lack moral courage. Your lunches and dinners are renowned for the excellent wines and liqueurs you serve in abundance.'

'You have had that experience of them, haven't you?' asked Lady Astor thoughtfully.

'Thank you, yes.'

'You think I ought to close my cellars, do you?'

'Logically, I see no other course.'

'Very well,' retorted Lady Astor, 'barley water for you at my table from this on; my butler shall have his orders this very day.'

CHAPTER 13

Some Critics and Some Friends

In the period 1927 to 1931 Lady Astor made friends with some remarkable men and was also subjected to acrimonious attack. There is a legend of South American origin that George Bernard Shaw was first drawn to her when he read that she ejaculated 'Rats!' while listening to a rubbishy speech in the House. This interjection enormously amused him; he never forgot it and liked recalling it. His name first appears in the Cliveden Visitors Books under date Christmas 1927. We have an early glimpse of him in the St James's Square house as seen through American eyes. Lady Astor was entertaining at tea in the drawing-room a little crowd of American visitors when Shaw was announced. She came forward to welcome him and he asked: 'Who are all these people?' Making one of her bogus introductions, she replied: 'Those on the left are Austrians and Bulgarians, and those on the right are Czecho-slovakians. None of them can speak a word of English.' Shaw seemed a little nonplussed, but when somebody whispered: 'We are all Americans,' became immediately his normal outrageous self. At this time he was seventy-one. As his topsy-turvy parodoxes, enunciated defiantly in his soft Irish brogue, cascaded over the assembly, he was asked whether he believed what he was saying. Lady Astor replied for him: 'Of course you don't believe a single thing.' She liked Shaw for several reasons. His conversation stimulated her, as her retorts to it stimulated him. Her spirits rose, she became immensely animated as she returned him tit for tat. It was her substitute for champagne. Besides this reason for finding Shaw's company a wonderful tonic, she admired him as a genuine reformer, who wanted to see done many of the things she had always advocated. Underneath his banter and extravagances she knew he was an honest good man.

There is a photograph of him on the terrace at Cliveden, dressed in his usual costume of Norfolk jacket, knickerbockers and stockings, his stalk-like body flowering with his bush-beard, and crowning all a cloth cap. He is doing his best to please his hostess by entertaining Rhodes scholars invited for the afternoon. By this time of his life he had made it a rule not to attend social functions, but she had managed to get round him. Indeed, we find that she got him to accompany her when visiting institutions in which she was interested, such as the Nursery Schools, founded by the great reformer Margaret McMillan. At one of them he is recorded to have asked a group of children: 'Have you read any of my plays?' 'No,' they replied. (They were all under five.) 'I am glad to hear it,' said he. She also roped him in to make a speech at Plymouth and open a hostel given to the University College of the South-West by her husband and herself. The occasion was one when he let his sense of humour run away with him. He was, of course, the last man to make the sort of formal speech required, thank the donors, and expatiate on the good which the hostel would do. He went, however, further in the opposite direction than one might suppose possible even for a licensed wit. He was dressed in a neat black suit, as if to do honour to the occasion, a subtle touch. He said: 'The extraordinary devotion of my friends Lord and Lady Astor to the city of Plymouth has always been a source of astonishment to me because I have never been able to understand in what way the citizens have deserved it. I have a strong impression that a large number of them resent it extremely. Lord Astor is evidently carrying on a struggle against the inevitable consequence of his own public spirit. After a few more years I believe he will be the most unpopular man in south-west England. Possibly, however, those who come after him, his sons for instance, if they abstain from doing anything for the people of

Plymouth, and make as much money as they possibly can, may restore the popularity of the Astor family.'

And he went on: 'Many of you may think I am an enthusiastic advocate of university education, whereas I am fully convinced that English university education is destroying civilization and has for some centuries been making decent government and decent life for the people impossible.' His conclusion was: 'The thing to do to these venerable institutions, particularly Oxford and Cambridge, in spite of the beauty of many of their buildings, is to raze them to the ground and sow the foundations with salt. If it is too much trouble to knock them down, use them as asylums for lunatics.'

This roundabout way of thanking the donors and encouraging the students, when considered afterwards in cold blood, was thought far-fetched by some of his auditors, but at the time, carried away by his high spirits, they enjoyed watching the gambols of the irrepressible old dramatist. There was still more, for not yet content with his jocularities, he turned to Lord Astor and addressed him thus: 'I am very glad that the name of the university will always be associated with Lord Astor. I have a very large knowledge of the revolutionary world, not only in England but in Europe, and the most extreme Communist I have ever met is Lord Astor. I have said to friends of mine who call themselves Communists and who indulge in a deal of curious and antiquated worship of Karl Marx: "Why do you bother about Marx, why don't you go after Lord Astor?" but they are too old-fashioned.'

It fell to Lady Astor to propose the vote of thanks to G.B.S. If she had not expected him to go the whole hog on such an academic occasion, she was not unduly surprised, and was certainly very glad to have been spared a dull speech by somebody else. Her reply was just right. She said that there were few people who could speak as he did, and perhaps it was as well for the world that there were.

She grew really attached to him. He retained her affection till his death, over twenty years later. What was the tie between them? It has already been suggested: a mutual stimulation and a mutual respect for the depths of each other's character. She egged him on to the extravagances and paradoxes, which seemed to make life worth living for him. They roused all the fun in her, loosened her tongue and gave her a sensation of intoxicating well-being. She did not read his plays or attempt to grasp his economic theories, though she summed up his ideas once very aptly by saying: 'His greatest gift has been in breaking down things.' But the friendship between them was not intellectual; it pertained more to the realm of magic and art. He was a man of genius; it was an incomparable pleasure to mingle with his spirit. That magical feat she achieved because she understood the art of talking to him.

Their amusing relationship is glimpsed in an account of how, in May 1930, she threw herself into his humour at Nottingham, to which town they had motored one morning from Buxton to attend a public function at the County Hall. The reporter of the *Nottingham Evening News*, a young man called Shaw, described what happened when he sent in his card with a request for an interview. 'When G.B.S. had read my card, Lady Astor came out and told me: "Mr Shaw says I am to inform you that the real Shaw is in there, so you must be an impostor." However, G.B.S. then appeared with a mischievous expression and said good-morning. I asked him when last he had visited Nottingham. He replied: "It is not for me to remember that. Surely the people of Nottingham cannot have forgotten so momentous an event." Which reminds one of the occasion when a lady approached him and asked: "Are you Shaw?" To which he replied: "Generally, but not invariably so." That was the extent of the interview, for he proceeded to enter into a bantering discussion on nationalization with Lady Astor as they walked towards his beautiful chocolate-coloured Lanchester.'

A popular vote taken at this time declared Lady Astor more indispensable to the world than G.B.S. In the debate of a Yarmouth society, the members discussed which of six notabilities – Lady Astor, Viscount Cecil, Marconi, Mussolini, Bernard Shaw or Sir John Simon – if voyaging together in a balloon, should be jettisoned in an emergency to secure the safety of the others. Though this was nine years before Mussolini became a menace to peace, it was agreed straight away that he be pitched out first. In a final ballot, to give the order in which the rest should be sacrificed, it was voted that G.B.S. go overboard before Lady Astor.

At Christmas 1928 Shaw stayed at Cliveden for some weeks and composed the greater part of *The Apple Cart* there. Lord Astor has told me that after dinner Shaw used to read out scenes, as he wrote them, and how amusing it was, for he could change his tone and expression to suit the various parts. He had a model of an apple cart and horse, and this he rolled into the room. His manner was most engaging. According to Edward Angly, an American, who was staying at Cliveden at the time, Shaw insisted that he should be seated at his hostess's right at lunch and dinner, a privilege, he said, which he demanded more as a compliment to the arts than to himself. The previous Christmas he had been invited for three days, but stayed three weeks. When reminded of this by Lady Astor (which she did more than once), he replied that it was because of the length of his stay that he had been invited a second time. In the course of the readings he explained that the play was not unconnected with his belief that Labour would win the next election (as in fact it did in May 1929, five months later). One of the characters, the American ambassador, wanted the amalgamation of England and America, an exaggerated version of Lady Astor's wish for the two countries to be united in indissoluble friendship. The play contained praise of England, put in King Magnus's mouth, praise which Shaw as a rule was very chary of. 'G.B.S., you are getting some sense in your head in your old age,' she declared. On Boxing Day, continues the same American informant, Shaw was Santa Claus in a party for the whole Cliveden staff and their families. He was so suitable for the part that he required no make-up. 'You look like Santa Claus, even though you've got the manners of the devil,' she told him fondly. He enjoyed himself immensely in the rôle as it gave him scope for his fancy. 'The lies he told the youngsters, his blue eyes alight, appeared always plausible to them.'

The Apple Cart was translated into Russian and its première was in Moscow in June 1929. Taken as a skit on democratic government, it was very popular with the Communists. The next chapter will give an account of Shaw and Lady Astor's visit to Moscow in 1931. The success of *The Apple Cart* accounted in part for the warmth of his reception there.

With Baldwin's defeat in the general election of 1929, the second labour government came in. Ramsay Mac-Donald, who had lived down the ridiculous charge of being a Bolshevist, became Prime Minister again. It was Lady Astor's fifth election campaign at Plymouth. Before going down there, she addressed the Conservative Association at Luton. In the course of her speech she entertained her audience with some characteristic sallies. To combat the Socialist view that everyone was equal she said: 'If we parents cannot guarantee the equality of our own children, how in Heaven's name is the state going to guarantee a general equality? I have one boy who could sell a horse without legs; and I have another who couldn't sell the Derby winner. It is absurd.' And then she ricochetted to another point in criticism of socialist M.P.s: 'What I notice in the House of Commons is that the men who want to run the business of the country are never men who run any business of their own.'

A voice: 'They'll never do worse than you.'

Lady A: 'Never mind. Let them do as well.'

She went on to say that she wasn't against Socialism and was asked: 'You'd be glad to join the Labour party?'

She replied: 'There is a great deal about the Labour party I like. But what I dislike are the humbugs. I can't stand humbugs.'

A voice: 'What about Baldwin and Churchill?'

Lady A: 'Don't think there are no humbugs in the Conservative party. There are. But our policy is not a policy of humbug.' And towards the end of her speech she made this *mot*: 'If people tell me that I'm a thief and a liar, I don't mind, because I'm not. But if they tell me I'm a nuisance, I hate it because I am.' She knew well how she tried her own party and said a few days later: 'If any woman in any other party had attempted to do what I have done in my party, she would not be allowed in it for long.'

Continuing to speak for the Conservatives in the weeks before the election campaign began, she said at Stockton in support of its member, Harold Macmillan (the present Prime Minister): 'I admire a man who is courageous enough to let his mother-in-law speak for him. How many men are there who would dare to do that?' (It appears that the Duchess of Devonshire had been down to Stockton to speak.) In praise of Macmillan she said that she had heard him speak once at Plymouth for one and a quarter hours on derating, a pretty dull subject in itself, but he made it so interesting that 'I could not hear the sound of a pin dropping nor the slightest snore, though I listened for both.' Praise could go no further.

During the election campaign some of her sayings were very true to character. 'Public life is in some ways a nuisance, in some ways a privilege. It is a privilege to say what you like without being afraid of losing your job.' 'Every single thing I told the Conservative die-hards that they were wrong in not doing, the party has done since.' 'Labour does not want to send children away from home; no woman does. Yet I would rather send my son to Timbuctoo with a job than have him at home without one.' (Timbuctoo stood for absolute remoteness in her vocabulary, yet not so far that a fleeing brewer would be safe from her there.) And another saying: 'I am a sporting character really. I love gardens and out-of-door life and adore knitting.'

The fight at Plymouth was touch-and-go this time in

spite of her great popularity, because of a swing towards Labour greater than she had experienced before in her career. There was the affair of Mr Chalmers' hat. He was manager for the Labour candidate, Mr Westwood. The two of them ran into her once outside the Town Hall. She remarked to Mr Westwood that if he got in, it would be with the help of the Liberals. He clapped her on the back, saying: 'We shall win, Liberals or no Liberals. Don't lose your temper, although you are going to lose your seat.' After this exchange he moved on with his manager, Mr Chalmers. A crowd of his supporters nearby began to sing 'The Red Flag'. Whereupon she struck up the National Anthem, in which her supporters joined. Mr Chalmers did not take off his hat when he heard the National Anthem. She called on him to do so, but he paid no notice. Whereupon she stepped over to him and knocked it off, or so it was reported. The episode caused some excitement in the country and discussion in the press. She denied that she had knocked his hat off. She had tried, had a swipe at it, but failed. His hat was only tilted. This, in fact, was shown to have been the case; she had foozled her shot.

The campaign continued. Mr Westwood is reported as saying: 'Well, we have handed Nancy a ticket this time. You see, she's lost her temper something awful. When I drive through her meetings she calls me all sorts.' He was looking out of the window at some American warships, which happened to be in the harbour on visit. 'Perhaps they have come to take her home,' he said hopefully. 'Now listen to me, I went up to her the other day and called her a temperance humbug, that's what I said.' 'What did she call you?' asked the reporter. Westwood lit a cigarette and forbore to answer. 'You think you will win?' the reporter said. 'Can I win?' cried Mr Westwood. 'I could have a red Plymouth tomorrow if I wanted, only the police came to me and said: "Westwood, you are keeping Plymouth good."'

As one sees from this, Mr Westwood was a character. Lady Astor, with her taste for characters, grew to like him very much. But she had to fight him and did so in grand style. There are excellent pen-pictures of her hard at work. The best are two articles in the *Daily Express* of 28 and 29 May. 'Lady Astor stood completely alone in the courtyard of the worst tenement in the worst street in Plymouth, a Communist stronghold, and glowered at balcony on balcony above, packed with more than a hundred shouting, shrieking, hostile women. "So you are a pack of Bolshies, eh?" she challenged, waving her umbrella threateningly. "Better get away, Lady Astor," I warned. "Leave this to me," she said. She danced up and down outside the tenement with her umbrella at the present. "They say I drink gin and bitters," she cried, and pointing to a woman who had been shouting herself hoarse, demanded: "You up there, how many gin and bitters have I had with you?" Somehow or other she won them over. When she left in her car, the crowd shouted: "Good old Nancy." She went to a house where photos of Mr Westwood were in every window. "Who is that?" she asked the woman who opened the door. The woman said, the Labour candidate. "Come over here," said Lady Astor. They talked and she came back to the car. As we were rounding the corner, we saw the woman taking down the photos of Mr Westwood.'

One should not, perhaps, take this account too literally, but it certainly is not untrue of what we know of Lady Astor's character. The article ends: 'Lady Astor will win this election. They dare not vote Socialist. "Why, you never know when her ladyship will come into your scullery and put it across you," said a woman to me.'

In the course of the election she said many amusing things, some of which have been preserved. When touring the poorer quarters of Plymouth she entertained the crowds with stories circulated by her opponents to discredit her. As she told the stories she laughed outright. 'They have been telling people that in the last election five years ago I used a beer lorry to speak from, told the workers they ought to have beer and held a glass of beer in my hand. They are even spreading the old story that my four sisters and I appeared in tights in a Broadway musical turn called The Gibson Girls. But they have also accused me of living so luxuriously that I have two maids to bath me.' As usual, she punished hecklers. 'Are you a Christian?' a man asked her. 'I'm trying to be one. How about you?' 'I'm trying,' he echoed, beginning to be at a loss. 'Well, it's going to be a trying job,' was the rejoinder that routed him. And to another man who said: 'Don't you think mothers ought to stay at home with their children?' she replied looking at him with mock concern: 'I think children ought to stay at home with their mothers.' No heckler had a chance against her. She was so much better at heckling them than they were at heckling her.

As was anticipated, she won, but it was a narrow shave. It seems that at the last moment a man-of-war came in and the sailors all voted for her. She got 16,625 votes to Mr Westwood's 16,414, and so rode out the storm which sank her party.

It was Bernard Shaw who introduced to her Lawrence of Arabia, who was then forty. He had enlisted in 1922 in the Air Force and now in 1929 was serving in a camp near Plymouth under the assumed name of Shaw and with the rank of aircraftman. Besides G.B.S., he had other distinguished friends, including Lionel Curtis and Philip Kerr (Lord Lothian) with whom he passed some of his time off from duty. It was thus that he came into Lady Astor's orbit.

On December 1930 a question about him was asked in parliament by Mr Malone, M.P., who wanted to know, in view of the allegations at a Russian state trial that in 1927 he was in England and mixed up in a conspiracy against the Soviet government, where in fact he was at that date. The answer given stated that in 1927 he was not in England but in India. Lady Astor then asked: 'Is it not true that Aircraftman Shaw is leading a quiet, respectable and useful life?' There were cries of 'Hear, hear' and laughter and shouts of: 'That's more than you are.'

A close friendship had developed between her and

Lawrence, all the more strange because he did not care for the society of women. Their characters were apparently very different. She was ten years older than he and a person living much in the world. He was a recluse, who shrank from the world's contact, and yet by that very shrinking was as much in the public eye as was she. He was a man of letters and the strangest of eccentrics, the secret of whose disgust with normal life has puzzled people ever since. She had a great appetite for life, much plain good sense and detested humbugs and *poseurs*. What was it, then, that made it possible for them to like each other. One has to bear in mind that by 1929 Lawrence had recovered a good deal from the nervous breakdown he suffered after the Arab campaigns. Then, shocked, disappointed and physically exhausted, he had contemplated suicide and the fear of it was one reason for his enlisting in 1922 in the Air Force. The hope that a daily round of discipline and dull routine would steady him was realized. By the time he met Lady Astor he was approaching normality and found himself at ease in her house. It was restful for him to be able to drop in. He kept some of his books there and sometimes would read quietly. He was not fond of meeting other guests, but when he found the atmosphere congenial could be very amusing. If, for instance, Bernard Shaw was asked, there would be great fun, a sparkling conversation, wherein he was just as brilliant as Shaw or Lady Astor. Thus she was able to get a peep of him as he was before his breakdown. The present Lord Astor has told me that in their house Lawrence was relaxed and easy, fond of children, patient with young people, sometimes very witty, sometimes playing practical jokes, a different man altogether from the shrinking and uncouth eccentric he appeared to many people.

Yet it would be wrong to think that his friendship with Lady Astor rested principally on such foundations. The key perhaps is to be found in the gravity which underlay both their characters. She regarded him as a hero, who had had extraordinary adventures and who by the force of his personality had won the admiration of many eminent men and many humble men, but who for one reason and another had suffered a grievous psychological wound. That he was a wounded hero greatly appealed to her. One of her strongest characteristics was an impulse to succour the unfortunate. When to these reasons for his attractiveness is added her respect for people with great intellectual gifts, one may begin to understand why the wide differences between them were no bar to a deep friendship. That he, on his side, became attached to her was partly because she was a strong woman. He was a type of man who leans on strong women and finds a refuge in them, as also was Bernard Shaw. There are people who would account for both Lawrence's and Shaw's feeling for her by their fundamental need of a mother to go to. Lawrence may also have felt in harmony with her because instinct told him that, contrary to appearances, she resembled him underneath. Had she not also her fastidiousness, her need of withdrawal, a shrinking which in his case made him a recluse, in her case drove her into the hurly-burly in an attempt to cover or relieve her heart? Was she as sure of herself as appeared? Had she not also her despairs? The answers to these questions cannot be known. But she said this much to me: 'When Lawrence was stationed near Plymouth he used to come in often and see us after dinner. If interested, his conversation was brilliant, but he was often silent. I used to ride pillion on his motorcycle and go long distances very fast. He liked it because I could balance without touching him. My last ride with him was only a fortnight before his fatal accident.' When one considers, it was an astounding thing that a woman of her age and station should ride madly over the country behind a disguised hero. Was it the wild horses of Virginia over again, love of daring adventure for the excitement of it? Perhaps, but perhaps there was a deeper need.

In 1935, some five years after she had first met him, he died. He was buried without military honours at Moreton in Dorset. The reporter of the *Daily Telegraph* saw the scene thus: 'The Prince of Mecca, to whom kings and statesmen had listened with respect, was laid to rest in an obscure English churchyard, without mourning, without flowers, under an alien name. The plain elm coffin lay on trestles before the altar bathed in blood-red light from the east window. All was strange and incongruous, yet fitting. Quiet though the funeral was, the few mourners were all celebrated persons. The pall bearers included Sir Ronald Storrs and Eric Kennington, the artist. Augustus John was there in rough tweeds with a flowing scarf. A blackbird's song was heard during the service. At the graveside Winston Churchill wept. Grass from Akaba was strewn on the coffin. There was only one bunch of flowers – lilac and forget-me-nots placed on the grave by an unknown girl. Lady Astor was present. He had died on her fifty-sixth birthday.'

Another remarkable man with whom she made friends was Gandhi, when he came over in 1931 for the Indian Round Table Conference. Lord Lothian introduced him to her. Before she met him, she tended to think that the Indians' agitation for home rule was overdone, as they had nothing serious to complain of. In a book published in 1932 called *Entertaining Gandhi* by Muriel Lester, who was Gandhi's hostess during his visit, the author records how when he first came to Lady Astor's house she called him a humbug in her teasing way and declared his policy was only destructive. He listened patiently as she ran on and then asked whether she would like to listen to him or would rather go on talking. This sort of direct plea for fair play always appealed to her. She immediately asked him to say what was in his mind and promised not to interrupt. He then told her the whole story of the national movement in India and won her over. As in 1931 it was considered by many Conservatives, including Churchill, to be practically treason to sympathize with the Indians in their desire for independence, her sympathy for them is a revealing fact.

After this talk, Gandhi told his secretary that he would like to see her again, if it could be arranged. Hearing of this some of his entourage protested that as she was a Conservative, it would be a waste of time. But he knew her better. 'That may be,' he said, 'but it is enough for me that she loves humanity.' On her side she felt that he was a great man. She called him 'the wild man of God,' classing him with Elijah and John the Baptist. In fact, she understood him as well as he understood her. Before he returned to India, where he had been so often imprisoned by the British and was to be imprisoned again, he came on her invitation to the house several times. Her maid Rose Harrison has told me that he used to sit with his spinning-wheel on the floor in the drawing-room. Yet, it was characteristic of her that she could also see him in a humorous light. Thus, at a later date, when speaking at Lincoln, she informed her audience that once at some public meeting he 'was holding onto his clothes. I believe that is one of the problems of the East. What should we do if we had to hold onto our clothes all the time? No wonder they don't get anywhere'.

In April 1930 a bitter attack was made on her by Harold Laski, Professor of Political Science at the University of London and a member of the Fabian Society's Executive, who was considered by the Labour party to be the leading political theorist of the day. Labour had now been in power for a year and had run into troubled waters. In October 1929 Wall Street collapsed and the great American depression began. Six months later its effects were being felt in England. There was a sharp rise in unemployment and a financial crisis, which was to lead the following year to the formation of the National Government, a sort of coalition under Ramsay MacDonald. This was the background of the Laski attack. In his view nothing but left wing Socialism could save England. Compromise with capitalism was impossible. A revolution, not violent yet uncompromising, was in sight. Lady Astor, who had always stood for compromise, co-operation and common sense in negotiating settlement of differences, seemed to him to have no conception of the fundamental issues.

His attack was contained in a long article published on 19 April 1930 in the *Daily Herald*. He began by an attempt to discredit her with her own sex. Of her first election in 1919 he said: 'Why she was elected it is difficult to say. She had done nothing for women's emancipation. She had no special knowledge of any social or political problems. But she was rich and entertained lavishly and was just the person required for a Tory member.'

He goes on: 'It would be difficult to argue that Lady Astor has made any mark in the House. Her attitude is of the type that in New York makes a millionaire's wife notable for smartness in repartee. Her speeches are generally amiable, but do not display any direct familiarity with the things of which she speaks.' He admits that she is a good Tory democrat, but alleges that her democracy is of the sort where a great lady is being kind to the poor. He has to allow that it is impossible to dislike her, 'for she is sincere and good-natured, but the trouble is that her sincerity is so uninformed.'

The diatribe continues, Laski professing astonishment at her catholicity which can embrace 'a professional éminence grise like Lionel Curtis, to whom daylight is unknown, and an agitator like Ellen Wilkinson, who abhors the shadows', and asks what in fact was her political philosophy. He sums it up as '*noblesse oblige*; compassion for the poor; a half regret that they do not work harder; a determination that they shall not drown their sorrows in drink; a yearning for a proper understanding between capital and labour, whatever that means; a feeling that with a little kindness we can conquer the world'.

Next comes a description of a party at 4 St James's Square. 'I suppose that no new lion has ever come to London without being at her house. In one corner you can see Mr Guedalla polishing his latest epigram; in another the Sitwell family is trying to be mistaken for the Lake poets; in another still is Lord Cecil looking like a Laudian archbishop. It is endlessly good fun. It gives the socialist attendants a consciousness of recognition, while the aristocracy is able to feel the full limit of its generous condescension.' As for the intellectuals, he supposes that the evening is so delightfully brilliant, that they take what is only electric light for the sun.

The gravamen of the attack comes at the end. Lady Astor does not understand what class distinction really is. A revolution is in progress and the revolutionaries do not want to come to terms with the Conservative element in society, but intend to destroy it. 'She really thinks that the Tory party means to unite the classes in a great national fellowship of mutual benefit. For her a declaration of goodwill is equivalent to the realization of justice.'

This was what Lady Astor looked like to an intellectual of the extreme left. Her compassion, charity, reasonableness were all rubbish. The masses were not deceived. They intended to abolish her and her kind.

Professor Laski's opinion of Lady Astor was not shared by the Labour party as a whole. A month later, Ellen Wilkinson published this in the *Evening Standard*: 'It is eleven years since Lady Astor put Englishwomen in her debt by standing her ground in a parliament "of men who looked as if they had done well in the war", as she put it. If she cannot get what she wants by logical argument, then she tosses that overboard and gets there anyhow.' And she added later: 'Lady Astor knows a good deal more than most of her critics about political affairs. She has learned them at what is one of the best schools of contemporary politics, the dinner table at 4 St James's Square. Her biggest political drawback is that nothing can prevent her laughing at pompous fools.'

As we know, Ellen Wilkinson was only one of many members of the Labour party who appreciated Lady Astor. Her old friend Jimmy Thomas was Lord Privy Seal in the MacDonald administration of 1929. Members of that Cabinet were frequently at her house. The Laski attack (by no means the most grievous she was to suffer) is thus seen in perspective. He turned on her the full weight of his broadside because he wanted to extinguish Labour's regard for her. He thought her a threat to his theory that no compromise with capital was possible. She was a dangerous siren. 'She is the perfect instrument of the aristocracy', he declares in the same article, 'for persuading the people they have nothing to complain of.'

This attack did not deter her from siding with the weak and defenceless. We find her at this time campaigning for the more humane slaughtering of animals and for preventing boys under sixteen from working underground in mines. The few who wanted to abolish the death penalty had her support, for it shocked her humanity, the strongest argument in her opinion for its abolition. In this and other subjects close to her heart, she saw no reason for restraining her humour. During the hanging debate she brought down the House with this sally: 'Sometimes the best men lose their tempers and murder their mothers-in-law, and why more drunken husbands have not been murdered is an absolute mystery to me.' A private bill of hers to protect prostitutes from being convicted for soliciting on the evidence of a policeman failed to pass its second reading, and her constant advocacy of a measure to raise the school leaving age to sixteen had no result. But these disappointments did not cause her to abate her efforts for the improvement of social conditions. In November 1929 we find her laying the foundation stone of the new training centre attached to the McMillan nursery school at Deptford.

Margaret McMillan, after labouring for many years with her sister Rachel among the poor in Bradford, moved to London in 1903 and founded a nursery school at Deptford, the object of which was to care for slum children under five, left to play in the streets when their mothers went out to work. Such children were under-nourished, contracted diseases, and were damaged both in body and mind. The nursery school gave them a good start in life. But in spite of the importance of her work, Margaret McMillan could get no grant from the London County Council and had a great struggle to maintain the nursery. Lady Astor, hearing about the school, paid a visit to Deptford. With one of her flashes of intuition she perceived that, if the nursery school system was to grow as it deserved, a centre in which nursery school teachers could be trained was a necessity. She brought Lord Astor down to Deptford and he agreed to build a training centre. It was the foundation stone of this building that she came to lay in November 1929. Of all the Astors' many charities, this was one of the most constructive. It enabled the nursery school movement to spread over England. Many thousands of children of the poorest classes have greatly benefited. It has remained to this day Lady Astor's favourite charity. Now at long last nursery schools have been recognized by the state and are in receipt of grants.

Though Lady Astor's heart was much engaged, she did not allow the formality of the foundation ceremony to restrict her droll manner. As she slapped on the mortar with the silver trowel, she exclaimed: 'This is the best part of the ceremony, making mud pies. I hope no union officials are here. I never saw a man laying bricks but that I thought I could do it better and quicker.' And afterwards in her speech on the advantages of nursery schools for children, she said: 'Truly the children who come here are more fortunate than the children of the West End, who have to bear the horrible monotony of being dragged through the parks from two to five o'clock by their nurses.'

Despite all setbacks, she never let an opportunity slip to argue for restriction in the sale of liquor. With the second Labour government of 1929 she again thought that she could count on more support than under the Conservatives and again was disappointed. In May 1930 when beer and excise duties came up for discussion, she turned on Mr Snowden, the Chancellor of the Exchequer, for being lukewarm. The higher the duty, the better for temperance. But it was from her own side that her remarks drew the hottest fire. Winston Churchill, in one of his most bantering and lively moods, called it 'nothing less than brazen' in the face of the ghastly muddle of prohibition in America, that she should continue to support the anti-drink campaign. She misjudged even her own sex, for which of them 'would not prefer a mild word spoken across a husband's tankard to the finest temperance harangue by her'. As she had so little support in the House for her temperance views, she had continually to stand up alone to pummelling of this sort. The House laughed but it could not help admiring the game way she took the punishment. The fact was that she enjoyed the fight. She did not mind being laughed at, and that was how she seemed to get the last word.

But in the case of the Ashes she was left without an effective retort. On some public occasion she rashly stated that the reason the Australians had beaten the English that year in cricket and retained the Ashes was because the English eleven drank and theirs did not. This observation caused an immense hullaballoo. The press and her mail were full of protests from every quarter. The matter was taken up with comical seriousness. Investigation showed that in both the cricket elevens there were teetotallers and in both men who drank, so that there could be no connection between drink and victory or defeat. She got it hot from both sides. The English team was incensed at the charge of insobriety; and the Australians' annoyance was no less, for it was an insult to say, they cabled, that they had won only because the other side was drunk.

But if the cricketers were angry with her, Lady Astor could take comfort from the fact that earnest teetotallers looked to her for guidance and approbation. There is extant a letter from one such man, an open letter which was published in November 1930 in the *Yorkshire Telegraph*. It begins: 'Dear Madam, picking up a magazine six or seven years old, I came across an article written by you entitled "England and the Dragon", in which you condemned the sale of alcohol. You, madam, with a great income and an assured position in life, can well afford to denounce the drink trade. But I, a lifelong teetotaller, am compelled by lack of income and indifferent circumstances to earn my living in a pub.' And he goes on to ask her indulgence not only for himself but for all those who like him are forced to serve in bars. On reading this letter, suited both to amuse and touch her heart, she may have recalled how Naaman, the Syrian, asked Elisha's indulgence, should he be obliged to bow in the house of Rimmon, and how Elisha replied: 'Go in peace,' and, supported by this biblical precedent, have granted the writer the indulgence he desired.

CHAPTER 14

The Visit to Moscow

Labour's victory at the polls in 1929 was in part made possible by the subsidence of the extreme anti-Bolshevist feeling which had caused its downfall in 1924. A cartoon which appeared in *Punch* three months before the 1929 election accurately reflects the change. John Bull says: 'This impossible Bolshie,' and the Bolshevist: 'This impossible bourgeois,' and then both together: 'Well, my friend, what about business?' Russian trade was possible, even if Russian principles remained anathema.

In December 1925 when condemnation of the Communist system was being voiced so strongly, Lady Astor, talking to unemployed and disgruntled miners in Durham, said: 'If any fit out-of-work man among you believes that Russia is paradise and is prepared to live under Bolshevik rule for two years, I will pay his passage to Russia.' The idea, of course, was to make the British Communist look silly; no man would volunteer to go. But in this she was mistaken. In the course of the next few weeks she received quite a bundle of replies to her offer. She had further explained that she would not only pay the man's fare, but his wife's and children's too. But he would have to make enough money in Russia for the return fares. Altogether thirty applications or enquiries were received. In the end a man called Morton of Liverpool was chosen. He and his family left for Russia in the summer of 1926. The press made a big feature of his going. It transpired later that Morton was a more confirmed Communist than Lady Astor supposed and that the project was not exactly the test which she had had in mind when she first made the offer. In December 1926 Morton was reported in the

English press as saying in Moscow that he had never been so happy before in his life. Russia was altogether a much better place than England. This caused some merriment. Lady Astor was laughed at for having made the wager. 'The man who called Lady Astor's bluff' was one of the newspaper headings.

Now, four and a half years later, she herself decided to pay Russia a visit, relations with the Communist régime having, as stated, become less strained. It came about through Bernard Shaw. He was invited to Moscow because his plays were all the rage there, particularly *The Apple Cart.* They were interpreted as favouring Communism and decrying democracy. His ideas, in fact, had little connection with Communist politics, as he always remained a Fabian Socialist, but the Russians thought his sympathies were with them, and as they looked up to him as a very great writer, they wanted to make much of him. Not only did they fail to give full weight to the difference between his Socialism and their Communism, but they had no suspicion that he adored amusing himself at others' expense and that it was imprudent to take almost anything he said quite literally. That he was the great farceur of the Western World, who had emerged from the Emerald Isle to break down all beliefs by laughter, did not cross their minds.

On accepting the invitation to visit Russia in July 1931, he stipulated that he be allowed to bring a party of friends with him. So anxious were they to see him that no difficulties were raised. This gave him the opportunity for his first joke at Russian expense. Instead of selecting some colleagues from the Fabian Society, earnest Socialists with a liking for Communism, like Laski, for instance, he chose friends who were in the Conservative party, and not only that, but rich capitalist or landowning aristocrats, the very type which the Bolshevist revolutionaries had killed off. These friends were Viscount and Viscountess Astor, and their party consisting of the Marquess of Lothian, the Hon. David Astor aged nineteen, and Charles Tennant, a Christian Scientist and kinsman of Lord Glenconner. The

Astors, it seems, were delighted at the chance of visiting Soviet Russia, very little known at the time, and hoped they would learn what would be useful afterwards when discussing Anglo-Russian relations in parliament. They did not, however, realize all the implications of going with Bernard Shaw nor guess the embarrassments involved.

Sokolikof, originally one of the conspirators who accompanied Lenin when he went into Russia to lead the revolution, was Soviet ambassador in London. He knew the Astors quite well, having been a guest in their house, but seems to have imagined that, as left wing Conservatives, they might be converted to Communism after seeing Russia. Perhaps, too, as friends of the great Communist Shaw, they were themselves already more Communist than appeared on the surface. Accordingly he granted them passports.

En route at Berlin they met Maurice Hindus, an American from Harvard, well known as a Russian scholar and author of books on Russia, who offered to help them, as he was going to Moscow himself, and joined them in their reserved carriage on the Berlin-Moscow express. Later, in the dining-car, Hindus pointed out no less a person than Litvinoff, the Commissar of Foreign Affairs, who happened to be returning from a visit to Germany, and introduced Shaw and the others to him. He spoke English and before they reached Moscow they were on friendly terms with him. They had been warned in London to take plenty of provisions, as no food would be obtainable on the train or in the stations at which it stopped. They found this was not so, however. Both the restaurant car and station buffets were well stocked. It leaked out afterwards that this had been arranged by the authorities to impress them. Normally no food was for sale in either. As the buffets were much better stocked than shops in Moscow, the Russian passengers on the train seized the opportunity and bought up everything. The English party, of course, did not guess the significance of this. Lady Astor, however, is said to have been startled by the sight at one station of a gang of bare-footed women working with shovels on the line, heavy work only fit for able-bodied workmen. They were in fact forced labour, farm workers conscripted as railway navvies. But she was assured they were volunteers, working happily for a good wage. The sight of them, however, gave her pause.

When the train drew up at the Moscow terminus a great crowd was waiting. There was a guard of honour and a brass band. Members of the Foreign Office, reporters, photographers, delegations of authors and representatives of the proletariat surged forward. It was Shaw they were meeting, not his friends. As he appeared in the doorway of his special coach, the crowd burst into wild applause, reported the *Daily Herald* of 22 July 1931. Shaw smiled with pleasure and waved his hat in happy abandon. He had never had a reception like this on arrival at a town in his own country. Bowing and delighted, for he was rather vain, he made his way between two lines of Red soldiers to the exit where a car was waiting for him. The others followed, but no one paid any attention to them, even to Lady Astor (a new experience for her), for all eyes followed Shaw's movements. Outside the station the courtyard was packed with thousands of people waving banners. From thousands of throats went up a shout hailing Shaw as leader of a Western World about to embrace Communism. With the soldiers' help the visitors reached their cars and were driven to the Hotel Metropole, where the best room was reserved for Shaw, while Lady Astor had a small one on the top floor. He was in wonderful spirits. It was a film-star welcome. But as he was well aware that it rested on a partial misunderstanding, for he was not exactly what they deemed him to be, his enjoyment was double, half for the acclaim, half because of the game of make-believe. It was hard to say which he enjoyed the more, the flattery or the knowledge that he was fooling them (not because they were Communists but because he fooled everybody). He was in the mood to say the most outrageous things, and said them during the nine days of the visit and on return home. He never told the Russians what he really thought.

His first adventure was not planned. The hotel lift stuck four feet below the level of the ground floor which it had overrun. He and Lady Astor had to be dragged out through an aperture. It was said that the lift man had lost his head from excitement. Shaw's first public statement is thus recorded: 'We are staying only nine days. I would like to stay nine years but we are busy people. I know a lot about Russia already, of course. Why, I was a Socialist before Lenin was born.' The Moscow press was full of articles on how at various times he had made favourable statements about the Soviet Union. It was admitted to be not quite certain whether he was in favour of evolutionary or revolutionary Socialism, but it was assumed that if he held the first, the heretical view, he would soon see that the Russian revolution was the only road for the salvation of mankind. When the substance of the articles was explained to him, he did not contradict their assumptions, for they added to the humorous mystification with which he liked to surround himself.

The programme arranged by the Soviet authorities (for the visitors were state conducted from first to last) was an ordinary round of sightseeing to begin with. First Lenin's tomb in the Red Square. They were invited to jump the queue, which was immensely long, and taken straight to view the corpse in the glass case. Then to see what remained of the crown jewels. The best had been sold. The visitors at first imagined they were all the jewels that the Tsars had possessed. Lady Astor observed that she had more jewellery than that herself.

Soon after their arrival she received a telegram from a certain Russian professor named Krynin, who, as a counter-revolutionary, had fled the country and was living in America. He had left his wife and children behind and asked her to plead with the authorities to allow them to join him in New York. Her nature being what it was, she immediately tried to do her best. Commissar Litvinoff had been agreeable on the journey and helpful since. She would approach him. The account goes that she took the opportunity at a reception given by the British Embassy to go up to him on the terrace, where he was talking to a knot of people, and half kneeling, say: 'I come to you as a peasant before the Tsar' and hand him the telegram. Such was the story in the American press and the allegation that she knelt made a bad impression. This was certainly an exaggeration. By this time she knew Litvinoff quite well and had, no doubt, rallied him in her bantering manner. She evidently presented the telegram in the half jesting way which was habitual to her. He replied politely, it is said, that unfortunately he could do nothing, as the matter was outside his jurisdiction. It seems that no further action was taken.

The programme continued, the visitors being shown what was thought suitable they should see. Thus, at a collective farm, all was in good order, and at a village where no alteration had been made since Tsarist times were only mud huts, excessively dilapidated. At an electrical works, the men protested to Shaw against the lies spread in England that there was forced labour in the U.S.S.R. His reply was characteristic: 'I wish forced labour would be established in England; then two million English unemployed would find work.' The *Pravda* reporter followed them and in that newspaper Lady Astor was made to pay plenty of compliments to the régime. The visitors had, of course, exposed themselves to such misrepresentations, which when copied into the English and American papers did them no good.

Learning that the Astors were fond of racing, but neglecting to inform themselves that Shaw was not, they took the English party to see trotting races. 'We were told', wrote Lord Astor in some notes he made of the trip, 'that in celebration of G.B.S.'s visit an attempt would be made to defeat the world speed record for trotting over a certain distance. After the race it was announced that this had been done.' The visitors believed in the genuineness of the record until, soon afterwards, the stewards offered to break another record. But if the Astors had grown sceptical, not so Bernard Shaw who, very bored with the racing, had fallen fast asleep in the grandstand. While Lady Astor fanned him to keep the flies off, the crowd gaped with admiration at the sage in slumber, in no way disappointed that their efforts to amuse him had fallen flat, since it was proper for a sage to doze, and, anyway, it was a great privilege to behold him, his head on his breast nestling in his beard. Lady Astor's solicitude in fanning him also went down very well. David Astor tells me that beforehand G.B.S. had said: 'I am the only Irishman who has never been to a race meeting.'

Nevertheless, when Lady Astor asked to see Mrs Morton, widow of the Liverpool man she had financed in 1927, and who had died in the interval, she was not granted permission. The authorities were uncertain what Mrs Morton might say. Some years later she managed to extricate herself from Russia and turned up at Cliveden, where she and Lady Astor had a heart to heart talk. Her experiences had been very painful. Lady Astor was proved right in the end.

Shaw wanted to see Krupskaya, Lenin's widow, for he had admired Lenin in his day. At first the authorities made difficulties. They did not refuse outright, because they were making a pet of G.B.S., but pretended that she was not at home, had gone off somewhere, could not be got hold of, would be away some time. The fact was that at the moment she was out of favour and they feared she might disillusion Shaw. However, when he pressed the matter, he and Lady Astor were driven to her villa in the country where she had been all the time. But the authorities must have warned her to be discreet, for nothing of importance was said, though she was greatly flattered and pleased by the call.

Shaw's seventy-fifth birthday fell on 26 July. To celebrate it, a great reception was given, at which he made a speech in his best irresponsible style. He first drew a picture of weeping relatives clinging to the members of his party and begging them not to go to Russia, where they would meet their deaths, probably from starvation. 'We brought away large parcels and baskets of food, bedding and even tents, so as to make sure of having a roof over our heads. But the moment the train crossed your border, we saw our mistake and dropped everything out of the carriage window.' He expressed great confidence in Russia's future. 'When you go a little further, you can carry the experiment to success, as I hope you will. Then we will follow your example.' And pointing to the Astors and Lord Lothian and describing them as enormously rich people, capitalists and landowners on a huge scale, he said: 'You mustn't blame them, they can't alter the system, but the British proletariat will alter it.' This sort of thing, reported in England, looked very bad in cold print without Shaw's twinkling eyes and quizzical smile. One has to remember, however, that most things Shaw said had some truth tucked away in them. In this case it would seem that he foresaw a great future for the Soviet, an opinion not shared in 1931 by most observers in England, who expected its collapse.

The tourist rush through the sights continued and some picture of it may be gleaned from American correspondents. Shaw was photographed on top of a giant Tsarist cannon-ball. When told that the old church nearby was being demolished because the Tsars used to worship there, he said: 'I think the Russian government had better have a five-year aesthetic plan,' and added in his levelling way: 'If a revolution like this had happened in America, they would have looted everything, whereas the churches are still as they were.' Here a newspaper adds: 'Lady Astor interrupted: "If you stand there soliloquizing, we won't cover the ground." And she led him away by the arm.'

At the Hermitage gallery Shaw was bored, for he had hardly more interest in painting than in horses: 'We marched past acres of pictures but they all looked alike to me,' he grumbled. The anti-theological museum, located in one of the churches, pleased him, and he studied with interest the exhibits, arranged to illustrate the alleged crimes and deceits of the Russian Church throughout its history. He declared to Lady Astor who could not help being shocked at some of the irreverent things she saw, that it was an attack, not on Christianity, but on the priesthood. 'How I wish I could get Martin Luther back here from the dead!'

Meanwhile Stalin, like a great panjandrum, sat invisible in the Kremlin, a fortress he rarely left. None of the foreign pressmen had ever seen him. Fully cognizant, of course, of the visit and daily informed of what Shaw said and did, he became so curious to meet him that, departing from rule, he invited him to the Kremlin. G.B.S. asked leave to bring his party with him and this was given. They had all to promise, however, to keep secret what might be said as long as they remained in Russia.

Traversing the passages of the Kremlin leading to Stalin's inner sanctum was like being in Sing Sing, said Lady Astor afterwards. She had felt a ruthlessness in the atmosphere outside; she had seen the road which led away to far Siberia, a road of despair; had caught a glimpse of a frightened old priest in a church. In the maze-like corridors of the Kremlin she listened for the groans of tortured men. However, when they were at last ushered into Stalin's presence, they found a neatly dressed man in uniform and long boots, who shook hands with them in a friendly manner. Litvinoff was also present, looking untidy in his shirtsleeves, a contrast to his immaculate chief. A conversation of some length then ensued, but seems to have been confined to trivialities, for afterwards Lord Astor, when making his note of what transpired, could remember nothing of importance, except that Churchill, then out of office, was the subject of some of Stalin's questions, who wanted to know whether he would regain his position and influence. In a letter which Shaw contributed to the press on his return to England he wrote: 'Stalin asked why Churchill was so anti-Russia. I said he had a bee in his bonnet and was hopelessly old-fashioned. But Stalin was not satisfied with this reply. He has a high opinion of Mr Churchill's ability. We told him that he need not worry, because Churchill would probably lose his seat at the next election and anyhow would never be Prime Minister.' (This was a bad shot, for in the election three months ahead, of October 1931, Churchill was elected, though for the next nine years he remained out of office.) But as Lady Astor once remarked: 'Of course, Shaw knew nothing whatever about politics.'

'We came away from the interview impressed,' noted Lord Astor, 'by Stalin's quickness and lucidity and were surprised, too, that he had a sense of humour.' What he thought of them is not on record. But evidently he rated them high enough and useful enough to spend an hour or more talking to them. On the party's return to the hotel, the reporters and foreign correspondents crowded round and asked questions. David Astor has described to me the amusing scene. Shaw brushed the newsmen aside and slowly mounted the staircase, a huge flight of marble steps. The reporters followed, begging him to tell them what happened in the Kremlin. Ignoring their pleas, he continued his leisurely ascent. At the top he halted, turned round, folded his arms like a ham actor and said solemnly: 'You want to know what happened? Well, I'll tell you. We discovered that Stalin has big black moustaches.'

On 3 August 1931 the party was back in England. On the way Shaw made a statement at Warsaw to the correspondent of the *Chicago Tribune*. 'I am a confirmed Communist. I was one before Lenin and am now even more so after seeing Russia. Dictator Stalin is an honest and able man. There is no starvation in Russia. Workmen there are happier than in other countries.' Though Shavian Communism was different from Russian Communism, he seems in this instance to equate the two. Other remarks of his at this time, however, suggest that the main impression he carried away from the visit was the formidable growing power of Russia. For in other sections of the American and

English press he is recorded as saying at Warsaw: 'Russia has put her house in order, and we western capitalist nations have got to look out because we are not doing so. It is a very serious thing. It is all silly nonsense about Russia being a failure.' After this he relapsed into his normal banter: 'I very much like black bread and cabbage soup. They agree with me and I had plenty of both.'

The remarks he made in commendation of Bolshevist rule, and the compliments which *Pravda* alleged that Lady Astor had paid, sufficed to raise a storm of criticism in England. G. K. Chesterton led it in an article published two days before their return. It begins thus: 'Shaw would long ago have become a grand old man but for his desperate attempts to remain an enfant terrible.' He had devoted his life to furthering Socialist ideas, and at the same time undermined them by his paradoxes. 'Nevertheless, there is something impressive and touching about the entry of the veteran Socialist into the first real Socialist civilization.' The irony was, however, that he had entered the world of Socialism at the moment when it had ceased to be socialistic. The great dissipator of illusions, he had himself become the victim of the illusion that Russia was the scene of a Socialist victory, when in fact it was the scene of its defeat. The so-called dictatorship of the proletariat was the negation of the Socialist vision. This and other gibes were embarrassing for the Astors. If Shaw was a dupe, were not his friends also, or why had they joined in so nonsensical an excursion? Shaw made things worse by an address he delivered on 7 August, four days after his return, at a summer school run by the independents of the Labour party. it contained such passages as: 'The success of the Russian five-year plan is the only hope of the world.' 'Capital punishment is absolutely abolished under the Soviet, though there is shooting for political offences.' And he told with apparent approval of how the Bolshevists arrested 1,000 people suspected of hoarding German notes and shot two of them in each of the principal centres of population. He also remarked: 'I want to say one word about Lady Astor. She said they could not do without God and they must come back to religion. There is no need for them to come back to it; they are full of it. The whole institution of Communism is necessarily religious.'

This remark told in favour of Lady Astor, but a section of the public held the view that in going to Russia with Shaw and expressing there, as was reported, opinions favourable to the Soviet régime, she had forfeited her right to be considered a Conservative. An article which had appeared in *Pravda* and was published in the *Daily Worker* of 8 August gave several examples of such opinions and told against her. One of the London papers put her situation this way: 'Lady Astor is having a hard time just now with the force of criticism directed against her for going to Russia. She has declined to express her views on the Soviet. The only reference to her which Lord Astor has permitted himself is that she never during her visit expressed herself as other than against the principles of Communism.' Seeing the way things were, Lord Astor had advised his wife to refuse press interviews till the storm blew over.

When the controversy over the Russian visit was at its warmest, Winston Churchill published an article in the *Sunday Pictorial* of 16 August, in which he ridiculed G.B.S. and Lady Astor, a piece of writing which, exhibiting as it does his style at its richest and most mordant, must have been composed with great care. Both as a little known Churchillian composition, and as highly relevant to the matter in hand, quotation from it will be found rewarding. He begins by declaring that G.B.S. and Lady Astor have at least one quality in common. 'They like to have everything both ways. Thus Mr Bernard Shaw is at once a wealthy and acquisitive capitalist, and a sincere Communist. His spiritual home is Russia, but he lives comfortably in England. He couples the possession of a mild, amiable and humane disposition with the advocacy and even glorification of the vilest political crimes and cruelties. He indulges all the liberties of an irresponsible chatterbox babbling from dawn to dusk. He has laughed his sparkling way through life, exploding by his own acts or words every argument he has ever used on either side in any question, teasing and bewildering every public he has addressed, and involving in mockery and discredit every cause he has ever championed.'

Churchill now turns from 'the nimble antics of this double-headed chameleon' to consider the character of Lady Astor. 'Similar, though different, contradictions are to be observed in Lady Astor. She reigns in the old world and the new, at once a leader of smart society and of advanced feminist democracy. She combines a kindly heart with a sharp and wagging tongue. She accepts Communist hospitality and flattery and remains Conservative member for Plymouth.'

Coming to the Moscow visit he has this: 'The Russians have always been fond of travelling-shows and circuses, and here was the world's most famous intellectual clown and pantaloon in one, and the charming Columbine of the capitalist pantomime. So the crowds were marshalled, thousands were served out with their red scarves and flags, Commissar Litvinoff, unmindful of the food queues in the back streets, prepared a sumptuous banquet, and the Arch-Commissar, Stalin, the man of steel, throwing open the closely guarded sanctuary of the Kremlin, and pushing aside his morning budget of death warrants and *lettres de cachet*, received his guests with smiles of unaffected comradeship.'

Churchill's argument is that there was something idiotic about the visit of these two English people, both so humane whatever else they were, who saw no harm in colloguing with abominable and treacherous villains. Who were these men with whom they dined and laughed, whose compliments they received and returned, and for whose wickedness they showed no indignation? What was the Soviet really like? He replies with a denunciation in the classical style: 'Here we have a power actively and ceaselessly engaged in trying to destroy civilization by stealth and propaganda and, when they dare, by bloody force. Here we have a state, three million of whose inhabitants are languishing in exile, whose intelligentsia have been methodically destroyed, a state nearly a million of whose inhabitants have been reduced to servitude for their political opinions, and who are rotting and freezing through the Arctic night; toil to death in forests, mines and quarries for indulging in that freedom of thought which has gradually raised man from the beast.'

In reflecting on these words we must bear certain things in mind. At the end of the 1914–18 War, Churchill, then Secretary of State for War, had sought to overthrow the Bolshevist revolution by supporting the White Russian invasion, a project which had failed and whose failure had had an adverse effect on his career. During the succeeding ten years he had watched the Soviet tyranny gradually consolidating itself and viewed it not only as an infamous but as a menacing world event. That two persons, both internationally celebrated but for neither of whose talents he had appreciation, should visit Moscow and delude the world into supposing there was something to be said for Stalin and his gang, was shocking to him. He felt bound to hold them up to ridicule as irresponsible meddlers, the man as a doting old joker, the woman as a fashionable lady in search of a thrill. But his tremendous burst of words was putting it too strongly. The visit was not all that important. The spectacle of the old dramatist, the Fabian idealist, accepting with a pleased smile the plaudits of his Russian fans, did not really amount to much. What he said was the usual Shavian fireworks. It was less a political than a literary event. But ironically enough one interesting fact had come out of the visit. Stalin was reported as anxious to know whether there was danger of Churchill returning to position and influence. As for Lady Astor's share in the event, everyone knew well, including himself, that she had done no more than take the opportunity of a trip to Russia to see what she could see, accompanied by those indubitably honest men, her husband and Lord Lothian. No one with even the smallest acquaintance with her character could suppose that she condoned the cruelties and oppressions of the Soviet; Churchill himself did not even suggest it. What remained, therefore? That she had taken a short holiday in Russia.

Time always brings strange surprises. Nine years later Churchill, shortly before regaining office, was to urge the Cabinet to make an alliance with the murderous gang he now denounced, because Hitler's Germany was far the greater danger, and, his advice not being taken, Russia at first aligned herself with our mortal foe. When the scene changed and Hitler invaded Russia, Churchill himself was to visit Stalin and support him with all the means at his disposal. Had Russia not held and defeated the invading Germans, who can say what would have happened to us? But the climax of the drama was not yet. The régime which Churchill in 1919 sought to crush in its infancy; which in 1931 he ridiculed Shaw and Lady Astor for dallying with; which in the years of the Second World War he courted as England's ally; has now become every bit as dangerous as he originally conceived it to be. In such a whirligig the Shaw-Astor trip to Moscow has a very limited significance.

Had the public, particularly the Plymouth electorate, taken the serious view of the Moscow visit which Churchill took, Lady Astor's career might have been ruined. But the public had the sense to see that she was no different from the person they had always supposed her to be and whom they understood and enjoyed. When an individual who disapproved of her, inserted an advertisement in the press – 'A gentleman of Plymouth, conscientiously believing that Lady Astor should be opposed at the next election, would like to communicate with a gentleman willing to oppose her as an Independent Conservative' – the Conservative executive committee of the Plymouth (Sutton) division immediately met and passed a vote of unabated confidence in her.

During this same month of August 1931 the great financial crisis, referred to further back, reached its peak.

MacDonald, Jimmy Thomas, Snowden and other ministers of the Labour government, were of opinion that only drastic economies could save the country from the major calamity of bankruptcy. But a section could not face up to retrenchments which involved cuts in the pay of all government employees and even, indirectly, in the dole to the unemployed, and deserted MacDonald. Convinced that the budget must be balanced, he had to turn for support to the Conservatives and Liberals, and form the coalition, termed the National Government. To obtain the country's endorsement of his actions he went to the polls, fixing October for the election. Thus it came about that Lady Astor had to contest Plymouth for the sixth time. The proposal to run an Independent Conservative candidate fell through. She was faced only with a Labour opponent. Throughout the contest her energy was as great, her wit as fresh and entertaining as ever. Noticing at one point a group of men studying the racing news, she hailed them with the tip: 'If you want a winner, back me!' Another man shouted to a heckler not to overdo it. 'Say what you like, she's a sport, she takes it all in such good part.' Among the working class her visit to Russia could do her no harm, and this may partly account for the fact that she got in with a majority of over ten thousand. Evidently the Conservative voters thought it all nonsense that she had praised Communism. They understood her too well. For twelve years she had been representing them and for nine years before that had been working among them. They knew where her heart was. It was not in Russia but in Plymouth. What utter rubbish had been talked! So they returned her for the sixth time with the largest majority she had ever had.

CHAPTER 15

The Fable of the Cliveden Set

When the National Government assembled after the election of October/November 1931, Lady Astor was a woman of fifty-two years of age. There was no sign that she was losing her ability to hold the House, not the smallest indication that members were getting tired of her drolleries. The *News Chronicle* of 1932 has: 'Lady Astor is one of the few refreshing personalities in this parliament. She has the power of retaining her own vivid personality when she is speaking. "She is hopelessly wrong there; I would get up and tell her so, only it's not worth it," whispered a Tory, referring to a point she was making. "I wish you would," jeered a Liberal in front of him. "She would knock your head off." It was quite true. She hit out at her interrupters to such purpose that none interrupted a second time.'

While increasing years might, indeed, be assumed to have strengthened the temper of her mind, it was more surprising to observe how physically fit she remained. She was still the out-of-door Nancy Langhorne. Her maid, Rose Harrison, who entered her employ in 1929 and is still in it, said to me: 'Her ladyship always had a cold bath every morning when she got up about 8.30. She then played a game of squash, and after that had a hot bath. Then I brought her her tea. By eleven she was dictating letters to her secretaries. She can dress in five minutes. I never had to dress her. Just buttoned her dress at the back and tied her shoelaces. Normally she used only foundation cream and powder. In all my time she never went to a beauty shop, or at least only once, the time when David Metcalfe, the little son of the Prince of Wales's equerry, hit her face by mistake with a golf club. Her cheek was terribly bruised and she had to go to have her face made up as she was dining out that night. It was a blow that would have laid up most people. But she made no fuss about it.' This happened in June 1934. The small boy was swinging his mashie too close; the upswing caught her face. The press of the world was immediately alerted that Lady Astor had a black eye. Some American papers, not informed that it was Fruity Metcalfe's boy who had done the mischief, invented the story that she had been punched by a youth from whom she was attempting to recover her ball which he had picked up. Her entry into the House of Commons with the black eye was received with cheers. She is recorded to have said: 'As long as it is not taken as a sign of connubial infelicity, I don't mind.' An M.P. said to her solemnly, as he assessed the damage: 'My word, Nancy, what must the other bloke be like!'

In the early summer of 1933 she was spending as much time as possible on the golf links near her house at Sandwich in Kent, practising for the parliamentary golf handicap. She reached the semi-finals, when she found herself drawn against the Prince of Wales. Her handicap was twenty, his twelve. They were by this date, on excellent terms. He was thirty-nine years of age and within two and a half years of his catastrophic reign of eleven months. She was one of the many who believed that with his modern outlook and popular appeal he would be just the king required in a period of social change.

The match took place on 5 July 1933 at Walton Heath, a course which she knew very well and which favoured her style, but on which he had not played and whose features in some ways did not suit him. He gave out that he particularly disliked a crowd of spectators, but a huge crowed assembled, as was inevitable, for it was not every day that one could watch the Prince of Wales playing a match against Lady Astor in the semi-finals of a famous competition. The Prince was very nervous. He drove well, but his putting got worse and worse until on one green he took four. Just before the turn he was two down and seemed to be going to pieces. Lady Astor, who did not want to beat the heir to the throne under such embarrassing circumstances, sought to calm and cheer him. She was always very good at cheering people and in this case was so successful that he pulled himself together. He drew level and when she lost the seventeenth hole, he won the match, two up and one to play. The Prince, always partial to gay clothes, wore a blue check shirt, grey plus-fours, check stockings and black-and-white shoes. She was smartly but soberly dressed. 'A very close game,' said he, when speaking next week at a golfing dinner. 'May I add that I found my opponent a very charming companion.'

On the morning of the match Lady Astor's daughter Phyllis suddenly confided to her mother that she was engaged to be married to Lord Willoughby de Eresby, son and heir of the Earl of Ancaster. For the public this news was even more interesting than the golf match with the Prince. A grand London wedding, the event of the season, was anticipated. But five days later Lady Astor announced: 'We are not going to have a large fashionable London wedding. Such weddings have really become dreadful. There is nothing private about them. They shock you. My daughter wants to be married quietly in the village church.' Arrangements were accordingly made to have the marriage solemnized in Taplow church, a couple of miles from Cliveden, a charmingly rural spot. But a quiet wedding with just a few friends turned out not to be feasible. In the end it was found necessary to invite five hundred guests. Wedding presents flowed in from royalty, the nobility, members of parliament, ambassadors, celebrities, feminists and sportsmen, people who had stayed at Cliveden or been entertained at St James's Square. The newspapers gave a list of the presents, the most notable of which was jewellery from Lord Astor, which included a diamond tiara. Among the lesser presents were some that added that amusing touch which in some form or another always seemed to impinge upon whatever Lady Astor did. That the Marquess and Marchioness of Titchfield gave a waste-paper-basket was perhaps not more than original, but there was certainly a droll antithesis in Captain Abel-Smith's six whisky decanters and Mrs Winston Churchill's water jug.

Though Lady Astor was unable to have the quiet wedding she first planned for her daughter, she resolved that at least it should be teetotal. Only soft drinks would be served. There would not even be champagne for the toast to the bride and bridegroom. It was as if she sought to capture a primeval innocence that would accord with the summer day, the lovely grounds of Cliveden, the long view from the terrace down to the river, and the church at Taplow, close by which lived her friend, the poet Walter de la Mare, in whose pastoral verse these beauties are embalmed. Who could have guessed that the name Cliveden in a few years' time was to stand in many people's minds for what was sinister, alarming and secret?

Legends tended to gather round Nancy Astor as she grew older. Sometimes they took the form of false accusations, as we have already found and will be finding again further on in this chapter. But sometimes they were just amusing folklore, true to character or atmosphere, though not to fact. As an example there was the statement made in April 1935 by the mayor of Pittsburgh, U.S.A. He declared on a public occasion that she received an income of £20,000 *a day* from her real estate in New York. The London *Evening News*' comment was: 'This preposterous statement reached London today. Since then Lady Astor has been pestered by friends asking her if it is true. "It is a complete canard," she said. "I don't own a single acre of real estate in New York." And she added: "I am staggered by so sweeping a statement. It sounds to me like a tale from the Arabian Nights." ' That was it. There was always an air of the Arabian Nights about her. The Arabian Nights, though fabulous, reflect Arab Baghdad better than does sober history; a fabulous history of Lady Astor could be written and might turn out the truest picture of her.

Fable pursued her everywhere. Thus Professor Boulton of the University of California gave out that fur was not the foundation of the Astor fortune. The truth was, he said, that John Jacob Astor I, when after fur, met a trapper called Cartier who said he knew the spot in Deer Island, off Maine, where Captain Kidd had buried his private treasure. John Jacob bought the secret for a thousand pounds down, found on the island a wonderful cache of gold and jewels, which he sold in England for a million and a half. After thousands of people had given credence to this story, it leaked out that Boulton had invented it as a way of testing the critical acumen of his students.

A different sort of folklore is the invented reply to the heckler. Here is an example, which does credit to the man who made it up, taken from the American weekly *Time*: 'After Lady Astor had spoken at some length about how the National Government had given women jobs, a droop-moustached male voter boomed: "That's enough of your boloney! The government's failure to cure unemployment has forced many a British girl to take to the streets." "That's enough from you, walrus," replied Lady Astor. "One thing I am certain about is that no street girl would have lowered herself to go with you. Now, sit down, walrus, and shut up." ' Lady Astor wrote to the press and absolutely denied this story, but if a fake, it is a very good fake.

There is a great corpus of temperance folklore. The following example differs from most others because it rests on a misprint. 'I think my most beautiful memory of Lady Astor,' wrote someone in the *Daily Herald* of 1936, 'is the report in a newspaper that she was once seen coming down the gangway of a ship with a jaunty red nose in her hat.'

On the drink subject, A. P. Herbert's complaint cannot be missed: 'When Lady Astor starts a campaign to close the pubs, it is called idealism. If I plead for the pubs to be kept open till midnight, it is propaganda for the brewer.' (Incidentally the repeal of prohibition in the States in December 1933 was a hard knock, as she had felt so sure, and said in public so often, that it would be permanent. But she never gave up her own efforts and we find her fighting a bill in 1934 which proposed to allow drinks to be served in restaurants till midnight.)

Another thing which statistics showed to be partly folklore was that Lady Astor by constant interruptions in debate, in the form of questions, queries, contradictions, wranglings with members, personal remarks and objections, was longer on her feet than any other member. In this connection Isaac Foot's, the Liberal member's, remarks on her interruptions should be recalled. On 18 May 1934 he stated on a public platform: 'I said to Lady Astor once when we had to go to a committee of the House: "Of course, you will have to look after your interruptions." "Well," she replied, "that's all very fine, but Mr Bernard Shaw says that my interruptions are better than my regular speeches." ' Mr Foot went on to admit that he agreed with this. 'I think she can say in a flash what many others try to say in an hour's ratiocination.' If she could say in a flash what took others an hour, how could she be accused of being always on her feet, wasting the House's time? Someone took the trouble to add up the columns of *Hansard*, over an average period, which recorded what was said by her and other leading members. It was found that while 145 columns were filled by Lt. Commander Kenworthy, 93 by Churchill, 79 by Ramsay MacDonald, 71 by Lloyd George, 58 by Baldwin and (the best comparison) 47 by Miss Susan Lawrence, Lady Astor filled only 24. The figures finally disproved the myth that she chattered. In point of fact, it is on record that in 1934 there were people to declare that she had been talking too little lately. The *Sunday Chronicle* in December of that year addresses her thus: 'It must be many months since you were heard in any of your famous political trouncings. Public life is the poorer for your silence.'

In the later years of the thirties, however, far from fading from the scene, Lady Astor was destined to be caught up in the major controversy of the period, and because of her views on foreign policy, to be suspected of intrigues undermining the authority of the government and exposing the country to grave peril. In consequence of this suspicion she and her associates were denounced both in England and America with a bitterness far exceeding anything she had had to endure before. These accusations, which had no substance whatever, were a further example of how the fabulous attached itself to her.

The dominating fact of the thirties was the rise of Hitler. By January 1933 the Nazi party had seized power. The problem was what did that signify. It was round this question that the controversy raged. Was the emergence of the Nazis the inevitable result of the Treaty of Versailles, a treaty which had been so harsh that it had created a fanatical counter movement? Could the animosity of a reviving Germany be softened by concessions? Ought one to be fair to the Germans? Or were the Nazis an exceedingly dangerous growth which should be rooted out at once? Which was the more dangerous, Nazi Gemany or Bolshevist Russia? Should we disarm in token of goodwill or build up our forces to counter the threat? Such were the elements of the controversy which lasted from 1933 till the eve of the Second World War.

The Astors, as we have seen, belonged to a liberal set among the Conservatives. Their ideas on foreign and dominion policy had been set out for years in the *Round Table* quarterly. Lord Lothian, Geoffrey Dawson of *The Times*, Lional Curtis, the inventor of dyarchy, the device by which in the twenties it was hoped to bring India a step nearer self-government, were well-known figures in the Astor group. They were firm believers in the ability of the League of Nations to bring Europe back to prosperity and insure justice and peace for the future. The Germans' withdrawal from the League in December 1933, ten months after the Nazi party came into power, was a great shock. Efforts must be made to get them back. This could only be done by satisfying their reasonable aspirations. Fair play would restore their confidence in us. Lord Lothian who, on the British side, had been one of the artificers of the Treaty of Versailles, regretted what he had helped to do. The Germans had been punished too severely. It was not yet too late to make true friends of them.

These views, characteristically liberal, were also inspired by emotion. The prospect of a Second World War was abhorrent. How dreadful to conclude that the hundreds of thousands of young men who had given their lives in the previous struggle had failed, despite victory, to ensure a lasting peace! It was the bounden duty of the survivors to save the new generation from the catastrophe which had wiped out so many in the last. It was a debt owed to the dead, a sacred debt. When Lady Astor thought of her many friends who had been killed, she felt all means should be sought to stop Europe from sliding into a second holocaust.

This was the attitude towards the problem of resurgent Germany which governed the thinking of most of her circle. It fell in well with her character. She had always believed that problems could be solved by reasonable negotiation. Hearts were not won by threats but by love. That was the road towards a permanent European settlement.

Churchill was the great protagonist of the opposite view. He believed that the Nazis were actuated by a maniac ambition, which could not be placated by fair dealing, and must be warded off by strength. Russia was an abominable tyranny and potentially a great danger. But she was far off and backward. Nazi Germany was next door and a modern state. She was rebuilding her armed forces as fast as she could. Our army and air force had gone downhill. Their rehabilitation should begin at once.

The Astors' circle did not deny that Germany was a potential danger, but thought that she would stop rearming if Britain led the way in a disarmament agreement. In February 1933, immediately after the Nazis obtained power, Lady Astor signed a letter for the press along with a dozen others – some Labour, some Liberal – urging air disarmament. If Britain took the lead in this, an international settlement would be in sight.

This remained her policy throughout – international agreement instead of an arms race. It was the policy favoured by the majority of the nation, which had had more than enough of war. The National Government under Ramsay MacDonald pursued this policy, as did Baldwin when he headed a Conservative government in 1935, and Neville Chamberlain who succeeded him in 1937. For all his personality and eloquence, Winston Churchill failed to persuade these Prime Ministers, their parties, and the nation behind them, that their policy was wrong. But though the Astors' conception of how Germany should be handled was substantially the same as the government's they were suspected of being too well disposed towards the Nazis. A fiction gradually took shape that they were actually pro-Nazi. As we shall shortly see, this fiction gained wide credence. A quantity of specious arguments were produced to support it. It was made out that a conspiracy was being hatched at Cliveden, which would deliver England into the hands of the Nazis. For a short time Lady Astor was thought of as a traitor. It was a curious scare, and very unpleasant for her.

In the summer of 1936, the first suspicion began to be voiced. *Time and Tide*, Lady Rhondda's weekly, which had always supported Churchill, issued a warning that dangerous views were held by some important English people and mentioned by name Lord Londonderry, the Earl of Dudley and Lady Astor. These and others in influential positions, fascinated 'by the surface tidiness of the Fascist regimes in central Europe, stand for a rapprochement with Germany. To some of them, Hitler, the dreamer, the visionary of the mystic face, a non-smoker, a non-drinker, the anti-Bolshevik, is becoming almost a fuehrer, almost, we should say, the fuehrer.' The article concludes that there is no hope of coming to a settlement with the Nazis.

Lady Astor, realizing the seriousness of the allegation, thought it prudent to reply to the article by a letter in its next issue. She defended her position thus: 'I have desired to restore a sense of security in Europe by treating Germany as an equal. I have worked for the reversal of the policy of goading her people and rulers into restlessness by trying to keep them in a state of inferiority.'

Though by the spring of 1937 Hitler had greatly increased the strength of his army and air force and was displaying an ever-increasing intransigence, she still thought that the best way to control him was through the League. She opposed the Anglo-Russian alliance against him advocated by Churchill because it would supersede the League and substitute force for persuasion. Europe would be again divided into two military camps.

In November 1937 the storm broke. Lady Astor had small reason to think that her views on how to meet the German menace were unpopular. In November 1935 when, after Ramsay MacDonald's retirement, Baldwin had appealed to the country, she had to face her constituents in Plymouth again. They found her views on Anglo-German relations quite satisfactory and returned her for the seventh time. But in the two years that followed, the German menace had become much more threatening. Fewer people believed in the power of the League to manage Hitler; there was less trust in the efficacy of concessions and appeasement. A scare blew up that England was in great and growing danger. And the people to blame were not Baldwin and his ministers who had refused to take Churchill's advice, but a clique more powerful than the Cabinet, the group of politicians and others who gathered at Cliveden, over whom Lady Astor presided.

The scandal was started in a Communist newsletter. Anthony Eden, Foreign Secretary, had just resigned because he disagreed with the weak stand which Chamberlain, who had recently succeeded Baldwin in the premiership, was taking against Hitler. The story was put out that Lord Halifax, who had taken Eden's place and who went to see Hitler in November 1937, had tried to buy German friendship by promising him a free hand in central Europe and also by a promise to return the colonies lost after Germany's defeat in 1918. The people backing Halifax in this negotiation were said to number, among others, Lord Londonderry, Lord Lothian, Sir Alexander Cadogan and Lady Astor. The allegation was that these people, supported by *The Times* directed by Geoffrey Dawson and the *Observer* under Garvin, papers owned by the Astor family, all met at Cliveden, that they overawed the Cabinet, which was split on what policy to pursue, and were concocting a pro-Fascist plot against Socialism and Communism. Hitler, assured that he would not be interfered with in his designs against Austria and other European states, would undertake not to strike westwards and would go against Russia. England would sell its honour and buy its safety by allowing him to smash democracy.

With the publication of this fairy-tale the witch hunt was on. Two cartoons by Low in the *Evening Standard* of December 1937 show what sort of talk was going the round. In the first of them Chamberlain stands on a tight-rope with a balancing pole, the pole being Halifax. At one end of the pole sit Dawson, Lothian and Lady Astor, labelled 'The Shiver Sisters'; at the other end are three persons with a placard: 'Blimp Bros. No concessions and the devil take the hindmost' who represent those who backed Eden. The second cartoon, published on 3 January 1938, showed Goebbels, as a ballet instructor, teaching four girls to dance, the girls being labelled Lothian, Dawson, Garvin, Nancy. The Low cartoons were, of course, no worse than the more or less good-humoured caricature to which all politicians are constantly subjected. But they showed how the wind was blowing and were followed by graver insinuations. On 28 February 1938, for instance, at a mass meeting in Hyde Park, the Labour M.P. Mr Barnes spoke of 'this country having now got to a position when we must have society ladies determining our foreign policy. The foreign policy of this country is no longer settled by the Cabinet in Downing Street but at the country home of Lady Astor at Cliveden.'

This was followed by extravagant articles in the general press. *Reynolds News*, under the heading BRITAIN'S

SECRET RULERS, declared the country was being ruled by the Cliveden Set, which had compelled Eden to resign and Chamberlain to assassinate the League of Nations. Lord Halifax was described as politician No. 1 of the Cliveden gang. All these conspirators had financial reasons for wanting to support the Axis.

The attack was not confined to the gutter press, for by now a lot of people believed that Cliveden was the scene of a conspiracy. Even so experienced and well informed a person as Harold Nicolson, misled by the emotional atmosphere, had some sarcastic things to say in *Newsletter* of 12 March 1938. In support of Eden and in reference to his resignation, he wrote that Lord Londonderry had 'waved the swastika aloft for years' and Lady Astor 'fought bravely for Hitler and Mussolini.'

On 23 March 1938 Low published a third cartoon in the *Evening Standard* depicting the Shiver Sisters. The caption has 'To mark our leader's recent successes, a party was thrown at the Cliveden nest. Nancy took the salute from the loyal troops officered by Ladies Lothian and Grigg. Old Mother Shaw was most amusing, and Nancy's editors, Frau Garvin and Frau Dawson, obliged with a spirited rendering of the Hitler war song.' The picture shows Lady Astor taking the salute from the porch at Cliveden, as her associates goose-step past. Shaw in a bonnet is crawling along the ground in front of them, apparently engaged in some Shavian clownery.

By now Hitler had taken Austria and was moving into position to threaten Czechoslovakia. At moments of national alarm traitors are always seen in every bush. Upton Sinclair, the novelist, headed an article in the American press with WE HAVE TRAITORS IN OUR MIDST and aroused feeling in the States against Lady Astor.

Stafford Cripps, carried away by the violence of feeling in the air, threw common sense to the winds when on 27 March he denounced the Cliveden Set in terms which he must have known very well could not be substantiated. 'They are the people who got Viscount Halifax to go to

Germany behind Eden's back. They are the people who have been entertaining Ribbentrop and making friends with many other Nazis. They are the people who are running the policy behind Chamberlain and they are the people who would like to see Britain a Fascist state as well. Chamberlain must go.'

Wild personal abuse of the Astors now appeared. Under the caption WHO'S WHO IN THE CLIVEDEN BARONAGE, the *Tribune* on 25 March described Lord Astor as a vulgar plutocrat who derived his money from an ancestor who sold spirits to the Indians. Lady Astor's divorce of Gould Shaw thirty-four years back was resurrected to prove that she was a disgraceful person. It is astonishing that the perpetrators of this sort of stuff could have hoped for credence. But passions were running so high at the moment that there were people to swallow it.

During the five months this blistering campaign had been on, Lady Astor in what public speeches she made continued to reiterate her view that war could be avoided by coming to terms with Hitler. But appeasing Hitler did not mean approving of him. 'I abhor Hitler and Hitlerism,' she said while on a short visit to the States early in 1938. 'I have no friendship whatever for the Nazis. I deplore the whispering campaign against me, which has now started in America.' The agitation had not shaken her nerve nor caused her to alter her view that a *modus vivendi* was still possible with Hitler, an opinion that many people in England still held, including the Prime Minister, Mr Chamberlain, and most of his Cabinet.

Not only was she undaunted by the attacks made on her, but her high spirits and humour remained as before. On 12 April 1938 an amusing scene was witnessed at the door of her London house. It was lunch time. A reporter on the look-out for copy saw arrive Lord Halifax and Geoffrey Dawson, two of the arch-conspirators of the mythical Cliveden Set. 'Lady Astor', he writes, 'came flitting down the steps of her house and said to me: "A lot of nonsense is talked about the Cliveden Set! They say we're spies or something." Pointing to Halifax and Dawson, she went on: "I am giving them lunch, that is all. What's dreadful in that? They are my friends." And to Mr Dawson she said: "Come on, Geoffrey. We had better pose nicely. The Cliveden Set caught in the act!" Another photographer had now come up and asked Geoffrey Dawson his name. "Ribbentrop," he replied. The three then went laughing into the house.'

On 28 April, when addressing the Scottish Liberals at Glasgow, Lord Lothian took the opportunity of exploding the fiction of the Cliveden Set. 'May I refer briefly to a widespread story about the intrigues of the so-called Cliveden Set, said to be pro-Fascist, to exercise malign and sinister influence over the Foreign Secretary and the Prime Minister. The whole thing is a mare's nest originally invented by the communist editor of the *Daily Worker* and spread in pamphlets issued by the Communist party. There is no such set. There has to the best of my knowledge never been a meeting of the supposed principals to discuss foreign policy. On the very date meetings are alleged to have been held at Cliveden, I was in India and Lord and Lady Astor in the United States.' And he ended his speech by repeating that if only a settlement with Hitler could be reached, risk of a world war would instantly disappear. He had come to realize, however, that our first object must be air parity. Only then would negotiations have a good chance of success. He had moved from his former standpoint, which he used to put this way: 'We cannot hope to stand up to their unreasonable demands till we have rectified their reasonable grievances.' Rectification of grievances unbacked by force would not, he now saw, preserve peace.

The Scottish Liberals were perfectly satisfied with his statement, for no one who had even a small acquaintance with the character of the Astors and their record, and knew how people of all shades of opinion were guests at Cliveden, could possibly imagine them as leaders of a secret cabal. They had advanced their views on how to meet the German menace openly in speeches, conversations and the like. An attack on them by the extreme left, launched at a moment of crisis when rumours of all sorts were receiving credence, sufficed to set a snowball of calumny rolling.

After letters to *The Times* and the *Daily Telegraph* by Lord and Lady Astor a week later on the lines of Lord Lothian's speech, the agitation died down. No more was said during May, June, July and August, but the Munich crisis of September 1938 revived the agitation. The Astors and their friends saw a justification of their policy in the assurances of peace which Mr Chamberlain brought back from the famous meeting with Hitler. A few days later Winston Churchill rose in the House to protest against the assumption that Chamberlain had succeeded in arriving at an arrangement. On the contrary, he said, 'we have sustained a defeat, an unmitigated defeat.' There were ministerial cries of 'No, nonsense', for the government was immensely relieved by Chamberlain's assurances. 'The noble lady cries "Nonsense",' continued Mr Churchill, looking at Lady Astor. 'The terms which the Prime Minister has been able to secure by all his immense exertions and by all the anguish and strain through which we have passed (Ministerial cries of "peace, peace" and cheers), the terms which he has gained for Czechoslovakia have been that the German dictator instead of snatching the victuals from the table has been content to have them served to him course by course.' As his speech went on, Lady Astor interjected: 'Don't be rude to the Prime Minister.' Churchill turned to her and said: 'No doubt Lady Astor has been receiving very recently a finishing course in manners.' The Labour party took this up and shouted that the finishing course had been from von Ribbentrop.

Though the bogey of the Cliveden Set had really been laid, the intense feelings of anxiety, dread and waning hope at this terrible moment in England's history sufficed to resuscitate it. New facts were unearthed to support the suspicion that somehow or other Lady Astor and her friends were hand in glove with Hitler. The case of Lindbergh, in 1928 the first to fly the Atlantic, was cited as proof. When in England after his famous flight, he had been taken up by the Astors and stayed at Cliveden. A dauntless young fellow, his character was boyish, his education meagre. Turned by his feat into an international hero, he was lifted too far out of his mental plane and did a number of stupid things, including the acceptance of a decoration from Hitler. The story now went that in the summer of 1938 he told Chamberlain that Germany had 10,000 war planes as against England's 1,500, because Hitler asked him to frighten Chamberlain and so cause him to continue his policy of appeasement. Lindbergh was a friend of the Astors; Lindbergh was an agent of Hitler's. What more need be said? Though this story was a fiction of the most improbable kind, it gave powder and shot to the Astors' critics. But their case was so flimsy and lacking in evidence which could bear examination that it fizzled out, though the crisis worsened.

A long article, which Bernard Shaw published in the American magazine *Liberty* in April 1939, after Hitler had broken his Munich promises and taken Prague, did more to clear Lady Astor both in America and England than anything said in her defence heretofore. Written when Shaw was eighty-three years of age, in a straightforward prose, whose cogency is not weakened by the paradoxes from which normally he could not refrain, it not only winds up the Cliveden Set imbroglio, but also provides a valuable portrait of Lady Astor by a man who knew her very well and was the most celebrated writer of the day. The article is prefaced by a letter to the editor, in which Shaw remarks that the Astors had become the representatives of America in England and any attack on them was in fact an attack on America. 'As they have gained that position slowly by being a transparently good couple, and not only on account of the irrepressible vitality of Lady Astor, it is important to genuine good relations between the two countries that the American press should stand up for Lady Astor.' The article itself contains the following: 'I have been at Cliveden. I have spent weeks there. I am a frequent visitor at their London house. I have met there all the aristocrats and die-hard Conservatives. At Cliveden you meet everyone worth meeting, rich or poor, and of every point of view. You meet the Duchess of Atholl and also Ellen Wilkinson; you meet Colonel Lindbergh and Charlie Chaplin, whose dislike of Nazi rule is outspoken to a degree. You meet the Marquess of Londonderry, so much to the right as to be an embarrassment to the Conservative government, and you meet me, an implacable Marxist Communist for nearly sixty years. If I wanted, I could prove that Cliveden is a nest of Bolshevism or indeed of any other sort of bee in the world's bonnet.'

Shaw's reading of Lady Astor's character now follows: 'She has no political philosophy and dashes at any piece of kindly social work that presents itself, whether it is an instalment of Socialism or a relic of feudalism. In the House of Commons she is the most vital member and was certainly the most disorderly until her disorder became a national institution.' And he goes on: 'Lord Astor spends his substance lavishly on public welfare in Plymouth and his life in doing public work and getting no credit for it.' Shaw then points out, what apparently had not given pause to those slandering the Astors, that though the family owned *The Times* and the *Observer*, two of the most influential papers in the country, whose editors, as frequent visitors to the house, knew that the Cliveden Set legend was a grotesque invention, the papers never bothered to explode it. Why? Surely the two editors should have come to the rescue of their principals? But the policy of both papers was never to put forward the interests of the Astors, and even in this case they kept to the rule, 'an extaordinary paradox if the Astors were the sort of persons they are alleged to be.' And Shaw ends: 'As for deep and Machiavellian plots for the subjection of the human race, with Virginian Protestant Nancy conspiring with Hitler, I should find it far easier to suspect Roosevelt of conspiring to revoke the Declaration of Independence. I hope I have now succeeded in substituting credible portraits for the phantasms of the Cliveden legend. Never has a more senseless fable got into the headlines.'

But though the charge of conspiracy was laughed out of court, the claim stood that the views of Lady Astor and her circle had been proved wrong by the course of events. It had not been possible to come to terms with Hitler, the attempt to appease him had been vain. In this same month of April she contributed an article to *Forum*. In it she admits that her view of the foreign situation may have been wrong. 'But it was right to try to the uttermost for peace.' Even now war was not inevitable. Nevertheless 'it may only be postponed. But who, standing in his place, would not have tried, as Chamberlain tried, to hold the wolves of war in leash?' This introduces a different argument in support of Chamberlain's actions. Respite was necessary before closing with Hitler because Britain was not ready to fight him. Chamberlain was not cringing before him at Munich but craftily gaining time to rearm. This argument, as an *ex post facto* argument, had an appearance of truth. England, alerted to Hitler's intentions at last, would be able to fight him if she rearmed with sufficient speed. Good had therefore come out of Munich. It had cleared the air. We now clearly saw what we had to do. But it cannot be said that this argument rehabilitated Chamberlain. At Munich he was thinking not of gaining time to prepare for a war with Hitler, but of appeasing Hitler so that he would not go to war; and he thought that he had succeeded.

This, of course, remains a point of controversy. I believe, for instance, that the present Lord Astor's view is somewhat different. He has told me that those who knew Chamberlain well, as he did, thought that when he went to Munich he was suspicious of Hitler's good faith and that this suspicion was not removed by what happened there. He returned to England in a divided mood. He had assurances of great moment which might be true, but in his heart he wondered whether they were. When he waved the famous paper and said to the yearning crowd 'It is peace in our time', it was more a gesture than a declaration of his firm belief. What followed was curious. He found that his message, delivered rather as a statement of what had been agreed than of what would certainly take place, was accepted as the latter and was so enormous a consolation to the thousands waiting on his word that he was suddenly acclaimed the saviour of his country. This heady dose of adulation for an old man, who had never had much acclaim, dispelled his inner reservations and convinced him that in fact he had salvaged peace. He was deceived, not by Hitler, but by the emotional admiration of his own countrymen. Not until the seizure of Prague six months later was the spell they cast on him lifted. This interpretation is, on the whole, more damaging to Chamberlain's intelligence than the other. But whether he was deceived abroad or at home is not of first importance to discover. That he was deceived determined the issue. We lost another six months before we really buckled to.

But all the governments since 1933, when Hitler came to power, had been as mistaken about Hitler's character. He was insatiable from the start, because from the start he wanted the whole world. There had never been even a chance of arriving at a *modus vivendi* with him. There had been only one way to deal with him. He had to be forced to give up his ambitions. A rapid rearming after 1933 by England and France could have obliged him to do so and prevented the Second World War. But neither the British government nor the British people were willing to face rearmament. Given that psychological fact, the Second World War was inevitable. If Lady Astor and her friends had not been influential, they could not be blamed for holding the mistaken views which were so widely held. But they were influential and must share the blame with those responsible for misleading the general public. That Winston Churchill understood Hitler's real character, a fantastic character, exceedingly difficult to gauge, for it belonged more to the realm of nightmare than the reality of sober men, was enormously to his credit. But in fact it made no difference at the moment, for in the face of so general a public opinion he was powerless, until the truth was demonstrated by events. It is thus that the catastrophes of history happen. Most men do not know a devil when they see one.

But though Lady Astor and her friends cannot escape the blame which attaches to all those prominent people who supported the policy of appeasement, which made war inevitable, the suspicion that she and her friends forwarded that policy for sinister reasons and were powerful enough to overawe the Cabinet was an hallucination born of the troubled hour. Unsupported by even a scrap of evidence and contradicted by all the known facts and probabilities, the allegation would appear an utter absurdity, did it not allow us a glimpse of the imagined world in which some people supposed her to live. Her own comment on the affair, in an article called LADY ASTOR INTERVIEWS HERSELF, published on 4 March 1939 in the *Saturday Evening Post*, has that illuminating touch which, as Isaac Foot remarked, enabled her to get to the root of things in a flash. 'My compatriots must have lost their sense of the ridiculous if they swallow this nonsense about my directing cabinet policy.' What did they take her for? She was just a woman like any other. 'But I am supposed to have more power than had Queen Elizabeth, Marie Antoinette and Cleopatra combined!'

Here are the Arabian Nights again, here the legendary world she was supposed to live in. It seemed quite natural to credit her with the powers of such personages because she was Lady Astor.

CHAPTER 16

Later Years and Retirement

Though the commotion over the Cliveden Set had been far from pleasant, Lady Astor could look back on other happenings without dissatisfaction. Thus in the George VI coronation honours of the summer of 1937, just before the attack on her opened in November of that year, she was made a Companion of Honour. *The Times* commented that it was very appropriate for one who had rendered so much public service. Birmingham had already made her an Honorary D.Litt. and now in November 1937, at the very moment when it was being alleged that she was working for the destruction of England, Reading conferred on her a similar degree. When asked to respond on behalf of the other honorary graduates, her speech was gentle and winning, and revealed a humility poles away from the conception of her as a dark manipulator of state affairs. She began by declaring that to receive the degree was enough, but to be asked to speak for others so much more distinguished than herself was too great an honour. And she ended what was both an amusing and a charming address by saying: 'If one wants to be famous, one should attach one's name to learning. I myself have no desire for fame, for when I entered public life I had to leave fame and gratitude behind. I am very much touched by the honour conferred on me, for in public life one is seldom honoured, unless one is an exceptional character. Most of the politicians of the lower rank like myself find it rare to be in the company of such learned men and women.'

One might think that here she was feigning modesty, but it was quite characteristic of her to speak thus of learning, and I have often heard her say the very same, particularly in her frequently repeated expression: 'I know my betters.'

Another event to which she could look back with pleasure was the election of her eldest son, the present Viscount, to represent East Fulham in the Commons in the 1935 general election. When addressing the voters there on his behalf she remarked in her usual happy vein: 'If you return him to Westminster, you will be as unique as Plymouth, which returned the first woman, for he will be the first young man in parliament who has got his mother in the House to look after him.' The Astor family was very strongly represented in the Baldwin administration of 1935. In the Commons, besides Lady Astor and her son, there was her brother-in-law, Major J. J. Astor, now Lord Astor of Hever, her son-in-law Lord Willoughby de Eresby and her nephew Ronald Tree. With her husband in the House of Lords, the family had a representation of six in parliament, which no other family could equal. As the sun of the six she shone the more. She had become, as Robert Bernays, M.P., wrote at this time, 'the best-known woman in England after the Queen. You might as well try to keep Bernard Shaw out of the newspapers as Lady Astor.' Visitors to the Commons, he says, always want her pointed out to them. 'What is the secret of her hold on the public imagination?' he asks and opines that it is the romantic story of her arrival from Virginia 'to impose her personality on a reluctant gathering' of Englishmen. Her achievement had enough of the miraculous to keep the public continually wondering. They half expected her to look extra-ordinary, like Mr Maxton, for instance, with his sallow features, compelling eyes, and black hair hanging over his collar. But when they saw her, neatly and quietly dressed, with little make-up and with twinkling rather than mesmeric eyes, they concluded that the miracle was the greater.

Such marks of esteem as the C.H. and the D.Litt., all go to show how fanciful to the great majority were the allegations against her. Public confidence was also demonstrated by Plymouth, which elected her husband and herself Mayor and Mayoress in 1939. The citizens had pooh-poohed in 1931 the charge that she was a Communist because she had gone to see Stalin with G.B.S. The opposite charge that she was a Nazi seemed no less fantastic. If there still remained people who were doubtful of what went on at Cliveden, the appointment in April 1939 of Lord Lothian as British Ambassador at Washington must have set their doubts at rest. That he, well known to be her greatest friend, and who had been accused of being the leading pro-Nazi of them all, should be chosen as the best man England could find to persuade the Americans to come in against the Nazis, was the final refutation. His period of office was very short, for he died in December 1940. He was a remarkable man, the quietest and most self effacing of Lady Astor's close friends. The description of him written by Mr Kingsley Martin, the well-known left-wing journalist and editor of the *New Statesman*, from whom flattery was not to be expected, carries much weight. He wrote in December 1940: 'Lord Lothian had as much charm as any man I have known in public life. He was an aristocrat, an intellectual, and a man of good will. He always hoped that his good will would conjure away the illusion of evil in others.' His mistaken estimate of Hitler was partly due to his having too open and generous a mind. There was no suspicion in his nature. 'He had that natural optimism of temperament that suits so well the English gentleman.' Lady Astor greatly admired in him these very qualities, and emulated them herself. He did not live to see the Americans join in the struggle, but he helped to set them on the road to the alliance. During his term of office they ceased to be indifferent onlookers and became sympathetic friends.

At the outbreak of war in September 1939 the Astors placed the site of the 1914–18 Cliveden hospital again at the disposal of the Canadians, who built a new hospital on it. Lady Astor herself took thought how she could best serve the needs of women and children, such as their evacuation from areas likely to be bombed. Throwing herself into the emergency with her usual fire, she drew attention in parliament to harassing stupidities, which were legion at that moment of makeshift and improvisation. She spoke up for the soldier and sailor, and their wives. She urged vigour and speed, denounced hesitation and laziness. She watched for abuses, unfairness, oppression of the common man, and standing for broad good sense held up to ridicule the paltry and ineffectual. In war a woman finds it hard to make her voice heard in the din of what is essentially a male occasion. But with unabated spirit she concentrated on what she considered her particular rôle, 'the gingering up of the government' as she had always called it.

She took a decided line in the crisis of April 1940, when after the false calm of the phoney war Hitler suddenly struck at Norway. On 11 April, Winston Churchill, now First Lord of the Admiralty, addressed a hushed Commons, warning members that the invasion of Norway was the first move in Hitler's grand strategy and that it was impossible to tell where he would strike next – Holland, Denmark or directly at England. Chamberlain had begun to feel the wind. He had ridden out Munich, the seizure of Prague and the invasion of Poland, but confidence in him as Prime Minister was declining. He was nearly seventy-two and not in good health. Had he the force to lead the country in war? Was he putting the right men in the right places? Lady Astor had long been his faithful supporter, as we know. But she now began to doubt him. After Churchill had sat down on the 11th, she said in the debate: 'People are beginning to feel that Mr Chamberlain is not the wisest selector of men. Duds must be got rid of, even if they are one's dearest friends. And if there is a sweep, it should be a clean sweep and not musical chairs.' On the Sunday the *Observer* said that she had the pluck to express the smothered conviction of the House. On 8 May there was a Labour motion of no confidence in the Prime Minister, which was supported by thirty-three Conservatives including Lady Astor, while sixty abstained from voting. Two days later he resigned, Churchill taking his place at the head of a coalition government. In voting against Chamberlain she put duty before friendship. She liked Chamberlain but believed him unfit for his job; Churchill was not a man she got on with easily, but she thought him the right man to lead England at the greatest crisis in her history.

As member for Plymouth for twenty years and now its Mayoress, she rightly felt that she should devote as much of her time as possible to work in that great naval port. Her house on the Hoe was so close to the harbour that the warships seemed to anchor right under her windows. She sought to identify herself yet more with the population and resolved that if Plymouth became a target for the German bombers, she would stay and see it out. A major assault of the kind seemed inevitable, when the Germans began methodically to bomb the chief bases, and sure enough it came in March 1941. The gallantry with which she faced the ordeal forms a fitting last chapter to her public life.

It was on the night of the 20th of that month that an attack began, which lasted several weeks and caused greater devastation than bombing in any other city. It so happened that King George VI and Queen Elizabeth paid Plymouth a visit earlier that very day. The Astors conducted them round. They inspected the city and the air defences and spent some time in the docks and the poorer quarters, talking to the people and enquiring after their needs. Lady Astor gave them tea in her house. Their train was due to leave at 6 p.m. and when they were about to enter their car to drive to the station, a man elbowed his way through the cheering crowd with a live crab in his hand. 'Where are they?' he panted. 'Mr Cload has sent it for the King.' Enquiries were made. Yes, the King was expecting a crab from Mr Cload and it was popped into the royal car. The explanation of this singular gift, it seems, was that two hours earlier Mr Cload, a ship's chandler, had been presented to the King. As he shook hands, Lady Astor had asked: 'What about a fresh crab, Mr Cload?' He replied: 'The ship is out now, but should be back before Their Majesties leave. I'll see they get a crab.' For many years it had been the custom for every member of the royal family who visited Plymouth to accept the gift of a live crab from Mr Cload. While the King and Queen were at tea with Lady Astor, Mr Cload stood on the quay, looking anxiously out to sea. His boat came in just in time, the best crab was selected and a man sent hot foot to find the King and present it.

Two and a half hours after the royal departure, the bombing began. Mr Ben Robertson, the American writer, was staying with the Astors and has described what happened in his book *I Saw England*. 'At 8.30 p.m. we had eaten some chicken and stewed rhubarb and the cakes left over from the royal tea party, when the sirens started and the guns began to thunder. From the very start there was something about the intensity of the whole which made us think that this was it. We had all the tubs in the house filled with water and saw that spades were handy. The maid Rose said: "Lady Astor, I must tell you, I have a sailor boy visiting me." "Tell him to stay," said Lady Astor.'

Ben Robertson describes how they watched the bombs falling in the distance, and then 'we heard a stick of bombs coming nearer and nearer and fell flat on our faces by the hall door.' The explosion covered them with glass from the broken windows of the house. 'The air warden ordered Lady Astor to the basement. There she talked about Virginia and her childhood and the tobacco fields and about Rose Harrison, her maid, saying that Rose and she had worked together for thirty years and that Rose was the only woman in the world who would put up with her, and that she was the only woman in the world who would put up with Rose. Rose said: "Lady Astor is the kind of woman that takes understanding. I was three years getting to understand her." Lady Astor said: "Rose, I have never understood you." Someone came in to say that an incendiary was on the roof. "Come on everybody," called Lady Astor, "get the sand-bags. Where in hell are the buckets?" From this we were up and down the stairs. Once she stopped by a blasted window to look at Plymouth, which for miles was a blazing fire. Her eyes filled with tears and pushing back her steel hat she said: "There goes thirty years of our lives, but we'll build it again." '

I asked Rose Harrison to tell me about this famous occasion. She is a small, strong woman, as brave as a lion and very independent. With her bluff manner and Yorkshire accent, she is more like a devoted retainer than a fashionable lady's maid. She said: 'The first incendiaries fell at 8.30, the bombs at 9. Her ladyship was standing near the hall door. A bomb fell nearby and she had splinters of glass in her hair. Someone told us we must go into the shelter. An American journalist, Mr Ben Robertson, was with us. In the shelter I spent the time picking bits of glass out of her ladyship's hair. Mr Robertson was taking down notes for his book and some of the things I said come into it.' She then quoted the Astorism given by Mr Robertson, but in a neater form and truer to Lady Astor's style: 'Nobody would keep Rose but me; nobody would stay with me but Rose.' And she went on: 'We came out of the shelter. There was no glass in the windows, no light in the house. Her ladyship was dead beat and went to her bedroom and slept, with all the windows blown out.'

(The present Lord Astor once said of this: 'That didn't bother my mother, for she always slept with the windows wide open, summer and winter.')

The next night the bombers came again. 'Her ladyship went out to dinner and the raid came when she was away,' Rose Harrison told me. 'She and his lordship went round the town during the bombing. When she came back to the house, she was in a state of nerves over the harm the raid had done and at the danger I had been in. "I will never leave you again," she said to me. It was 2 a.m. before she went to bed in the rubble of her bedroom. She refused to leave Plymouth afterwards. Those things were too hard for his lordship, who never quite recovered from the strain.'

Rose Harrison spoke with some emotion. These two nights had drawn her very close to Lady Astor, perhaps closer than she had ever been. She said to me suddenly, as if in some sort of exculpation, 'Her ladyship is a very determined woman, but so am I. But there is no malice in her character. No matter what quarrel we might have, she was just the same soon afterwards. We had many quarrels, though I always gave her place as a lady. I remember once after a quarrel that I went to his lordship and said: "I am sorry, my lord, but I have been rude to her ladyship, but she was very rude to me first." His lordship said: "What are we going to do with her, Rose?" I said: "Well, my lord, I don't know what the cure is." '

This shows as well as anything could what the two women were like who sat in the shelter that night, the one talking of old days in Virginia, the other picking the glass out of her companion's hair. They were very well suited to each other, and well suited to support the occasion, which was terrifying but did not terrify them.

The morning after the first raid reporters got a statement out of Lady Astor. After she had told them what we already know, they asked what was the strangest sight she saw that night. She replied: 'At the height of the raid I saw a man who walked along calmly exercising his two dogs.'

Of Lady Astor's sang-froid on the second night when she and Lord Astor went round the town, it was reported: 'Lady Astor escaped injury last night, although she worked much of it in the shelters. The townspeople call her marvellous in the way she went from shelter to shelter throughout the attack, giving encouragement and help.' Her encouragement was sometimes to make people laugh. Noticing a man taking a nip to liven his courage, she remarked: 'You see that man standing there? Well, he can drink a couple of bottles while another man is looking for the corkscrew.'

The bombing continued night after night. But though

her house was badly damaged, she did not move out of the city or go back to Cliveden. She set herself to keep up the hearts of the people. There were insufficient shelters for the poorer class. She had more hastily erected. When families were driven out of their houses, she arranged other accommodation for them and saw they were fed. Early in May Churchill came on a visit and remarked: 'Their houses are down, but their spirits are up.' Maintaining their spirits was the first of her duties, she said. A photo in the *Lady* shows her telling children to keep their chins up, and suiting action to the words holding a small boy and pushing up his chin.

The sufferings of the Plymouth people were very great. Many fled the city and took refuge where they could. Refugees at first could find nowhere to sleep. Fortunate ones got permission to settle down for the night in a barn. Others trudged till they were tired out and slept in the fields. It was this tragic situation that Lord and Lady Astor grappled with. Gradually order was evolved from chaos by planned evacuation, billeting, etc. The press has enthusiastic accounts of how magnificently she rose to the occasion. The practical side of her nature had full scope. After her wit, perhaps her chief talent was a rough and tumble knack for getting things done. Her popularity, great before, increased. To say that she was venerated by the common people is not an exaggeration. She seemed to them to be everywhere and available to everyone. She listened to the poorest man with the same attention she paid to admirals. Her flow of spirits was inexhaustible. To cheer the people she had dances on the Hoe and might be seen herself taking a turn with a sailor. Bands played gay tunes and martial music. Wherever she showed herself there was jollity. The people said: 'The bombing was cruel, but her ladyship made it all right.' They looked on it almost as an adventure.

Lady Astor was now a woman of sixty-two. Yet she found the strength throughout the war to do two jobs – to carry out her multifarious duties as Lady Mayoress of a city which was the hottest spot in all embattled Britain, and as M.P. for the same to attend regularly when parliament was sitting, so as to bring the needs of her greatly suffering constituents to the notice of the government. She would sit in the House, participating in debates in her usual way by question and interjection, and then catch the midnight express for Plymouth, where she would get to work in the morning, apparently as fresh and energetic as ever. And this was not the end of her activities in the Second World War. There was the Canadian hospital at Cliveden. In the First World War, when she was neither Lady Mayoress nor M.P., she had made a practice of visiting the hospital twice every day and succeeded in getting into personal touch with a big proportion of the thousands of wounded who passed through it. Her inclination now was to do the same, but this was utterly impossible in view of her work at Westminster and Plymouth. Nevertheless, when parliament was not sitting, she divided her time between Cliveden and Plymouth and managed to establish at the Canadian hospital the same happy relations with the wounded as in the former war. This provides the answer to a question sometimes asked – what did Nancy Astor do during the 1939–1945 war? She worked from morning to night, and often far into the night, at her duties in London, Plymouth and at the Canadian hospital, a threefold task which would have proved beyond the power of most women of her age. But it did not overtire her. Her spirits remained as buoyant as ever. She even found time to go speech-making on occasion round the country.

Taught by experience of war, she could not hide her regrets that she had once thought the League of Nations would be able to maintain peace without military backing. In a speech at Cheltenham in September 1942, she said: 'When the admirals and generals and those who had been round the world warned this country not to disarm, politicians did not take their advice. This was not one person's fault,' she went on, thinking of poor Chamberlain, who after an operation in July had died in November 1940, a tumbled-down idol. 'After the last war we were all striving after peace. The trouble was that we didn't understand Europe or the world as the admirals and generals did. I am afraid that I was one who was against those who didn't want us to disarm.' After this confession, she went on to say that she had learnt wisdom from her mistakes and was not going to make the mistake now of believing that the Russians could be relied on. 'They are not fighting for us, but defending themselves.' We should be as careful about them as we should have been about the Germans. This remark about a Russia that had become our ally was much criticized. At the moment the general public was as deceived about the Russians as it had been about the Nazis.

In November 1942, ten months after the Americans had entered the war, the B.B.C. thought it might brighten up the Brains Trust if Lady Astor and Bernard Shaw appeared. When told there would be a number of Americans present, she agreed and managed to persuade Shaw to come. At the start of the session the question-master warned the audience that as G.B.S. had for years been trying to reform the English by skilfully directed insult, they would have to look out. So would the Americans, for the question was what did he think of them. At this, his eyebrows bristling, Shaw sat up straight and said: 'I am eighty-six; I shall only speak for two minutes. You ask me what does England think of America. I tell you, that's easy, England doesn't think of America. England thinks about England. The English take the greatest possible care to avoid knowing anything about what they are doing. Napoleon said "A man who knows where he is going doesn't go very far." So you can always trust an Englishman.' After Lady Astor had rattled off some of her best stories against Churchill and for the Virginian Negroes, a young American officer, one of several in the audience, asked Shaw's advice on how to make the most of their visit to England. The sage's reply was: 'My advice to you gentlemen is – never miss an opportunity to make the English feel thoroughly ashamed of themselves.'

It was in this lively style that Lady Astor continued to promote Anglo-American friendship. The following anecdote, which she related in a speech at Plymouth, further illustrates her endeavours in this field. 'When I was leaving my house in Plymouth Hoe the other day I encountered an American soldier – drunk. I dragged him into the drawing-room and put him in an arm-chair, where he fell asleep. When Lord Astor came in, he found the visitor and waited for him to wake up. After a while he opened his eyes and murmured: "Where am I? Can I get a drink in this hotel?" He couldn't!'

Bernard Shaw was constantly to be found at Cliveden. In 1944, aged eighty-seven, fragile but wiry, he was at work there on an ABC of Politics. 'People know the XYZ of everything, but they don't know the ABC,' he remarked over his porridge at breakfast, so a journalist who was staying at Cliveden recorded. He might be seen walking in the park with cane, cap, gloves, knickerbockers, Norfolk jacket and camera. Returning fresh and rosy, he would duel with William C. Bullitt, American ambassador to France till 1941. If Winston Churchill was mentioned he shied off the subject. Somebody asked – what about Frank Harris's biography? He pronounced this judgment: 'Harris wanted to write a book about Christ, but he was afraid it would be unpublishable, so he wrote about me instead. He knew quite a lot about Christ but nothing about me.' When Lady Astor was in the room, his conversational somersaults became yet more giddy. Legend insisted that she had washed his beard during the Moscow trip. It was as white as snow now. He was immensely attractive. The Cliveden guests generally included American generals and admirals. He knew exactly how to entertain the top brass. His appearance was all they had hoped for. But perhaps it was his geniality which won them most. Like Lady Astor, he didn't quite hit it off with Churchill. Perhaps he did not feel a match for him. There is the famous exchange which gives Churchill the last word, rather a chestnut but worth repeating. G.B.S. sent him two tickets for the first night of one of his plays with the message: 'Bring a friend – if you have one.' To which Churchill replied: 'Prefer to come second night – if you have one.' That is championship sparring, as is the no less famous exchange between Churchill and Lady Astor. She: 'If I were your wife, I'd put poison in your coffee.' He: 'If I were your husband, I'd drink it.'

At the end of 1942 Lord Astor gave Cliveden to the National Trust and endowed it, so that it could be maintained for ever at his expense. His sole condition was that he should be allowed to live there and his heirs if they wished to do so. In making this benefaction, he not only threw open the house and gardens to the public, but also preserved in perpetuity the Cliveden woods, one of the most beautiful of all the reaches of the Thames, which, had he sold them to speculators, would probably have been cut down and the land resold for building sites. He expressed the hope that, if later on his descendants decided to leave the house, the government would use it, as he had used it, as an international meeting place.

By the time the European war ended in May 1945, there had been no general election for nearly ten years. A dissolution was long overdue. As the conflict approached its end, selection of candidates for the constituencies began. The Conservative party at Plymouth was eager to adopt Lady Astor again. On 24 November 1944, the anniversary of her first election in 1919, the Bishop of Plymouth conducted a service in St Catherine's Church as a thanksgiving to God for her having represented Plymouth for twenty-five years. This must have been the most unique tribute ever paid to an M.P. When therefore in the following months she announced that she intended to retire from parliament and would not stand again, there was much disappointment among her constituents. She was retiring, she said, in response to her husband's request that she should. He had always acted as her chief-of-staff in organizing her election campaigns, and no longer felt able for the exertions involved. He was not physically the man he had been. The extra work, strain and anxieties of the war years as Mayor of Plymouth had worn him down. Moreover, he was not as interested in party politics as before. While Mayor, he had been out of touch for five years and was disinclined to re-enter the arena and work for policies for which he no longer had much feeling. He had become more radical and his views were less identical with hers than formerly. Always too liberal, too keen on social betterment to be a real Conservative, he had become wrapped up in the development of schemes which he had carefully planned. His model farm, for instance, took up quite a large part of his time. His wife, he felt, had had a splendid parliamentary career. Undefeated seven times, for a quarter of a century she had had free scope to express her ideas in parliament. He doubted if there was more she could do than she had already done. Furthermore, it was not certain that she would get in, for a Labour victory was thought not unlikely after ten years of Conservative and coalition ministries. By retiring now, she would leave the scene undefeated and at the summit of her reputation.

His decision brought her to a full stop. It was against her inclination but she had to accept it. She knew that she could not manage without him. Their partnership had been so close that it included every aspect of her public life, not only the fighting of elections but her speeches in parliament and her political entertaining at St James's Square and Cliveden. If he intended to withdraw his support altogether from what had been an intimate collaboration, a unity which had given the family its strength and influence, the edifice which they had built up together would collapse, for her strength alone was inadequate to support it.

The papers generally expressed regret. *John Bull*, which in Bottomley's time had attacked her so fiercely, now lamented her departure: 'If Lady Astor persists in her retirement, the House will lose its most historic figure.' It went on to praise 'her sublime audacity.' She had entered parliament 'like a gale of wind and for twenty-five years the gale had never subsided. Her *obiter dicta* would fill a volume.' The *Daily Mail* recalled a few of her sayings: 'Men are a menace to any country and until women take a hand there is little chance of real world peace.' And: 'The government believe in beer and more of it, but it doesn't seem to buck them up.' And: 'I make a point of going up to lonely-looking soldiers. One I spoke to the other day said: "Who are you?" I replied: "Never mind, come and have some lunch." '

The last day of the old parliament was 15 June 1945. In a speech of farewell she said: 'I leave with the deepest regret and the profoundest respect for the House of Commons. I don't think any other assembly in the world could have been more tolerant of a foreign-born woman, as I was, who fought against so many things they believed in.' She is also recorded as saying: 'I am heartbroken at going. I shall miss the House, but the House won't miss me. It never misses anybody. I have seen them all go – Lloyd George, Asquith, Baldwin, Snowden, MacDonald and the rest – and not one of them was missed. The House is like the sea and M.P.s are like little ships that sail across it and disappear over the horizon. Some of them carry a light and others don't. That is the only difference. I don't want to go and I wouldn't if it were not the wish of my husband.' They were both sixty-six. She had not had enough, but he had.

There followed a Labour victory at the polls and Churchill's displacement by Attlee.

Lady Astor had not visited the States since before the war and, longing to see her old friends again, set off there in a fruit boat in January 1946. The *New York Times* has: 'The Astors have arrived aboard a tiny steamer, six days overdue and battered by the Atlantic gales. The undefeated 66-year-old Virginian-born Viscountess immediately held court on the lonely pier. "I am an extinct volcano," she announced to the reporters. In a take-it-or-leave-it interview she discussed the British government, Ribbentrop, fresh eggs, the Bible, fruit, women, Russia, fur coats from gentlemen friends, etc.'

(At the Nuremberg trial Ribbentrop had asked that she be called as a witness in his defence. Needless to say, the court refused so ridiculous a request. In point of fact, she was in the Black Book, the list, drawn up by Ribbentrop on instructions from Hitler, which contained the names of the English men and women to be arrested as soon as the Germans occupied London.)

The reporters gathered that she had a Virginian aunt of ninety-five with whom she intended to stay. 'Any other plans?' they asked. In a stern voice she replied: 'I may run for Congress, what do you think of that?' She was wearing a mink coat, a hat trimmed with mink, a plain blue silk dress and light tan rubber galoshes, large earrings of sapphires and diamonds, gold chain bracelets and a rope of pearls.

At this time Churchill was also visiting America. 'Do you expect to see him?' they asked. 'He would hardly come to America to see me!' she replied. The Americans, as may well be supposed, were astonished at Churchill having lost the premiership after saving England. Was it a revolution? they asked her. 'The English,' she replied, 'are a very united people and even if they don't like their captain they won't sink the ship.'

If anything, she appeared freer and easier than when an M.P. She dressed down the reporters, but one of them said afterwards it was more fun than he had had for months. Her final remark to them as she got into her car was: 'Goodbye, you horrors.' Everybody was satisfied that their old Nancy was home again.

In high spirits she began a wide tour. At Miami they asked: 'What about Bernard Shaw?' Her answer was: 'I've just written to him to come over and bring Stalin with him.' Her aged aunt survived her visit only forty-eight hours. Her travels over the continent spread wider and wider. Her vivacity was unimpaired, she spoke her mind on all topics. She addressed several legislatures and universities including that of Columbia, her theme always that America and England must hold together, plan together and forget their differences to save civilization. 'U.N.O. is a great experiment, but who knows what the Russians are thinking of?' That was where lay the threat to the future. That was what made Anglo-American unity so essential. She was continually being cross-examined about Churchill, but did not foresee that the country would call him back to lead it against the Russian threat which she did foresee.

She was invited to the Pentagon by General Eisenhower, where she continued very savage with the press (to their delight) saying: 'I wouldn't trust the dogs as far as I could throw them!' But after roughly turning aside a photographer, she was sorry, saying: 'They have to do it for a living. If it wasn't for that I'd have killed them long ago.' But another reporter had better luck. She promised him an interview on her return to New York from Hot Springs. He gave her his word that he would report only what she said. 'No,' she replied. 'I'd rather you wrote what you think. If you write what I say, you'll go to jail.' One columnist suffered badly. 'What's his name, did he say? Pig and whistle or pig-sty or what?' To another one at Los Angeles she said: 'Get out of here, you buzzard, and bring the article back for me to see or I'll shoot you.' But her press was splendid.

She returned to England in May 1946, and was again in the States in the two following years. Her chief theme now was Russia. 'We have got to get Germany back on her feet. It is not only the decent thing to do, but is a matter of self-preservation. Germany is the strongest thing between us and Russia.' And at Tucson, Arizona, in March 1948: 'If we were to go after Stalin today he wouldn't have the chance of a snowball in hell. We must stop Russia before it's too late.'

At Houston the train pulled into the station at 7.15 a.m. Newsmen knocked at the door of her apartment. She shouted through the door: 'Go away. It's scandalous!

Woken at dawn! I'm an old woman, don't look pretty. Go away and read your Bible. Read Proverbs. Read what it says about virtuous women.' They persisted. At last she stuck her head out of the door. 'Can't understand all the tin cans laying about in Houston. I don't mean just Houston but all over the prairies. Filth and tin cans. What are they going to do about them?' 'Send them to England,' suggested a reporter. 'Well, fill 'em up first,' she retorted.

On 27 March she 'arrived in form,' it was stated, at Atlanta. 'I wouldn't let you interview me this afternoon if you were William Shakespeare,' she said down the phone to the representative of a ladies' paper. 'I know what you want. I've been a working girl myself. Call me later and now get off the phone.' Another Atlanta columnist had: 'Lady Astor had often squelched such people as Winston Churchill with the back of her hand. Her husband said of her: "My wife is apt to say what other people think and to say it without first having consulted a lawyer." When asked how she justified the claim that she had left the House of Commons a better place than she found it, she answered: "I had disagreeable qualities and a shameful audacity very much needed in that place." '

The Atlanta people were also much pleased with a retort she delivered at a public luncheon: 'If I gave you my day's programme it would make Eleanor Roosevelt look like a hitched horse.' This was as widely repeated as was an Astorism at the same lunch: 'During my twenty-five years in the House of Commons the Socialists did nothing but promise the kingdom of God without praying, and the good of this world without working.'

She seems to have let go on these American trips. The Americans, I find, have a robuster sense of humour than we have. It suited her. After all, she was an American. Appreciated though her humour was in England, it was relished even more in the States. Freed from her duties in the Commons, she was in real holiday mood among her own people. She could make what jokes she liked and be sure they would not misfire.

Her friendship with Bernard Shaw remained unimpaired. After his wife died in 1944 (a woman for whom she had a warm regard), he lived all by himself at the little village of Ayot St Lawrence, where she visited him at intervals. In March 1947, when he was ninety-one years of age, he was marooned by an exceptional fall of snow. Anxious about him, she set out in her car at once. When the car stuck in the snow two miles from his house, she got out and walked the rest of the way. She had with her a box of chocolates, lately sent her from America, for she knew well how fond of chocolates he was. He was enchanted when he saw her entering the snowy garden. They sat together eating the chocolates. After a visit to him the following year she said to some schoolgirls at Slough: 'Today I have been to visit a very young man of ninety-two, Mr George Bernard Shaw. His brain is perfectly clear. He has a terrific interest in everything and is never bored with himself for an instant. So cultivate your tastes, girls, and you will still be young at ninety!'

On 10 September 1950, while pruning in the garden, Shaw, then in his ninety-fifth year, fell and broke his thigh. He was taken to hospital where Lady Astor visited him. Three weeks later he was home again. But though apparently recovered, he was not able to throw off the shock of his accident. She went to see him on 31 October. On leaving his room she is recorded as saying: 'He is much weaker than when I saw him ten days ago. All he said to me was: "Oh, Nancy, what I want is to sleep, sleep." He is desperately tired.' She also said to a friend that day: 'No one can do anything for him. He is dying. He has lived ninety-four years and that is long enough for anybody.'

In the middle of the afternoon of 1 November 1950 he fell into a coma and died at dawn next day without regaining consciousness. Lady Astor was the only friend whom he was willing to see during his last days, and at his cremation she was one of the very few who attended, besides his housekeeper, secretary and niece.

With the death of Bernard Shaw the last of Lady Astor's

great men friends departed this life. She had lost Lothian, Lawrence and also Lloyd George, who died in March 1945. Of Lloyd George she said: 'He was more free from personal vanity and from side and snobbishness than any man I ever knew in public life. He was too great to hate or fear. He wanted freedom and a better world for all mankind. He was a most uncommon man. I am proud of my friendship with him.' And I have also heard her declare her opinion that the great social reforms which have changed the face of England are to be traced to his initiative, and in the long run may be seen as more fundamental even than Churchill's achievements.

Two years after Shaw's death, her husband died. The departure of this gentle and good man was for her the end of an epoch. She left Cliveden, where her eldest son, William, took up his residence as third Viscount, and bought a house in Hill Street, Berkeley Square, for the town house in St James's Square had been sold since it was no longer required after 1945 as a political headquarters. The Hill Street house remained her London address until 1958, when she moved to 100 Eaton Square, where she now lives.

CHAPTER 17

Postscript: Lady Astor Today

My acquaintance with Lady Astor dates from the middle years of the last war, when I became a friend of her eldest son, the present Viscount Astor. One of my earliest recollections of her is at dinner at Cliveden on 8 August 1945, to which her son invited me. Among the guests I remember were Peter Fleming, the well-known writer, and his wife. When we sat down to table I said to Lady Astor: 'I suppose you heard the extraordinary news on the six o'clock wireless?' 'No,' said she. 'What news?' 'The Americans have dropped an atomic bomb on the Japs at Hiroshima and wiped out the city.' There was dead silence for a moment at that end of the table. Lady Astor then declared that she didn't believe it and calling out to her husband at the other end said: 'Did you hear this about an atom bomb?' 'No,' said he. 'Where?' 'Mr Collis will tell you,' she said. 'Now then, Mr Collis, let's all hear about this bomb of yours.' At that date I was not used to Lady Astor's rallying mode and rather shyly repeated what I had heard at six o'clock. The news was received with incredulity, either because it sounded incredible or because I spoke too diffidently. It was assumed that I had got things mixed up. 'Well,' I said, 'if we listen at nine o'clock, that will settle it.' It was then about twenty minutes to. Lord Astor told the butler to bring in the wireless. During the interval I began to wonder whether indeed I had heard right and was relieved when the announcer repeated what was the most momentous statement ever made by the B.B.C. We had suddenly entered the nuclear age.

From that on I met Lady Astor every now and then. After her son succeeded to the title in 1952 I was more frequently at Cliveden and had opportunities of observing her when she was on visit there. A notable occasion was on 7 November 1953 when King Gustav of Sweden was staying the weekend. On getting to the house I found the porch in darkness and could not find the bell and knocked. No one came. I wondered if I had mistaken the day. But feeling about again, I found the bell, rang and at once all was illuminated. Mr Lee, the butler opened. When I told him of my predicament he was distressed. 'Lord Reith is expected any moment,' he said as he ushered me into the salon. 'I had better leave the lights on in case he too can't find the bell.' From the way he spoke one gathered that Lord Reith was not the sort of man he would care to ruffle. Lord Astor had barely received me when Lord Hailey, one of the weekend guests, came in. I had never met before this Oxford double first, the most distinguished member of the Indian Civil Service of his generation, now eighty-one and looking the old autocrat that he was. On his heels appeared Lord Reith, an immensely tall man, a sword cut across his face, a wild eye and a manner which had kept the B.B.C. in order when he was its Director-General. A few minutes later there entered Lady Astor, so much greater a public figure than either, her career behind her and no longer mistress of Cliveden, but with wit unblunted and in no way tamed by her seventy-four years. Presently Lord Astor was seen to go towards the door. It was King Gustav. He was on a private visit to England and had arrived at Cliveden without even a valet. He did not look more than fifty-five, though in fact was some ten years older. His air was that of a savant or professor. He is probably the most cultivated reigning monarch in the world. His manner of shaking hands was very natural; his face was kind and he was immediately likeable. Lady Astor and he had been friends from the time when she lent him her Sandwich house for his honeymoon. After the rest of the party had assembled, a move was made towards the dining-room. When passing Sargent's portrait of the late Viscount in the hall, Lady Astor remarked: 'I never cared

228

for it. He had a stronger face.' At the dining-room door Lord Hailey quoted a passage in Latin to cap what he was talking about. One felt that the first Viscount, who had filled house and garden with Roman antiquities, would have warmed to a guest who spoke Latin. The Pompadour panelling in the dining-room was, however, perhaps the happiest of all his purchases in the antique. The King passed to his seat at the foot of the table on Lady Astor's right. Though not indifferent to the elegant sophistication of the royal French style, his main interest was in early Chinese art, a subject in which the first Viscount had not dabbled, for in his day the vogue for it had hardly reached England. Anyhow, he was not the sort of man who would have cared for Chou bronzes or Sung stonewares. The later porcelains, however, he must have admired, as they go so admirably with a period French décor, as in the Pompadour room, but there were none there. King Gustav, well versed in considerations of this kind, is likely to have noticed the omission, but it was not a nicety which he would have cared to inflict on those present. He was on holiday, was fond of his host and Lady Astor, liked general conversation, and was perfectly suited by the English company in which he found himself. He had successfully broken down the barrier which hedges royalty, though his connoisseurship remained to isolate him somewhat, for he did not think about art in the same way as persons who had not studied it as deeply as he had.

Lady Astor was seated between him and Lord Hailey. Her manner to the King was a mixture of licence and respect. This sort of open friendliness with a trace of deference was what he liked about English society, for the knack of it was rare on the continent. I heard Lord Reith remark: 'It is interesting to reflect that England is perhaps the only country in the world where a king can put off all ceremony and just be a private gentleman.'

Lady Astor rarely allowed an opportunity of rebuking drinkers to pass. She had got into the way of taking a glass of Dubonnet herself, but declared it to be non-alcoholic, a fiction everyone was happy to accept. Lord Hailey, however, was drinking something stronger and presently she said: 'You are having too much. Being so long in India has demoralized you.' Like most people, he liked this sort of chaff from her and to keep it up said: 'India demoralized me? I see you suspect me of having lined my pocket there.' And they continued in this vein. Presently, to amuse the King, she began talking of her visit to Moscow with Bernard Shaw and related some of her exchanges with Stalin, which at the time did not find their way into the press, as the party had promised to keep secret what was said. The one I caught was this. 'I said to Stalin: "Your régime is no different from the Tsars'." "How so?" he asked. "Because," said I, "you dispose of your opponents without trial." "Of course," he replied.' Hailey observed that on the occasion when he met Stalin, he looked exactly like a Scotsman.

The mention of Shaw led to her telling the King this anecdote about him. 'I went to see him,' she explained, 'the day before he died. His mind was quite clear. As I sat by him stroking his head, he suddenly said: "That reminds me," and told me this story. "Mr X, a wealthy Italian, invited some friends to dinner. While they were having short drinks beforehand, his butler came in and whispered something in his ear. At this Mr X got up and said to his guests: 'I'm sorry, but I'll have to ask you to go home. There's a man in bed with my wife.' The guests expressed sympathy and prepared to leave. As they were dispersing the butler reappeared and again whispered to his master. Mr X seemed very contented. 'Don't go, don't go,' he called out. 'It's all right. The man has apologized.' " ' '

Lady Astor invited King Gustav to believe that these were Shaw's last words. It is improbable that he did. Nevertheless that 'the world's most famous pantaloon', as Churchill called Shaw, should have died with a joke on his lips, was not out of character.

After dinner Lady Astor continued to entertain her guests with stories, banter and all sorts of drolleries. Lord

Reith began to feel tired, because, as he explained to Lord Astor, he had been up all night, writing a report. 'I had a bath at 6.30 a.m. and have been hard at it all day. Do you think I could slip away before the King makes a move?' Lord Astor said that he would mention it to his mother. Perhaps she would get up. 'Don't tell her I'm tired,' Reith begged. He had the reputation of being tireless and was afraid of what she might say at his expense. But now Lady Astor's voice was heard: 'It is time for Your Majesty to get to bed.' King Gustav rose pleasantly, easily, and said goodnight to her, as she gave him a little curtsey.

It was at such weekend dinners at Cliveden that I continued, off and on for years, to meet Lady Astor. I made a practice of recording the next day a description of the scene and what she had said – or rather the few of her *mots* that I could catch. They came out without effort or premeditation, and in abundance for she rarely opened her mouth without making a lively remark. On the Saturday of the first week of May 1957, I was sitting next her at table and after listening to her anecdotes about well-known people, I said that it was her duty to preserve them for posterity by writing her memoirs. Her reply was: 'Anyone who writes an autobiography ought to be taken out and shot.' At the close of dinner I said to Lord Astor that I had been urging his mother to write her reminiscences. He replied: 'You ought to write her biography.' That was how this book was first mooted.

The suggestion had been made more than once that Lady Astor should write her autobiography. Publishers and editors had made her offers. She had played with the idea, but had put it aside for one reason or another. I think her main reason was that she knew she was without the necessary application. Her success in parliament and on the platform was not due, as has been shown, to prepared speeches but to her remarkable talent for improvisation. On her feet before an audience or surrounded by a circle of friends or with someone like Shaw, for instance, to set her going, her ideas flowed. To compose a book was out of her line. When an autobiography from her pen had seemed unfeasible, it was suggested that if she employed a ghost writer, who would take down what she said in answer to questions framed so as to cover the events of her life, and construct therefrom a narrative in the first person, an autobiography would result as lively as were the random utterances for which she was famous. This was tried about ten years ago but when a draft of some part of it was submitted for approval, both she and her husband declared it would not do. To write a biography was a new approach, but it remained to be seen whether she would lend herself sufficiently to the project to make it possible. After some hesitations and postponements she agreed to have talks with me in her new house in Eaton Square. These talks took place in the course of 1958. Alone they would not have sufficed for more than a short sketch. But as mentioned in my prefatory note, Lord Astor made available a quantity of information. This source, vivified by my personal contact with her at Eaton Square, and the previous meetings at Cliveden, has enabled me to overcome difficulties which in the past were found insurmountable by others and to put together what is here.

Lady Astor's home at 100 Eaton Square is a flat, but a very large flat formed by the first floor of No. 100 and of the next house and the one after it. She had never lived in a flat before. 'I don't like having to live in an apartment,' she said to me. 'What's my butler got to do without his own front door? I see people coming in at the door on the street or meet them on the stairs and I have no notion who they are, but can't ask them "Who are you?" I believe some are even Italians.'

For all that, the three big rooms of the flat I have seen – the dining-room, drawing-room, and boudoir – are quite palatial. On my first visit I had to wait in the drawing-room a few minutes and was able quietly to take in what was there, and admire how she had arranged her things, after the recent move from Hill Street. Most of the furniture, except the comfortable armchairs and sofa, was

Louis Quinze or Seize and stood up delicately on a French carpet. Eighteenth-century continental china of the highest quality and Chinese hardstone carvings in crystal or jade, stood with their reflections on polished tables. A Chinese carved lacquer screen was alongside the door. Part of the walls was lined with cases of more china and with book-shelves. On the west wall were English old master portraits and on the east Italian landscapes of the seventeenth/eighteenth centuries. I saw Ch'ien Lung birds in ormolu mounts on the chimney-piece, the sort of late Chinese porcelain that goes so well with French furniture, as the French discovered in the eighteenth century. A profusion of rare flowers was the finishing touch. When Lady Astor came in, she showed me the dining-room, furnished with the same luxury and taste. On my remarking on the beauty of the arrangement, she said: 'My niece did it for me. She is wonderfully good.'

Her niece no doubt did a lot, but Lady Astor's own taste is excellent. As in many other things, she had a natural flair for quality. She bought most of the porcelain herself and at one time, so Mr Barker of Spink's told me, was often in there looking at their Chinese hardstones, a place where Queen Mary was to be met, as the only sovereign in English history who made a collection of Chinese jade. During her crowded public career Lady Astor somehow or other found time to keep up an interest in the arts. If she touched on the subject in a speech, she had robustly sensible reflections to make. Her attitude, for instance, to Gertrude Bell's discoveries at Ur is typical. Gertrude Bell left £6,000 by will to found the first school of archaeology in London. A further £44,000 had to be raised. Lady Astor made a handsome contribution and, at a meeting in 1930 in the Central Hall, Westminster, in support, said: 'Men go to the east and their reputations go west. Gertrude Bell went east and the east came to Gertrude Bell. I have been consulting Colonel Lawrence as to what I should say about her and I only wish he could have been here to tell the meeting the things he told me about her great work.' And

233

in her amusing way she recalled that at the time when the revision of the Prayer Book was under discussion, a revision to which she was opposed, the Archbishop of Canterbury, whose proposals had been rejected, went home and consoled himself by reading Gertrude Bell's letters. 'I can't say I did that,' said Lady Astor, 'but I thanked God that we defeated the Archbishop.'

One recalls, too, how when she opened an exhibition of drawings, and photographs of American architecture at the Royal Society of British Architects in 1921, her speech contained the suggestion that architects should give up plastering houses with decorative mouldings and give more thought to modern materials and modern means of construction. This was an advanced view to express in England as early as 1921, for it was not till some years later that the modern plainer style became popular.

A third example of her flair for grasping what was in the air in art circles is the laughing remark which she made to Mr Cooling, when she visited an exhibition of Roger Fry's paintings in the Cooling Gallery in 1928: 'Tell Mr Fry I am disappointed. He paints a pig so that I can recognize it, his trees are like trees. Anyone would know those are rows of houses. It can't be good modern art because I am not mystified.'

She is the last person to think of herself as a connoisseur, but the interior she has created in Eaton Square is proof that her capacity is more genuine than that of the professed art critic who lives in rooms to whose ugliness he is insensitive, not so unusual a phenomenon as one might imagine.

On this first visit of mine, after she had shown me the dining-room she took me along to her boudoir, where on her desk the correspondence of the day and her engagements had been laid. Turning to me with a more formal air she said: 'What can I do for you?' her usual opening gambit with reporters or persons who have come to ask her help. I replied humbly it was about the book. She was immediately all kindness and, declaring that she had brought me from America some volumes on Virginia, she got down on her knees under a side table and dragged out six thick books – Katherine Jones's *The Plantation South* was one – and presented them to me, saying that they would give me the background for her youth. The nimbleness with which she executed this manoeuvre was remarkable, considering that she was in her eightieth year.

After we had sat down she said: 'When you come next, you must bring some of the Cliveden Visitors Books. If I see the names, I'll remember the faces; it will all come back to me, even if long ago.' The mention of the Cliveden books set her talking about people she had known. As she talked she became more animated. Some of what she said has been incorporated further back. Her way was to jump from one subject to another and from the past to the present and back again, dropping *obiter dicta* by the way. Thus: 'The welfare state may be the farewell state,' said she, meaning that people so coddled as we are now could not survive in this hard world. And she went on: 'For the first time in my life I find myself pessimistic. How can we hope to continue selling at the present rate our products abroad when other countries increase their exports?' 'Specialize on what only we can produce?' 'Yes,' she said, 'that's it. Machines and biscuits. Our biscuits are unique.' I thought of how the Chinese Emperors believed their rhubarb to be unique. It's like a weed now. Nevertheless, biscuits, there were secrets about biscuits. I had met Lord Palmer at Cliveden. Suddenly she seemed depressed. 'I don't feel that I have accomplished anything in life,' she said. One saw no need for such misgiving. Her life had been very full, fuller than the lives of most women obliged to earn their livelihood, much fuller than the lives of rich women who hadn't to work. Was it thinking that people drank as much as ever that made her feel that she had failed? Perhaps it was that she could not point to some great achievement, like Nurse Cavell's, Miss Pankhurst's or Margaret McMillan's. But her achievement, composed like a mosaic picture of a thousand little pieces, was a whole which has coloured the period.

As I said to start with, it is less what she did than what she was that made her. She touched so many things, as this book has shown, and whatever she touched was given more life. It does the world good when an original crosses its stage. A subtle transformation takes place. Clever men become cleverer, dull men less dull; lies less deceiving; pomposities are pricked; hatreds are seen as misunderstandings; melancholia is chased away; bunkum is shown the door; hope revives; the colour of flowers is heightened; one hears music. There are rare drugs which can thus transubstantiate; so can a few people.

Before leaving, I tried to fix a date to bring the Cliveden books, but it was impossible. 'Leave it to me,' she said. It was usual, while she was parting with a guest, for some story to come into her head. In this case it was one of her Irish stories. 'A Belfast Protestant,' she said, as we went towards the door, 'fell seriously ill when away from home and when unconscious and evidently dying, was given extreme unction by a Catholic priest. He recovered consciousness just before he died and his last words were: "To hell with the Pope." ' She tends to be caustic about the Irish. On another occasion she said to me: 'As long as the Irish sat in Westminster they had a grievance and an audience. When they left the House they lost both. An Irishman without a grievance does not make sense. With no grievance and no audience Ireland is forgotten.' She also likes to repeat a remark of Shaw's to Stalin when they were in the Kremlin. Stalin asked: 'How do you account for England getting possession of so much of the earth?' To which G.B.S. replied: 'I'm an Irishman and know nothing about England.' And she adds: 'Whenever Shaw did not want to answer a question he always said he was an Irishman.'

The next time I came to Eaton Square I brought some of the Visitors Books. She welcomed me with her half shy, half hardy glance, but seemed a little distracted, as if she was in a hurry and had a lot on hand. 'What can I do for you?' she asked as before. 'The book,' I murmured. 'Come on,' she said, sitting on the sofa. One of the massive Visitors Books was placed beside her. I drew up a chair. She began skipping over the pages. 'Look at all these names!' she said dismayed. However, as she read on her interest was aroused. Arriving at Queen Alexandra's signature, she remarked: 'She was very beautiful, but her sister-in-law, the Duchess of Connaught, was the most intelligent of all the royal women. And she was also the most modest. When I said to her: "You must get tired of opening bazaars," she replied: "That's all I'm fit for." '

Turning another page she noticed the name of Sylvia Pankhurst, which reminded her of a retort made to a heckler by Sylvia's sister, the famous Christobel Pankhurst. She said: 'Once when Christobel was addressing a meeting a small weedy heckler shouted: "Don't you wish you were a man?" Christobel replied: "Yes, don't you?" '

The name of her old friend Lloyd George now caught her eye, under date of May 1921, and she recalled an amusing remark he had made about Curzon, as Foreign Secretary. 'One moment he is as easy and charming as could be. The next he is receiving a foreign ambassador as if he was a Basuto chief.'

In this way she continued to comment as she turned the pages. 'Lord Wemyss remarried at ninety-two. He was fought over by two women – William Robertson began life as a footman, the only case I know of a footman becoming a Field Marshal. – Philip Snowden, as a Labour leader, showed great courage in staying with me.' And coming on another royal signature: 'She was the biggest ass of the lot.' Of Margaret McMillan of the nursery schools she said: 'She changed the thinking of England about children. She first came to see me after having a dream that I would help her. At the opening of the nursery training college which we built for her at Deptford, her speech was listened to with such rapt attention that everybody forgot that Queen Mary was present.'

She continued to talk in this way about one person and another. Sometimes she spoke with earnest intensity, never maliciously, always with bold common sense. Often it was lightly, with gaiety and relish for a comic situation, and she would hit out half in fun to puncture some make-believe, insincerity or bit of nonsense. She became very absorbed.

When it was time for me to go, she got up from the sofa and we moved towards the door. She seemed to break off with reluctance. In a very gentle voice she said: 'I have been so deep in old times that I feel lost now in the present. I don't know where I am, like the Bishop of Exeter.' At her mention of the Bishop's name she had a rush of high spirits and, as if immensely amused at the recollection, said with extraordinary gaiety: 'He couldn't find his ticket at the barrier when going for his train. The ticket collector said: "It doesn't matter." He said: "It does matter." The ticket man said: "It doesn't." The Bishop said. "It does because I don't know where I am going." '

We had reached the hall. Her mood changed. 'Why are you writing this book?' she asked. 'What's the good? Nobody reads biographies. I don't believe in them.' I made some lame excuse. She said: 'That reminds me of what I said to an Irish heckler once in New York. "You came to this country because you were hungry and you've been a nuisance ever since." ' With that shot she scurried down the hall and disappeared into her boudoir.

My talks with her continued in this fashion. I arrived by appointment, she always asked me my business, and after protesting that biographies were anathema, became animated and, without a pause to take thought, commented on persons and episodes in her history. Sometimes I asked her to confirm a story. Thus, a cousin of mine, Rosamund Tweedy, once related to me that she had heard the following exchange between Lady Astor and a heckler. Alluding to her jewellery the heckler said: 'You have enough brass round your neck to make a kettle,' and her instant reply was 'You have enough water in your head to fill it.' At my recalling this retort, Lady Astor was not displeased and agreed that she had made it.

The Cliveden Set rubbish still rankled a bit, particularly the allegation that she had ever liked Ribbentrop. 'He never came to Cliveden,' she said, 'but I asked him once to lunch at St James's Square in the early thirties. When announced he raised his arm, crying "Heil Hitler." I said: "Don't give us any of that nonsense here." I thought it was a joke, though of course he was serious.'

The subject came round to American visitors. 'Alfred Lyttelton suggested that I should invite the Henry Fords to Cliveden,' she said. 'He and his wife came and spent a fortnight. He loved dancing.' (Saying this, she hummed an old waltz and tapped with her toe.) 'He wanted to send for his private orchestra from New York. When he left he gave each of the children a Ford motor car. Mrs Ford lived very simply. She arrived at Cliveden without a maid and with only six trunks.'

That reminded her of a dinner in New York with the Roosevelts, to which the Vanderbilts came. 'At table I was put ahead of Grace Vanderbilt. She was rather cross, I could see. So I said to her: "The Astors skinned skunks a hundred years before the Vanderbilts worked ferries." ' This very loose summary of how the two families made their fortunes, and the precedence claimed therein by the Astors, mollified Mrs Vanderbilt, it appears.

In such fashion her reminiscences ranged backwards and forwards across the Atlantic. They also included anecdotes about the House of Commons. Just as I was leaving one day she came out with the following, her way of saying a pleasant good-bye. 'In the House the Serjeant-at-Arms once said to me: "I want to tell you that I've always been in love with you." "If I had known that, I'd have taken more liberties with you – in the House," was my reply. Another M.P., I forget who it was, said: "I always hated you, but could not resist your feet and ankles." ' On my asking her what reply she made to that, she said: 'It stumped me.' She was very merry and quickly told another tale which showed Speaker Fitzroy less gallant than the Serjeant-at-Arms. 'Once on a very hot day in parliament I came up behind the Speaker in his chair and offered him a peach. He said: "If you don't stop tempting me I'll have you put down." '

After this last bit of fun she began walking away from me down the hall. When she had gone nearly out of sight, she turned round and with finger raised said: 'I can't ask you to lunch. There is a reason. I forget what it is. But there is one.' Then she was gone.

In the talks which followed she returned from time to time to her first view that biographies were the devil and that in any case nothing in her life would interest the public. 'There are no scandals in it,' she said. 'Who will read a biography which is not scandalous?' It was no good my reminding her that for the last forty years she had been news: anything reported about her was read with avidity in the two hemispheres. 'They said all the wrong things about me,' she complained. 'I have only one interest, really, the Bible.'

During the period of the talks, in a moment of self-depreciation, I suppose, she wired to her son, Lord Astor, about the book. He was in Scotland. The wire, after the local post office had muddled it up, seemed to refer to some exciting intrigue. It read: 'Please tell Mr Collins to stop writing my wife.' It took Astor a moment to interpret it. The next time I entered her house, having been told of the telegram, I was a little apprehensive. Shown into the drawing-room to wait as usual, I presently heard a voice calling my name in the hall. Lady Astor entered. She had a bustling determined air. 'Come here,' she said, drawing me aside. 'I cannot let you go on with my life unless you pay a visit to Virginia. If Bill wants the book, he will have to send you there. That will make him think twice. You can't possibly write a book on me without thoroughly understanding my Virginian background. Everything of importance to me happened in Virginia.' She did not seem to expect a reply to this and sat down on the sofa. I drew up a chair beside her as usual, glad it had been no worse. Seated on the sofa, very upright and speaking in an earnest manner, she continued to explain what Virginia had always meant to her. During a pause I ventured to say that all the notable events of her career had taken place in England. That was the plot of the drama of her life; it was because she left Virginia that she became famous. At this moment the telephone rang and she went over to it. A friend was asking how she was. 'I'm all right,' she said. He evidently hoped to be allowed to see her, but she discouraged him. Then she said: 'I've got a man here who wants to write my life. You know more what I did in parliament than anyone else. Will you help him?' It appeared that he was willing to do so, and seemed inclined to continue the conversation, but she cut him short, saying: 'Will you get off the phone!' and hung up. As she returned to the sofa she gave me his name and number. He had been an M.P.

I took this episode to mean that I was forgiven and felt grateful to the gentleman for his timely intervention. On the sofa she continued to discourse on Virginia, as she took out of her bag some heavy gold bracelets and put them on. 'Most of my relations were very poor. They had not been able, like my father, to recoup their fortunes after the Civil War. Waldorf and I once went right down into the country to see some old cousins of ours, the Miss Gibbs. They had a delightful colonial-style house, with old silver and all that. But when we sat down to lunch, they handed round the dishes themselves. The fact was they had no servants. From that on, Waldorf looked after them. And it wasn't only the Miss Gibbs that he helped. He paid school fees for the children of other relatives. It's a curious thing, I was such a Virginian, that I felt almost a foreigner in New York, more foreign than I did in England.' And that reminded her of something. 'Winston Churchill once took me up in the House for being an American. At that time he didn't care for them as much as later. "Why can't you go back to America!" he exclaimed. "You're half American yourself," said I. "My American blood is French," said

241

he. "Ah," said I, "that explains everything." ' It was well known that she disliked the French.

I was now asked to stay to lunch. Her indulgence to even the most annoying kind of reporters has been mentioned. After she had said she wouldn't trust the dogs as far as she could throw them, she would excuse them because reporting was their means of livelihood. She had extended the same indulgence to me.

There was still a little time before her guests would arrive and she took up her reminiscences again. Her strong liking for Jimmy Thomas, the railwaymen's leader, has been mentioned, and how he was lent a house on the Cliveden estate. 'He was a great power in the country and could have had a revolution if he wanted. At Cliveden he met people with all sorts of points of view, which broadened his mind. He had never been in a big house before. His was a very endearing character. The cottage we lent him was the one with the gables on the bank south of the ferry. He had his wife and children with him. Our nanny asked: "What about the children? How can they be let play with the Thomas children?" But his children were much better behaved than mine.'

And she went on to say what very queer people sometimes stayed at Cliveden, pointing to the name of Ambassador Maisky in the Visitors Book. 'When he was coming downstairs one day he was overheard abusing his wife. It was rumoured afterwards that the woman was not his wife at all, but a person sent by Stalin to watch him. He disappeared not long after and was not heard of again.'

She was shutting the book, when her eye caught the name of Field Marshal Lord Montgomery. 'What about him?' I asked. Her answer was: 'Monty once said to me: "I don't like women members of parliament," I replied: "I don't like generals, with one exception, General Evangeline Booth." That settled him.' They were good friends.

In this connection one cannot resist quoting a *mot* which the present Viscount is reported to have made in 1950: 'If Mother hadn't been in the House of Commons, she'd have been in the Salvation Army, and that would have been worse.' The Salvation Army people interpreted this somehow or other as a slur on their organization and wrote in to protest.

The luncheon guests arrived and we went into the dining-room. As Lady Astor was sitting down she said: 'At Mirador my father used to say grace, but as likely as not, the moment afterwards he would shout at the servants: "Damn you, shut that door!" He had a quick temper and was a bit capricious. One night he'd say to the butler: "Never hand me port again." But next night, if the butler did not hand him port, he'd abuse him. To me he'd say: "Here's a dollar if you sing." Then he'd say: "Here's two dollars if you stop singing." Those Virginian days were the happiest of my life. In Virginia when I was a child, my black mammy made me spit three times over my shoulder when I saw a cross-eyed man, but when I came to England the place was so crowded that I had to give it up.'

It was delightful to observe with what ease and pleasure, though close on eighty, she presided over a luncheon party of eight. Her skill in keeping the table alive was as great as ever, her management of the staff as efficient as in the great days of Cliveden. I have never eaten such a good lunch. I said: 'Lady Astor, you have a marvellous chef.' She replied: 'He is an Austrian and I know is devoted. But to keep him up to the mark I threaten to denounce him as a Communist.'

In May 1959 Lady Astor celebrated her eightieth birthday at a family party at Cliveden. Shortly afterwards it was announced that she was to be admitted as Honorary Freeman of the City of Plymouth. The day fixed for the ceremony was Thursday 16 July 1959. Such occasions tend to be formal as a rule, but though all the proper formalities were observed in her case, she transformed by her personality an official function into a gathering of friends. She stayed at 3 Elliott Terrace, where nineteen years before she had braved the bombs of the German airmen. The house faces the Hoe, which may be described for those

243

who have not seen it as the top of a bluff overlooking the harbour, a spacious flat, wide and airy. From the roof of the house one may admire the splendid panorama of Plymouth's outer harbour with its moles, Drake's island, and the distant prospect of the Eddystone lighthouse. Immediately to the right is the Devonport dockyard, where battleships, cruisers and destroyers were repaired during the Second World War. When they entered and left the dockyard they used a buoyed channel immediately below the house, to which they were so close that they gave the impression of being immediately under the windows. It was from the Hoe that the men of Plymouth watched the Spanish Armada sail up the Channel on a following wind. The spot where Drake played his famous game of bowls has not been exactly located, but it was hereabouts. His reply to those who ran hurriedly to inform him that the Armada was sighted was not only an example of his sang-froid but of his common-sense, for he could best deal with it when it had passed by pursuing it downwind, instead of beating up to meet it. To the left of the Hoe is the Barbican, the ancient stronghold by the inner harbour, where to mark the spot whence the Pilgrim Fathers sailed to found New England there is an inscription, roofed over and with two small pillars, a modest memorial of a momentous event. Behind the house stretches the city, in great part rebuilt after the almost complete destruction of its centre by the German bombs, a new city of wide avenues, modern buildings and admirable facilities for all classes. One recalls Lady Astor's cry – 'We will build it again' – as she viewed the flaming devastation on the first night of the attack. During the latter part of her husband's tenure of the mayoralty the plans were made for the new lay-out. Work has been going on steadily for the last fifteen years and the job is now almost done, the late Viscount's most enduring memorial.

Lady Astor invited me to lunch before going to the ceremony, fixed for 3 p.m. When I got to the house, she introduced me to two figures of the Plymouth scene. They were concerned that she should appear to the best advantage on an occasion which rounded off her public career. In a couple of hours she would be on the platform receiving the freedom of the city. What ought she to say in her speech of thanks? It seemed a little late for her to consider this. Presumably her secretaries had already drafted a speech. But her two confidants knew well that it was one thing for her to have a written speech and another for her to deliver it. Accordingly, when she asked what she should say, they were full of suggestions, which they pressed on her, as if oblivious, which they were not, that only when actually on her feet and speaking did she compose her speech, which coming out of her head extempore might or might not be founded on what had been planned. Among several admirable suggestions was one that she should not fail to emphasize how she had always supported in parliament the interests of all classes in Plymouth, irrespective of their political party. She listened with indulgence and though she refrained from saying, as she had said to her coachman, Churchward – 'I am making this speech, not you' – one felt that what she would actually say remained hidden, even to her. She was in high spirits, though for a person of her age to address a large audience of prominent citizens was bound to be an ordeal. Anecdotes of all sorts flowed from her. She related with delight some of her American Negro stories, particularly the one when the parson asks the virgins in his Negro congregation to stand up, as he has some advice or other to give them. No one stands up, but presently a woman with a baby girl in her arms gets onto her feet. The parson remonstrates with her: 'I asked only virgins to stand up.' The woman explains: 'Little Lillybelle is too young to stand.' As usual, her mimicry of the Negro manner and expression of face made the telling very droll. I knew that she could also mimic to perfection all sorts of people she had met, but now she surprised me by mimicking someone she had never met – the Empress-Dowager Tzu Hsi. Suddenly she assumed the appearance of that famous personage when receiving the wives of the diplomatic corps at Peking. It seemed to me that everything essential for the understanding of the Dowager-Empress was revealed for a moment. As I had given as much thought to the interpretation of Tzu Hsi's character as to Lady Astor's, and had been less puzzled by the second on account of what I had divined of the first, the sudden and unattended coalescence of the two hit me like something supernatural. The great mimics, like the great artists, dumbfound us with a hidden touch.

As she ran on from story to story, and the time ran on, her friends became anxious. Would she continue talking until she had to leave for the Methodist Central Hall where the ceremony was to take place? Surely she ought to rest for a bit before setting out? She consented and accompanied us to the hall door. It was after two. She had to change her clothes and be ready for her sons, Lord Astor and Mr J. J. Astor, who were calling for her at 2.45 p.m.

The Methodist Central Hall was packed with notabilities. At 3 o'clock a side door was opened and, preceded by the mace and accompanied by the Lord Mayor, the Bishop of Plymouth and others, she was ushered to her seat on the platform. The Lady Mayoress, Mrs Washbourn, then presented her with a bouquet, saying how fond everyone was of her, a simple heartfelt statement which was very telling. There followed formal speeches by the Lord Mayor and two aldermen and the motion was put: 'That this Council desiring to acknowledge the eminent and distinguished services rendered to the City by Nancy, Viscountess Astor, C.H., and as an expression of the high esteem in which she is held by the Citizens do confer upon Nancy, Viscountess Astor, the Honorary Freedom of the City of Plymouth.'

Presently it was her turn to reply. The assembly had been waiting patiently for this moment. Their eyes had been fixed on her as she sat on the platform, a very small figure in a blue dress and hat, a pinched expression now and then flitting over her face, as if she was beginning to feel the strain. But the moment she stood up to speak, all trace of nervousness disappeared. At her first words the ceremonial gravity which had governed the proceedings so far was dissipated by a breeze of merriment and warmth. Pointing to her sons she declared that to speak in front of them put her on her mettle. Her stories came out one after the other, without other relevance than that they were very characteristic of her, were expected, and that not to have told them would have caused grave disappointment. Her *mots* were sprinkled in between, as when speaking of the achievements of women, she remarked that if Eve had not tempted Adam to be up and doing we should still be idling in the Garden of Eden. Her mood changing, she spoke earnestly of her late husband, saying that all he had done for Plymouth could never be added up. Becoming gay again, she wondered what advantages the freedom of the city would afford her. She had always wanted free rides on the buses, but supposed she would still have to pay. In her peroration she thanked the Council with deep feeling for the honour, saying that she had not expected it and then suddenly with a smile confessing that she had.

At the end Mr Freddie Knox, who had me in his charge, so arranged things that I was able to get quickly out of the hall and watch Lady Astor emerge from the main door, where the representatives of some working women's club awaited her with a bouquet. It was very revealing that she knew the names of many of these women and, pausing to speak with each, was able to give the impression that each had her warm regard. One woman with an ancient box camera asked her to pose, which she did, and, as the woman laboured with the contraption, stood quiet and happy and as if more honoured by this humble attention than by the city's freedom. The women were like persons transported; they murmured confusedly. Their evident devotion reflected what was the dominant feeling of all those present in the hall. The people there had been amused, but it was their emotion, not their laughter, which was the true measure of the occasion.

But Lady Astor's day was not finished. The city was

giving her a dinner at the Duke of Cornwall Hotel. I suppose about two hundred and fifty people sat down. Among those present was the Rt. Hon. Isaac Foot, one time Mayor of Plymouth and, as reported in its place, one of Lady Astor's opponents at her first election in 1919. He became a lifelong friend of hers. When I spoke to him before the dinner I was much struck by his gravity and charm. He knew her so much better than I and could have told me enough to fill many pages, more interesting than what I have written. But alas! my acquaintance with him dated from that moment and it was too late for me to profit by his advice. There are some others as qualified as he. A second volume, as full as this of detail, could easily be constructed from their reminiscences.

The eating done, speeches were made, much less formal than at the official function and which brought out more clearly the affection with which Lady Astor was regarded in Plymouth. A point in Lord Astor's speech emphasized this from an unexpected angle. The printers, though bound by the prevailing strike not to set up any type, were obliged by their hearts to print the handsome programme for the ceremony of the afternoon. But, as may be supposed, it was Lady Astor's speech which was awaited with the liveliest anticipation. It was really extraordinary how this old lady, who had already spoken at some length that day to the large audience at the Methodist Central Hall, was able to keep the diners, most of whom must have been in the Hall, in roars of laughter with her sallies, *mots* and stories. On occasion she wondered whether she was telling a story twice: 'Have I told you this story already today? Never mind, I'll tell it again.' Everyone was delighted, laughed as heartily as before. But it was not all merriment, for she had a dramatic move in reserve. She was wearing a diamond necklace, a long necklace of large diamonds that fell to her waist, which had been given to her as a present when she was Lady Mayoress of Plymouth by some person out of admiration for her services to the city. This necklace, worth thousands of pounds, she now took off and, requesting the Lady Mayoress to come up, hung it round her neck, declaring it a gift to be worn by her during her husband's tenure of office and by all future Lady Mayoresses of Plymouth thereafter. On receiving this truly munificent present, the Lady Mayoress was too overcome to say much, but the Lord Mayor, Mr Washbourn, was readier than she and presented Lady Astor with a free ticket *in perpetuum* on all the buses in the city, a jest much to her taste and an apt conclusion for this sketch of a life, throughout which fun has always been mixed with seriousness and high spirits, with affection.

Index

All Futura Books are available at your bookshop or newsagent, or can be ordered from the following address:
Futura Books, Cash Sales Department,
P.O. Box 11, Falmouth, Cornwall.

Please send cheque or postal order (no currency), and allow 40p for postage and packing for the first book plus 18p for the second book and 13p for each additional book ordered up to a maximum charge of £1.49 in U.K.

Customers in Eire and B.F.P.O. please allow 40p for the first book, 18p for the second book plus 13p per copy for the next 7 books, thereafter 7p per book.

Overseas customers please allow 60p for postage and packing for the first book and 18p per copy for each additional book.